Judicial Decision Making in Child Sexual Abuse Cases

Margaret M. Wright

Judicial Decision Making in Child Sexual Abuse Cases

UBCPress · Vancouver · Toronto

15 14 13 12 11 10 09 08 07 5 4 3 2 1

Printed in Canada on ancient-forest-free paper (100% post-consumer recycled) that is processed chlorine- and acid-free, with vegetable-based inks.

Library and Archives Canada Cataloguing in Publication

Wright, Margaret M. (Margaret Mary), 1948-
Judicial decision making in child sexual abuse cases / Margaret M. Wright.

Includes bibliographical references and index.
ISBN 978-0-7748-1264-1 (bound); 978-0-7748-1265-8 (pbk.)

1. Child sexual abuse – Canada – Cases. I. Title.

KEO1171.C45W75 2007 345.71'0253602643 C2006-906159-9
KF9323.W75 2007

Canada

UBC Press gratefully acknowledges the financial support for our publishing program of the Government of Canada through the Book Publishing Industry Development Program (BPIDP), and of the Canada Council for the Arts, and the British Columbia Arts Council.

This book has been published with the help of the K.D. Srivastava Fund.

Printed and bound in Canada by Friesens
Set in Stone by Artegraphica Design Co. Ltd.
Copy editor: Dallas Harrison
Proofreader: Stephanie VanderMeulen
Indexer: Patricia Buchanan

UBC Press
The University of British Columbia
2029 West Mall
Vancouver, BC V6T 1Z2
604-822-5959 / Fax: 604-822-6083
www.ubcpress.ca

This book is dedicated to the memory of two people who contributed in immeasurable ways to my personal and professional development and to the overall quality of my life: my mother, Aileen Durack Wright, and my long-time teacher, mentor, and friend, John M. Gandy.

Contents

Figures and Tables

Figures

Tables

Acknowledgments

This book has been a long time coming. I owe a huge debt of gratitude to a large number of people who helped to ensure that it was published. Mr. Justice David Cole OCJ initially suggested that I study Court of Appeal decisions and has consistently supplied me with updates on relevant court decisions. If there are errors or omissions in this book, they are in spite of his efforts to keep me educated and informed about the courts. John Krompkamp then facilitated my access to the Court of Appeal of Ontario files.

The first study reported in the book was conducted for my PhD research. I am grateful to my supervisor, Dr. Sheila Neysmith, for her wise advice and support during that time, to my committee members Dr. Patricia Evans and Professor Janet Mosher, and to my external examiners for that degree, Dr. Donald Bellamy and Dr. Sue Wilson, for their feedback.

I am also grateful to the Canadian Federation of University Women for awarding me funding through the Beverley Jackson Fellowship, which helped me to conduct the research.

This book could not have reached publication without the support and encouragement of my colleagues at the School of Social Work and Family Studies at the University of British Columbia; they saw me through some years of serious illness, kept my spirits up, and had faith that I could complete this work. Andrea Rolls, the manager at Victim Services, Ministry of the Attorney General, British Columbia, has been supportive of this project since I arrived in Vancouver. As well, Jean Wilson, Associate Director, Editorial, at UBC Press, has gone well beyond the usual scope of editorial duties. Without her dogged determination, this book would never have been published. The anonymous reviewers of the manuscript provided me with detailed constructive support and feedback that significantly improved the book.

Finally, I owe my personal and professional survival to the love and support of my incredibly patient partner, David Turner, who has read every version of the manuscript and been the biggest supporter of this work, and to our two funny, entertaining, and intellectually stimulating children, Caitlin and Carolyn, who were a great source of stress relief.

Introduction

This book is about child sexual abuse. It is a book for anyone interested in how courts work to resolve serious social problems. It is for those people who struggle to understand what happens in the courts and to make some sense of the process. It is also for those people who work with offenders so that they can see how the experiences of the sentencing process may have influenced the offenders' willingness to accept responsibility for their behaviour toward their victims.

In 1988, Canada passed a law designed, at least in part, to answer the public outcry about the number of cases of sexual abuse of children that were regularly appearing in the media. They reported on sensational trials, which included alleged satanic rituals and cannibalism and described allegations of the pervasive institutional sexual abuse of boys at the Mount Cashel orphanage in Newfoundland. The remedy for all of this suffering, arrived at by Canadians through our federally elected officials, was a legal one, consistent with the tone of the decade. The 1980s saw the passage of the *Constitution Act* and the *Canadian Charter of Rights and Freedoms*. Passage of both these statutes gave rise to a number of other new laws, including amendments to the *Criminal Code of Canada* that redefined sexual assault within a legal framework. The word *rape* was replaced with a continuum of sexual assault categories. This was done supposedly to reflect the range of sexually intrusive behaviours that could be considered offensive. Women's groups had fought for recognition of the harms done to women and children and largely supported legislative changes to recognize these harms through the mechanism of criminal law.

C. Smart and other feminists have questioned the utility of a "resort to law" as a means of achieving social change. The law is only one component of a social structure that must be examined in any attempt to encourage change. An exclusive focus on law as a solution ignores the multi-faceted reality of life in a complex society. However, deconstruction of the implementation of the law gives us insight into how some of our social systems perceive the offence, the offender, and the victim.

This book is the result of two separate studies in which I examined how the courts have dealt with cases brought before them and what effects the "resort to law" has had. In the first study, I examined child sexual abuse sentencing cases heard by the Court of Appeal of Ontario between May 1990 and June 1993. Analysis of the data in this study demonstrated that, although laws may change, interpretation of them is dependent on the social construction of child sexual abuse in the minds of the judges. Bill C-15 was passed in 1988, as noted above, to change how cases of child sexual abuse were tried. Its passage was a result of advocacy by women's groups and others concerned with the lives of children. These advocates wanted at least to convey the message that child sexual abuse is taken seriously by this society and that incidents of it will not be tolerated. The new law was designed to make it easier to prosecute child sexual abuse cases as well as to improve the victims' experiences of the process. I wanted to determine whether these goals had been met, and attempted to answer several questions.

- Which variables (e.g., relationship, duration of abuse, type of abuse, etc.) can predict the outcome of the appeal of the sentence? Which factors influence judicial decisions?
- Can the variability that seems to be present in all sentencing research be accounted for in cases involving child sexual abuse?
- Which issues are important to justices in these cases?
- How do they construct them?
- Is this construction indicative of a patriarchal world view that supports the belief that male reality is more important than other realities?

In this first study, I scrutinized the extent to which law is gendered from the point of view of how the Court of Appeal of Ontario made sentencing decisions. As well, I considered the degree to which patriarchal bias in interpretation of the law is supported by the medical and allied professions. Smart (1989, 34) has asked, "How does gender work in law and how does law work to produce gender?" I highlighted how gender themes weave their way throughout these cases, and I illustrated how judges and justices still retain notions of the privacy of the family in their consideration of the offender to a greater extent than the facts of the offence and the harm done to the victim. The study is an examination of the degree to which patriarchal norms influence interpretation of these laws in court. The results reinforce the recognition articulated by Dobash and Dobash (1992) that, without cultural change, legal change is window dressing.

In the second study, I examined similar cases in the period 1998-99. Using the same method, I analyzed all of the cases of sentencing after convictions for child sexual abuse. What stood out as the most noticeable difference between the earlier three years studied and that year was the change in the percentage of Crown appeals. In 1990-93, the appeals were almost equally divided between Crown appeals and offender appeals. In 1998-99, the Crown appeals were reduced to 4 percent, while 96 percent were offender appeals. Other changes were noticeable as well: for example, the number of appeals related to dangerous offender designations increased. However, much of the same patriarchal bias appeared in the use of mitigating and aggravating factors, as was evident in the first study. Also present was the relative invisibility of the victims in spite of an increased number of victim impact statements presented to the court. In this book, I analyze these findings in light of the expectations raised when the legislation was passed, and I raise questions about the utility of a legal method to resolve the social problem of child sexual abuse.

In Chapter 1, I provide background for passage of the 1988 amendments to the *Criminal Code* through a description of some of the news accounts of child sexual abuse in the 1980s. I go on to describe the results of the Badgley Commission and its influence on the law. I then consider the voices of critics of the law. In an analysis of the legal construction of child sexual abuse, I then review feminist writers' views about the failure of the law to represent the interests of women and children. I also explore the power of the medical profession as a maintainer of the patriarchal view of male-female and adult-child relationships, and I consider feminist challenges to the "common sense" and patriarchal constructions of the "typical" child molester. I then outline and discuss sentencing issues in cases of child sexual abuse in general practice, as well as critiques of the implementation of these laws. Finally, I raise questions stemming from the review of the literature for exploration in subsequent chapters.

In Chapter 2, I describe how and why I carried out the research. I chose sentencing decisions because of the richness of information about the offence, the victim, and the offender that comes out during that phase of the judicial process. Many cases of alleged abuse result in guilty pleas, in which case very little information is available in the trial transcript. Detailed information is available only through the sentencing hearing. This chapter contains accounts of attempts to study sentencing patterns in child sexual abuse and details the process by which I arrived at the methodology of the present studies. It explains how the first study began as an attempt to determine which factors in cases of child sexual abuse were important to judges in making sentencing decisions. It quickly became obvious to me that a study of trial judges' sentencing practices was not possible. What also became obvious when examining the cases available through the Court of Appeal of Ontario was that the variability in sentencing in child sexual abuse cases is considerable, that is, it is just as variable as sentencing has been found to be in general (Hogarth 1971).

I explain how the absence of any statistically significant predictors of a sentence led to an analysis of some of the processes of judicial reasoning and how they played themselves out in these cases. The relevance of the various actors in the courtroom drama is assessed in terms of their appearances in the cases studied. I discuss how the cases became the units of analysis so that I could consider influences on judicial decision making within the context in which decisions were made. Finally, I provide some descriptive demographic information, largely in chart form, to give the reader a glimpse of some of the background characteristics of the offenders, the victims, and the offences. There are also some details about the success and failure rates of these types of appeals and waiting times for appeals to be heard.

In Chapter 3, I reflect on expectations of the changes in the law and explore the ways in which courts have arrived at a characterization of the various types of sexual offences against children. I analyze the distinction that the courts make between penetration and non-penetration offences, how they arrived at this distinction, and what the implications of ignoring other significant factors surrounding the abuse, such as its frequency and duration, might be. Although the sexual assault laws passed in 1983 and 1988 do not contain any reference to "rape" or any emphasis on intercourse as a more serious harm, the Court of Appeal has articulated intercourse as a benchmark by which to establish sentence severity. This chapter contains an analysis of the continuing emphasis on penetration and the minimization of other forms of abuse as part of a patriarchal interpretation of child sexual assault.

In Chapter 4, I examine popular perceptions of men who sexually abuse children. These perceptions are based on stereotypical assumptions that portray these men as visibly deviant or demonic. Media portrayals present them as being "different." What happens when a "normal"-looking man comes before the court having been convicted of the sexual abuse of a child? How is his behaviour explained given that he looks like the rest of us? Judges and justices appear to have difficulty with this scenario and sometimes lose their focus on what the offender did in their attempts to understand who the offender is. I analyze the use of mitigating and aggravating circumstances and illustrate how the law is focused on the offender rather than on the offence or on the victim. I examine the tension between these two types of factors, and I illustrate cases that demonstrate how aggravating circumstances are downplayed and mitigating circumstances are emphasized, resulting in an unbalanced view of the offender. Finally, I outline the circumstances under which a balance is least likely to be achieved.

In Chapter 5, I illustrate that the victim is often overlooked or, in sentencing, mentioned as a sidebar, not as an integral part of the consideration. The victim's invisibility conjures up the image of a small child lost to the sight of the judge in front of an imposing bench. Her harm is seriously considered only in cases that involve penetration. She is most visible when she is being discounted as having been complicit with the behaviour and when her role as victim is being challenged. Victim invisibility goes beyond smallness in stature. Victim stature appears to be small because of how it is constructed relative to the stature of the male defendant.

In Chapter 6, I explore how judicial decision makers have depended on "experts" to help them understand the offenders and, by extension, the offences. Particularly interesting and concerning is how little attention is paid to the victim's input unless it is presented through the voice of a "medical expert." I examine the "production of medical definition" as it applies to this work. What influence do the medical/psychiatric and psychological reports have on the sentencing process? What is the construction of the offender in these reports? What role do other reports play?

Finally, in Chapter 7, I wrap up the findings of the previous chapters and raise outstanding issues. The chapter consists of a discussion on the implications of legal solutions to the social problems of children. I raise questions about which remedies are available to victims now that the appeal process has been constricted by the Supreme Court and scarce Crown resources, and I examine possible changes to the system that may be more realistically beneficial for children who have experienced sexual abuse.

Judicial Decision Making in Child Sexual Abuse Cases

1
Recent Events

On 1 June 2004, the news media reported the results of the sentencing hearing in the case of Judge Donald Ramsay in Prince George, British Columbia, *R. v. Ramsay* (2004). In his reasons for sentencing, Mr. Justice Patrick Dohm summarized the charges as follows:

> **Count 2 – The sexual assault of J.**
> The accused picked up J., an aboriginal/Metis woman, then 16 years old, off the street in Prince George. He took her in his truck about four miles out of town into the woods. There they agreed on $150 for sex. She took off her clothes, but when she reached for a condom he became enraged. He slammed her head on the dashboard, causing her forehead to bleed. After some struggle, she made it out of the truck.
>
> However, he caught up with her and pinned her to the ground. He slapped her across the face and proceeded to penetrate her with his penis as she cried. He got up, threw her clothes out of the truck and left. No money changed hands. She made her way back to the highway and hitchhiked back to town. Over a year later, J. struggled with the fact that the accused presided over a case conference concerning the custody of her son.
>
> **Count 3 – Obtaining for money the sexual services of H., a person under 18 years of age**
> The accused picked up H., then 12 years old, off the street in Prince George. He paid her $80 for oral sex and intercourse. Approximately three months later H., now 13 years old, appeared before the accused charged with various offences. The accused became aware of H.'s age and tumultuous past during the course of those proceedings.
>
> A month or more later the accused again picked up H. off the street and made references to her court appearance. They agreed on sex for

money. The accused paid H. a premium, $150, to simulate aggressive sex. The two got involved in a physical confrontation with respect to the transaction. Ultimately H. pushed the accused away and escaped out of the vehicle. He told her no one would believe her if she reported what had happened.

Count 7 – Obtaining for money the sexual services of A., a person under 18 years
The accused first picked up A., an aboriginal woman, when she was 14 years old. She was picked up off the streets and taken about four miles outside Prince George and down an isolated road. She provided oral sex to the accused in exchange for $80. This scenario was repeated four to six times while A. was from 14 to 17 years old. None of these encounters involved violence.

During the course of these encounters A. appeared before the accused several times. In court, the accused was made aware of A.'s background, including her fragile mental state, low self-esteem, limited education and her past with abusive adults.

Count 8 – Breach of trust
On either the second or the third of the encounters with A., the accused told A. that he would "let her off sentences" if she did not tell anyone of the encounters, thus creating an expectation that he would deal with her leniently in return for her silence. A. appeared before the accused in court eight times.

Count 9 – Obtaining for money the sexual services of C., a person under 18
At age 15, C., an aboriginal woman, appeared before the accused where, by her consent, she was made a ward of the state. The accused was made aware of her date of birth. Several months later the accused picked up C. off a street in Prince George and drove her to the same area as he drove A. She agreed to provide oral sex to the accused for $60.

She was performing oral sex and just near the end of the situation the accused wanted his money back. They struggled in the vehicle. He was attempting to overpower her with his hand in her pocket where the money was. He had her by the hair. She got away, naked. Before he sped away with her clothes still in the vehicle, he threatened to have her killed if she told anyone of the incident. She was not physically injured in the exchange. She later hitchhiked back to town. (*R. v. Ramsay* 2004)

Mr. Justice Dohm went on to say:

> The accused's conduct was utterly reprehensible. He freely engaged in sexual activity, including violence, with young women who were highly vulnerable because of youth, disadvantaged backgrounds and addiction. He sat in judgment on them for the very behaviour in which he himself was instrumental in causing them to engage, when he had full knowledge of their personal circumstances. For the administration of justice and for these young women a greater tragedy is difficult to imagine.
>
> It is difficult to imagine a more astounding example of the split personality phenomenon. No one can question that the accused has already paid a price for his crimes. He has lost his position as a previously respected judge and foreclosed himself from ever being part of the legal community again. He has brought shame on his former colleagues, on the judiciary generally, his family and on himself. I fully expect that his time in custody will be an exceptionally heavy burden; and on his release the burden will be with him still.
>
> But the principles of denunciation and retribution demand no less. His callousness towards those young women, his violence towards two of them, his conduct in discarding two like one might discard a pair of old shoes, and the resulting psychological aftermath, these are but a few of the appalling features of his crimes that emerge from the detailed statement of circumstances.
>
> These circumstances alone would justify a global sentence at the highest end of the range suggested by counsel. But in this terrible case there is the additional aggravating feature of the accused's position. From the circumstances agreed to by counsel it is apparent that the accused used his office both to solicit satisfaction of his perverted lusts and to shield himself from their consequences. In our society judges are the trustees of the administration of justice. One can hardly imagine a more infamous breach of trust. (*R. v. Ramsay* 2004)

The trial judge listed the factors that he considered favourable to the convicted judge:

- his guilty plea
- the Crown attorney's argument that Ramsay's early resignation from the bench should be seen as mitigating
- the offender's age

- character references indicating that the offender had had a "fine reputation" as a lawyer and a member of the community
- the offender's apology.

Mr. Justice Dohm also relied on expert input at sentencing: he cited a psychiatric report commissioned by the defence, which indicated that Mr. Ramsay was remorseful, unlikely to reoffend, and open to receiving treatment.

In discussing the seven-year sentence that he imposed, Mr. Justice Dohm said that "the Crown and defence have not only agreed on the facts, but also on an appropriate range of sentence, that being from three to five years imprisonment. But the court is not bound by the agreed sentencing range. Only where the range is, in the view of the court, reasonable and appropriate, and in keeping with the facts as presented, will a court be guided by it" (*R. v. Ramsay* 2004).

Because Judge Ramsay entered a guilty plea to the counts listed above, several other charges – including sexual touching of a person under fourteen years, invitation to sexual touching of a person under fourteen years, sexual assault, sexual assault with a weapon, threats or causing bodily harm, and procuring sexual exploitation of a person under the age of eighteen years – were dropped.

This is one of the few cases of child sexual abuse that has received detailed attention in the media. Because public discussion about these cases is relatively rare, the average person reading about this case would have little ability to put it into context. One person who could do so is retired BC provincial court judge Wallace Craig (2004), who said, "as a sitting judge and serial predator who victimized the most defenceless and vulnerable of women, Ramsay should receive a maximum sentence." Justice Craig was reacting to a *Vancouver Sun* editorial commending the sentencing judge, Chief Justice Patrick Dohm. In an op-ed column, Justice Craig pointed out that, in its lavish praise of him, the editorial

- failed to assess whether the "severity" of the sentence was even remotely on all fours with the "egregious" circumstances of the crimes and
- ignored the fact that a seven-year sentence may not be the de facto maximum for sexual assault causing bodily harm.

And he pointed out that "there is no doubt that *Regina v. Ramsay* is a benchmark precedent."

In further critiquing the sentence, Justice Craig went on to say, "but consider this: Ramsay's crime spree lasted at least 10 years and all the while he was one of Her Majesty's judges. His sentence was one half the maximum of 14 years." Justice Craig's concern, under other circumstances, might be one expressed by the Crown in an appeal; however, given that the Crown entered into a plea agreement with the defence and that the sentence was higher than that sought by the Crown, and given that the current Canadian legal climate does not encourage appeals by the Crown, it was being expressed in the media by a retired judge with no hope of any legal recourse. The potential legal precedent cannot be challenged.

This was a case that made it into the media; most cases of child sexual abuse do not. This case was atypical in that the offender was a judge; in many other ways, though, it was typical of what happens in courtrooms when sentencing decisions are made. What follows in this book is an account of many similar cases and an attempt to make sense of the sentencing processes in them.

The Legal Construction of Child Sexual Abuse

In 1983, the laws dealing with sexual assault were changed (Part V, *Criminal Code of Canada*), due largely to a persistent demand from women's groups that the old laws did not reflect the realities of sexual abuse. The aim of this legislation was to increase the number of reports made by victims of sexual assault, to increase the confidence of victims of sexual assault that their situations would be taken seriously and that they would not be further victimized by the process, to improve the processing of complaints of sexual assault by the police, and to increase the proportion of charges that could result in conviction (Ruebsaat 1985; Gunn and Linden 1993; Hudson and Roberts 1993). Some of the ways in which the law was supposed to improve confidence in the system were related to the recognition that women could be sexually assaulted by their intimate partners, specifically spouses, and that the corroboration requirements in cases of sexual assault were unrealistic and characterized women as being unreliable and likely to make false complaints out of anger. These requirements suppressed reporting of these offences. As well, there was significant recognition given to the fact that sexual assaults, particularly of children, are frequently so traumatizing that the victims cannot always be expected to be able to immediately report them (Gunn and Linden 1993, 152-53).

Research into the effectiveness of the criminal justice system in using these laws to meet their intended goals is sparse, but does exist. In general, the early research results indicated that there was an increase in reporting, with a particular increase in reports of child sexual assaults. The reports of assaults involved strangers less frequently than prior to enactment of the legislation and more frequently involved family members and acquaintances. In spite of the increase in reporting, "the conviction rate has probably not been affected by the legislation" (Gunn and Linden 1993, 153). Furthermore, "the rape reform legislation introduced in Canada in 1983 was successful in achieving one of the goals that inspired it. Ironically, its success was in attracting more victims into the system rather than in changing the way that the system responds to complaints of criminal sexual aggression" (Roberts and Gebotys 1993, 168). Gunn and Linden (1993, 154) conclude that passage of Bill C-127 was an acknowledgment of women's rights, but consistent affirmation of these rights cannot be guaranteed solely by legislation; Bill C-127 provides the framework that both allows and validates social change and is the first step toward meaningful change.

More recent research (Kong et al. 2003) indicates that the increase in reporting peaked in 1993 and has been declining steadily since that time. There are a number of possible explanations for this decline. Kong et al. connect it to a generally declining crime rate and to a reduced number of children in the overall population of the country. Others, such as Trocmé et al. (2002, 2), suggest caution in the interpretation of the decline: the number of substantiated investigations of sexual abuse decreased by 44 percent, from 3,400 in 1993 to 1,900 in 1998. This is consistent with decreases reported across the United States. Such a dramatic decrease requires careful analysis. While it could indicate that sexual abuse prevention programs and criminal charging policies may have acted to effectively deter sexual abusers, it is also possible that the same policies are causing victims and their parents to be less willing to report sexual abuse. This decrease may be the result of declining public attention to the issue after the enormous amount of attention that it received in the late 1980s. As well, child welfare workers have consistently reported problems with understaffing as reasons why the number of substantiated investigations has dropped. They also report reluctance by Crown attorneys who are also understaffed and insufficiently resourced to proceed with charges. Roberts (1996, 414) also reports that sexual assault allegations as a category of crime are twice as likely to be labelled unfounded: "We can observe that sexual assault victims who report to the police are more likely than victims of other crimes to have their complaints dismissed by the police as lacking sufficient foundation ... It is unlikely that having one complaint declared unfounded by the police, a victim will return to the criminal justice system." Research conducted and reported by Du Mont and Myhr (2000) supports the conclusions of Roberts.

Early Days

Immediately preceding and following passage of Bill C-127, many media reports presented compelling stories about the victimization of children. There were stories describing methods of "street-proofing" children to keep them safe. There were stories about new methods used by social workers and police to ensure an increase in the prosecution and conviction of those men engaged in the sexual use of children, and stories claiming that reports of child sexual abuse had doubled in the previous six months: "in every case, the child knew the perpetrator and the abuse had been going on for more than two years before authorities heard about it" (Hickl-Szabo 1984). In February 1981, a federal task force was struck, headed by Robin Badgley, a professor at the University of Toronto medical school, and comprised primarily of a number of medical and legal participants but also a journalist and a director of a daycare centre. The task force reported in August 1984 and recommended several changes to the *Criminal Code of Canada* that included the creation of new offences that would criminalize, among other things, sexual touching. Media comments after the release of the report emphasized the extent of the social problem of child sexual abuse and recommended passage of a new law to implement the report's recommendations. At the time, an editorial in the *Globe and Mail* commented:

> Sexual abuse of children is incredibly widespread in Canada and – like an iceberg – only a tiny part of it is above surface and recognized by the authorities or the public. This was the finding in the recent two-volume report on three years of research by the federally appointed Committee on Sexual Offenses against Children and Youth. The committee, which had been asked to determine the adequacy of laws and their enforcement in protecting children against sexual abuse, reported baldly, "On the basis of our findings, about some 10,000 cases of sexual offenses against children and youths, our principal conclusions are that these crimes occur extensively, and that the protection afforded these young victims by the law and public services is inadequate." (*Globe and Mail* 1984)

In assessing the committee's recommendations, the editorial went on to state:

> Many of these legal changes would be sound, but some are frightening. It would be sound to end the one-year limit on prosecution of sexual abuse. It would be frightening to permit conviction on the uncorroborated evidence of a single witness. It would be terrifying to have the laws of evidence changed to declare that "*every* child is competent to testify in court and the child's evidence is admissible," and that, "there be no statutory requirement for the *corroboration* of an 'unsworn' child's evidence." Any parent, teacher, or child psychologist knows that most young children pass through stages where they are unable to differentiate between reality and fantasy. (ibid.)

It is obvious in reviewing media reports of the time that most of them emphasized that the abuse was reprehensible but they had concerns, as evident in the editorial above, about how that abuse should be defined and prosecuted and possibly punished. Finally, some years after the report was tabled, Bill C-15 was passed in January 1988 and dealt specifically with sexual offences committed against children. The goals of the legislation were to

- provide better protection to child sexual abuse victims/witnesses;
- enhance successful prosecution of child sexual abuse cases;
- improve the experience of the child victim/witness; and
- bring sentencing in line with the severity of the offence. (Hornick and Bolitho, 1992, xiv)[1]

This book is a study of the last two goals. How are children and convicted offenders treated under this legislation? To answer this question, it is necessary first to look at the history of the legal management of child-adult sexual contact in Canada and to some extent in the British justice system.

History of Child Sexual Abuse and the Criminal Law

Child sexual abuse may have received a great deal of attention in the 1970s and 1980s, but sexual contact between adults and children was not a new phenomenon. There is a consensus in the literature that sexual activity between children and adults has existed historically and cross-culturally with varying degrees of acceptance. Its existence was not considered problematic; what was monitored were the boundaries within

1 Section V of the *Criminal Code of Canada* outlines in detail what constitutes a sexual offence against a child.

which adult-child sexual contact took place. In Roman civil and criminal law, the concept of *patriae potestas* or "power of the father" gave the male head of the household total power and control over the family (DeYoung 1982, 101-2; Foucault 1968, 135). Sexual assaults on the adult females or on the male or female children in the family were not considered offences against those assaulted as much as they were regarded as vandalism against the male's (father's) property. As such, the remedies involved paying damages to the injured party, the husband or the father (DeMause 1975).

Christian law represented a concern for the age at which sexual intercourse between adults and children took place. Canon law defined sex with a child less than ten years of age as invalid rather than illegal: it did not exist even though it actually happened (Rush 1980, 34). When civil law was separated from church law in England, the crime of statutory rape was created, in effect recognizing that sexual activity did take place between adults and children under the age of ten. If a man had sex with a female under the age of twelve, he could be convicted of a misdemeanour offence (Rush 1980, 34-35).

Historical studies of the sexual use of children are sparse and tend to concentrate on sexual activity with boys (Jones 1982). Quinsey (1986, 144) points out that the lack of commentary on adult sexual activities with young girls appears to reflect its "acceptance and ubiquity." Foucault describes a major change in social attitudes toward sexuality in the nineteenth century. This change was from a social framework in which sexual behaviour was expressed openly, and in which adult sexuality was open to the view of children, to a framework in which sexual behaviour was moved into a more private sphere, the home, and hidden from children. "On the subject of sex, silence became the rule" (Foucault 1968, 3). Parents were supposed to shield their children from the knowledge of sex and were expected to police them to guard against masturbation and other evidence of budding sexuality (Haller and Haller 1974; DeMause 1975; DeYoung 1982).

Changes in the Western view of childhood moved the controls over children into a more public sphere. Until the end of the nineteenth century, the concept of childhood was not well developed (Houston 1974; Platt 1977; Sutherland 1976; Rooke and Schell 1982). Because of this absence of status, children were dealt with as if they were the property of their parents and could be treated in any fashion, usually short of murder, that their parents deemed to be appropriate. The child-saving movement was aimed specifically at poor children because, as Rothman (1971) contends, the real concern in these efforts was not for the well-being of the child but for that of society in that these were really attempts to prevent the moral contamination of delinquency. Even after the child-saving movement, poor children were often treated as objects or as property, because poverty was considered to be an indication of abnormality (Rooke and Schell 1982). Therefore, the state or well-meaning people who were not poor could take charge of a child's life, usually by removing the child from his or her parents' home and placing him or her in an institution or foster home as a means of rescuing the child (Houston 1974). The rhetoric of the times compared institutions to family arrangements and found the institutional form of parenting preferable to that of the poor family.

In April 1893, legislation introduced in Ontario by J.M. Gibson, the *Children's Protection Act,* also known as the "Children's Charter" or the "Gibson Act," "reduced parents' right of property in their children and affirmed that from infancy, children possessed the rights of citizenship" (Sutherland 1976, 111). Sutherland has termed this time period one of "social optimism" (130). Yet, while the *Children's Protection Act* represented a turning point in the definition of children in Canadian society, many other factors mitigated against children's equal treatment vis-à-vis adults. Most of these factors related to acceptance of the primacy of the parent's role as well as to the secrecy surrounding and the taboo concerning discussion of sexual behaviour. The reduced right of property could be seen to be more applicable in poor families because of the closer scrutiny to which they were subjected. Their relative absence of power increased their "visibility."

In addition to this historical notion of children as property, we need to recognize that the concept or ideal of childhood that we hold today in Western societies is very different from the concept of childhood that existed in the late 1800s when the first federal legislation dealing with child sexual abuse in Canada was passed. Chunn (2002, 120) outlines some of this legislative history: "Although incest had been a penal offence in some provinces prior to Confederation, a federal statute had existed only since 1890, when the Canadian Parliament enacted a uniform criminal law ... Under the new law, incest involving grandparents, parents, and siblings was classified as a crime against morality carrying a maximum sentence of fourteen years of imprisonment. Two years later the 1890 law was incorporated virtually unchanged in Canada's first Criminal Code." Chunn goes on to contend that the prohibition against incest was part of a series of legislative and social attempts designed to strengthen heterosexual marriage. It also introduced some public oversight of what had been considered the private realm of the family, under the father's jurisdiction. Chunn considers the new scrutiny of the family to be part of the development of a budding welfare state. As many others have observed above, state oversight was often restricted to those members of the community who were most visible and, according to the beliefs of the times, most in need of scrutiny: the poor.

Smart (1999, 392) similarly analyzes the history of criminal justice interest in adult-child sexual contact when she describes the development of British laws and the construction of that society's definition of childhood:

> Sociologically speaking, it would seem that we can now easily accept the idea that the extension of schooling in this century changed childhood. However, the idea that extending the age of consent for girls from 13 to 16 years old in 1865 also changed the nature of childhood is less easily grasped. We tend to think that it was self-evident that a 13-year-old could not consent and was too immature for sex. In fact, this was not self-evident at all. Rather we ought to understand the extent to which the Criminal Law (Amendment) Act 1885 was part of a new construction of modern childhood. It created and extended a particular, historically and culturally specific, type of childhood to the age of 16 in much the same way as the Education Acts did subsequently.

When Smart challenges the incapacity of a thirteen-year-old to consent as "self-evident," she discusses the confusion that has existed for many years about men's motives for sexual contact with children, children's responsibility for such contact, and the possible harms that may result from that contact: "Their frame of reference was more attentive to the idea of inappropriate sexual contact – whether consensual or not – which they saw as morally harmful and exploitative. (This differs from the contemporary perspective which understands adult/child sexual contact to be psychologically damaging rather than morally corrupting)" (1999, 399). Smart examines the conflicting views of the child in her discussion of the "abused child as leper" versus the child as a "true" victim. She contends that to some extent this depended on the age of the child. She also contends that definitions of childhood victimization and adult offending were being created primarily by the legal and medical professions.

Medicine and the Privacy of Abuse

The medical profession has been identified as an agent of social control through which the mantle of privacy veils issues of violence in the relationships between men, women, and children and keeps them out of public scrutiny. The management of social problems by the medical profession ensures their "confidentiality" and to some extent their obfuscation. The average person is not expected to know what the physician, psychiatrist, or psychologist knows about someone. Nor is that person expected to understand the process by which that knowledge is achieved or to have insight into the dynamics of that person's functioning. Foucault (1968, 64) describes this view of medicine as the "confessional science" and outlines the medical profession's control over sexuality: "Through the various discourses, legal sanctions against minor perversions were multiplied; sexual irregularity was annexed to mental illness; from childhood to old age, a norm of sexual development was defined and all the possible deviations were carefully described; pedagogical controls and medical treatments were organized around the least fantasies, moralists but especially doctors, brandished the whole emphatic vocabulary of abomination" (36).

Gusfield (1992, viii), in an analysis of the medical profession's view of homosexuality, comments that "the medical metaphor is not as neutral and as amoral as it seemed in its inception." Gusfield advocates an analysis that highlights the way in which medicine conveys a particular moral message rather than simply reflects a natural order.

Smart (1989, 17) examines the interaction between law and medicine in the maintenance of patriarchal standards in male-female and male-child relationships and the power of law to "disqualify other knowledges and discourses." She examines how law as a profession turns to medicine as a profession for support of a phallogocentric construction of reality, and as a result extends its power: "We can see a form of cooperation rather than conflict and a process by which law extends its influence into more and more 'personal' or 'private' areas of life ... Hence law retains its 'old' power, namely the ability to extend rights, whilst exercising new contrivances of power in the form of surveillance and modes of discipline." Conrad and Schneider (1992, 278) support Smart's concern: "Our view of the medicalization thesis is that it is essentially about culture, focusing on the creation and use of categories and how this process constitutes, shores up, or challenges existing notions of reality." Medicine has exerted social control in the domestic sphere of life in terms of the regulation of sexuality and has defined what "appropriate" heterosexual relationships are. By defining what is "normal" in our society, it has contributed to the maintenance of power imbalances between men and women and between adults and children.

Medicalization of the Child Molester

With the dominance of the medical profession over the regulation of sex, as noted by Foucault, it is not surprising that some of the most widely accepted answers to questions about sexuality have been in the realm of biology. From Lombroso's (1911) early theorizing about the biological basis for criminal and aggressive behaviour, biological explanations have had a good deal of appeal. Biological explanations of men's aggression have been frequently cited to explain their dominance as well as their deviance. While some researchers have argued against this causal link, a great deal of effort has gone into attempting to prove one. The psychiatric community has been particularly active, if largely unsuccessful, in this regard, but much of the focus on treatment still revolves around the use of pharmacological agents: "The development of the selective serotonin reuptake inhibitors and other pharmacotherapies has moved the field more toward a bio-psycho-social model of etiology and treatment, and focused more attention on co-morbid psychiatric disorders in the treatment of sexual offenders" (Miner and Coleman 2001, 5).

Hucker and Bain (1990) report many problems in the study of a connection between sexual offending and levels of testosterone. These researchers indicate that the many studies that make claims to a link between hormone levels and aggression, sexual or otherwise, have not proven to be replicable and are plagued by small numbers of subjects and conflicting results. Studies investigating possible chromosomal abnormalities as an explanation for sexual offending have not demonstrated any correlation. Langevin (1990), on the other hand, indicates some confidence in studies that show a connection between temporal lobe impairment and sexually anomalous behaviours. He claims that, when recently developed imaging technology is used, there is some reason to believe that sexual sadists and pedophiles show different brain pathology in the temporal lobes. Langevin (1993, 70) is careful to point out, however, that the majority of men who sexually offend against children are not pedophiles but "conventional heterosexuals who offend for other, psychological reasons." He concludes that this is most obvious in intrafamilial abuse situations, but in cases of stranger offences he suggests that, although many offenders can be considered to meet the diagnostic criteria for pedophilia, a large number cannot: "Therefore, a child may be molested for reasons other than sexual preference" (1993, 74). It is clear that, in spite of the widely held belief that male sexual aggression against women and children is biologically based, prominent researchers who have been most actively looking for a biological explanation for the majority of sexual abuses have been unable to find it.

Other attempts have been made to explain sexual victimization of women and children from the point of view of personality theories or other similar psychological constructs. Erickson et al. (1987, 566), commenting on their review of this literature at the time, noted that it "perpetuated over simple and stereotypic descriptions of the psychological characteristics of sex offenders. Such stereotypic descriptions can usually be identified by liberal use of the article 'the' as in the rapist, the child molester, and so forth." Quinsey (1986; see also Becker and Quinsey 1993), a leading researcher in this field, also questions the utility of the search for causation in the personality of the offender. Over the course of several years, many researchers have attempted to develop a typology of men who commit sexual offences against women and children. These attempts themselves are a good indication of the way in which the professionals concerned viewed the problem. That is, they have seen the problem as centred on the personality or the pathology of the individual offender. Knight and Prentky (1990) have attempted unsuccessfully to develop a viable typology of men who commit crimes of sexual assault.

A relatively recent development in the literature on sex offenders in general is the contention that sex offending is a compulsive behaviour indicative of an addiction similar to alcohol abuse, drug abuse, and gambling. Carnes (2002, 2004) is the primary proponent of this approach. He believes that sex offenders find the behaviour pleasurable and exciting and develop a pathological dependence on it as well as a behavioural structure to support the addiction. Blanchard (1985a and b) contends that offenders become progressively more preoccupied with the activity and that their behaviour escalates in frequency and seriousness because of the addiction. There is no evidence, however, for the existence of this dynamic. Some researchers see this "addiction" as a form of obsessive compulsive disorder.

The focus in recent years has turned to what are termed "cognitive distortions" in sex offenders. This turn began, at least in part, when Yochelson and Samenow (1976) claimed that criminals think differently from non-criminals and that these thinking patterns are the primary source of their criminality. Those who have published in this area[2]

2 See, for example, Segal and Marshall (1985); Segal and Stermac (1990); Stermac, Segal, and Gillis (1990); Hanson, Gizzarelli, and Scott (1994); and Ward et al. (1997).

believe that how child molesters think about children, and their behaviour toward them are significant considerations in understanding child sexual abuse. Child molesters tend to believe that children are not harmed by sexual contact with adults, that children benefit from sex with adults, and that children can consent to sex with adults and are frequently sexually provocative. However, researchers in this area cannot say whether these beliefs produce the behaviour or whether the stated beliefs are a result of dissonance. That is, does the offender report the beliefs after he has committed the offence in order to rationalize behaviour that is otherwise difficult to justify? Are his reasons for choosing children related to them being easy targets, or does he really believe that they can consent to and benefit from sexual contact with adults? Harris, Rice, and Quinsey (1998, 96-97) indicate that, in terms of cognitive-behavioural treatment strategies, "just as was the case with pharmacological treatments, the data so far are consistent with the conclusion that agreeing to and persisting with treatment over the long term serves as a filter for detecting those offenders who are relatively less likely to reoffend, but the nature of the treatment (so long as it is not exclusively humanistic or psychodynamic) has little or no detectable specific effect on outcome ... The question of the effectiveness of cognitive-behavioral treatment of sex offenders will go without a scientific answer for many years to come." Other researchers explain cognitive distortions as something people do rather than have: "An important assumption of this approach was that cognitive distortions were a 'property' of the person expressing the belief and were also causally implicated in the commission of that person's offence. This individualistic approach in turn enabled or legitimized interventions based upon the assumption that the individual is susceptible to cognitive change programmes or should be subject to a management regime" (Auburn and Lea 2003, 282). These authors conclude that offenders use these distortions to manage their culpability for their offences.

Much of the literature on men who sexually abuse children infers that their criminal activity is quite different from that of other people. Some researchers are now disputing this inference, which obviously challenges the medicalization or pathologization of sex offenders (Simon 2000; Soothill et al. 2000; Smallbone and Wortley 2004). These researchers challenge the perception that sex offenders are a homogeneous group and that they are essentially distinct from other offenders:

> Although the circumstances or contexts in which sexual offending occurs may be different from those in which nonsexual offending occurs,

> criminological perspectives generally assume the same fundamental mechanisms to be responsible for both. Gottfredson and Hirschi's (1990) general theory of crime goes so far as to suggest that a single common mechanism – essentially a failure to exercise restraint over self-serving impulses – can account not only for most criminal behaviour but also for a broad range of irresponsible and risk-taking behaviour. From this perspective, paraphilias, sexual offending and nonsexual offending would be expected not only to co-occur but also to share a common etiology. (Smallbone and Wortley 2004, 176)

Sentencing Issues in Child Sexual Abuse

According to the Canadian Sentencing Commission (1987, 151), "the fundamental purpose of sentencing is to preserve the authority of and promote respect for the law through the imposition of just sanctions." Until the 1996 amendments to the *Criminal Code,* there was no "legislative statement of the aims of sentencing in Canadian law" (Manson, Healy, and Trotter 2000, 111) beyond maximum possible sentence length. Prior to that time, there were generally accepted "traditional" sentencing goals, utilitarian and retributive. Utilitarian goals are met by a focus on deterrence (general and specific), incapacitation, and rehabilitation. These goals emphasize the prevention of future crime committed either by the offender sentenced or by others in the public. Retributive goals focus on the concepts of retribution and just desserts and on denunciation. The emphasis is on the offence and on the need to censure and condemn the behaviour of the offender involved in it (Griffiths and Verdun-Jones 1994, 407; Manson, Healy, and Trotter 2000, 1).

Rehabilitation

There has been considerable criticism of the present correctional system as a useful agent of change. In the view of prominent Canadian researchers in discussing the rehabilitation of sex offenders,

> the best option in these circumstances of relative ignorance is to adopt treatments that (a) fit with what is known about the treatment of offenders in general, (b) have a convincing theoretical rationale in that they are motivated by what we know about the characteristics of sex offenders, (c) have been demonstrated to produce proximal changes in theoretically relevant measures, (d) are feasible in terms of acceptability to offenders and clinicians, cost and ethical standards, (e) are described in sufficient detail that program integrity can be measured, and (f) can be integrated into existing institutional regimens and supervisory

> procedures. The last point is of special importance because, to the extent that treatment fails to reduce recidivism, supervision (including denial of community access) has to take its place. (Harris, Rice, and Quinsey 1998, 97)

Brown (1991) and others make it clear that women's groups are disappointed with the track record of the traditional correctional system, particularly the institutional component of it. The success or failure of imprisonment to effect change in offenders has been the subject of considerable debate for some time. While the debate continues, few writers and researchers examine the culture of the correctional institution. That cultural environment is predicated on a form of macho masculinity in which sexism (Hansen 1993) and racism (Gittens and Cole 1994) are tolerated and even encouraged. Pro-social notions of co-operation and relationship are not valued or promoted in most institutional settings.

Denunciation

Ruby (1999) describes denunciation as an attempt by the court to express the abhorrence that society feels about a crime. According to Ruby, a sentence given under such a premise would be "inevitably harsh" (5). The Law Reform Commission of Canada (1974) described the attempt behind the concept of denunciation as educative. The sentence is supposed to reflect the societal value that holds the crime in question to be unacceptable behaviour. The Canadian Sentencing Commission (1987, 142-43) seemed to agree with the concept of an educative function but identified the same problem as exists, in its view, with deterrence: if the public never hears of the sentence or of the rationale for it, then there is no possible educational value. The commission also made the point that the public perception of seriousness of offences is more likely shaped by its perception of the harm done by the crime than by the sentence. A call for more appropriate sentences would then have to be accompanied by an explanation of the rationale for these sentences in terms of the harm done to the victims.

Deterrence

Deterrence as an aim of sentencing is usually divided into general and specific deterrence. In general deterrence, the public, or at least that part of it that might be tempted to commit a similar crime, is supposed to be deterred from committing crime by seeing what has happened to someone else who did. The Canadian Sentencing Commission (1987, 137) has observed that this form of deterrence may be undermined by a media tendency to report more cases of lenient dispositions. Specific deterrence is aimed at the offender himself being sentenced. The sentence is supposed to give that individual the message that his criminal behaviour has resulted in a personal cost that should encourage him to avoid similar behaviour in the future. Many theorists of and researchers in the effectiveness of deterrence have emphasized that deterrence is effective in preventing crime only if the potential offender perceives that there is a reasonable certainty of getting caught (Freidland 1990; Gibbons 1992). Since many people who commit crime are not caught, and since most are not caught for every criminal offence, the certainty principle necessary for deterrence to be effective has been seriously doubted, particularly for sexual offenders, who are believed to offend many times before they are reported or arrested.

Legislative Guidance

There have been many calls for sentencing guidelines in Canada. For example, Doob and Brodeur (1996, 376) argue that Canadians are not so concerned about lenient sentencing as they are confused by the process of sentencing. They frame the problem as one of disparity or variability in sentencing and conclude that without guidelines sentences "will, over time, no longer be seen as legitimate" (379). These authors see the problem as part of a more general lack of accountability and challenge the vagueness and difficulty of setting in motion what are perceived to be existing accountability mechanisms for judges' decisions, including appeals to higher courts. They argue that the current issue of disparity and the resulting discontent with sentences stem from the fact that we lack a sufficiently clear set of principles from which to formulate policy and practice.

Manson, Healy, and Trotter (2000) outline the history of the sentencing principles developed in the 1996 amendments to the *Criminal Code*. They question which principle, if any, has priority over the others: "What does this statement achieve?" (112). They go further to point out that, notwithstanding the principles in section 718, trial judges are "the principle [sic] instruments of sentencing" (122). In their presentation of *R. v. C.A.M.* (1996), they illustrate how primacy has been reinforced by the Supreme Court (122-23). For example, Mr. Justice Lamer stated that,

> As Iacobucci J. explained in Shropshire, at para. 46, ... [a] sentencing judge still enjoys a position of advantage over an appellate judge in being able to directly assess the sentencing submissions of both the Crown and the offender. A sentencing judge also possesses the unique

> qualifications of experience and judgment from having served on the front lines of our criminal justice system. Perhaps most importantly, the sentencing judge will normally preside near or within the community which has suffered the consequences of the offender's crime. As such, the sentencing judge will have a strong sense of the particular blend of sentencing goals that will be "just and appropriate" for the protection of that community ... The discretion of a sentencing judge should thus not be interfered with lightly. (Cited in ibid.: 269)

Manson, Healy, and Trotter (2000) question what would constitute an error in principle or a demonstrably unfit sentence. While the 1996 amendments created the expectation that sentencing processes might become clearer for everyone as a result of the statement of principles, using Doob and Brodeur's (1996) reasoning, it could be argued that the Supreme Court has narrowed the accountability of judges even further.

Feminist Concerns about Child Sexual Abuse

Some feminists do not share Mr. Justice Lamer's confidence in trial judges and have difficulty with the discretion that judges have in arriving at sentencing decisions. They dispute his claim above that judges' experience and position in the community situate them to make good decisions. Many women's groups who advocated for the changes in the law that came first with the proclamation of Bill C-127 and then Bill C-15 have expressed disappointment with the results of sentencing decisions since their enactment. Early on, after the change in the legislation, the works of Marshall (1985), Brown (1991), and METRAC (1992) focused on the gender bias that appeared in the processing of cases of child sexual abuse and was frequently most noticeable in the sentencing. Marshall (1985, 219) articulated these sentiments: "In cases where an assaulter has been found guilty, clear evidence that a crime took place is no guarantee that the judge understood either the nature of the crime or its impact on the victim."

The Manitoba Association of Women and the Law, in reviewing what it perceived to be stereotypical assumptions made by judges, found "judicial comment on sentencing that is overly sympathetic to the accused; minimizes or trivializes the offence; disguises or downplays the severity of the offence; [and] is overly concerned with the accused's background and the effect of the charge/sentence on the accused" (Brown 1991, xiii). Some feminists argued that, given the broader scope for the exercise of judicial discretion with respect to sentencing contained in the 1983 amendments, "there was a danger that many of the objectionable features of the offences would reemerge at the sentencing level. Examples of this might include: (1) an undue emphasis on the absence of penetration" (Ruebsaat 1985, 93). One of the primary features of Bill C-127 was removal of the emphasis on rape as the only real form of sexual assault. Critics of the legislation (Nadin-Davis 1983; Ruebsaat 1985) observed that, although rape was no longer specified as a charge, the underlying male view of the damage associated with sexual assault that it implied might be retained in the application of the new law. In fact, the presence or absence of penetration has become the benchmark in determining the sentence. According to the Manitoba Association of Women and the Law, "the crime of sexual assault does not require vaginal penetration, as did the former crime of rape. However, the system continues to downgrade the seriousness of the assault if there has been no vaginal penetration" (Brown 1991, vi). This minimization is reflected in a 1994 decision made in Montreal by Madame Judge Raymonde Verreault, in which she cited the absence of vaginal penetration as a mitigating factor in handing down a twenty-three-month sentence to a man convicted of having repeatedly sodomized his stepdaughter: "The accused spared his victim. They did not have normal and complete sexual relations ... vaginal relations to be precise, so she retained her virginity, which seems to be a very important value in her religion" (Reuters 1994, A2). Doob and Brodeur (1996, 382) refer to this case as an example in their discussion on judicial accountability. They indicate that the prosecution immediately appealed the judge's sentence, but "this judge was subsequently promoted to be the administrative head of one level of court in the province." They go on to describe the public outcry following the decision and the judge's subsequent voluntary leave from the court.

Some viewed the sentencing of men who molest children as seriously problematic: "Sentences for the sexual assault of children as for the sexual assault of women are often so low that they do not convey that sense of outrage felt by the general population. It would be unrealistic to suggest that harsh sentences alone will solve the problems of child sexual abuse. However, harsh sentences would serve to convey more clearly the message that the sexual assault of children is not tolerated in Canadian society" (Brown 1991, 52-53).

More recently, Canadian feminists such as Comack (1999), Chunn and Lacombe (2000), and Comack and Balfour (2004) have continued the critique of the criminal justice response to the social problem of child sexual abuse and other legislation dealing with sexual violence: "Critical legal theorists have argued that this business of criminalizing is much more complicated than it might first appear. Far from being an impartial and objective enterprise, law deals in ideology and discourse – through the meanings and assumptions embedded in the language that it uses, through its ways of making sense of the world and through its corresponding practices" (Comack and Balfour 2004, 9).

Feminist scholars have written extensively about the role that the law has played in remedying or allowing the abuse of women and children. Naffine (1990, 7) describes law as "deemed to be essentially an expression of masculinity, not only in its content but also in its modus operandi." She quotes Polan (1982) and MacKinnon (1983, 1987) as questioning the basic structure of the legal system, its hierarchical organization, its adversarial style, and its claim to and valuing of rationality and objectivity. Naffine goes further to conclude that "indeed law is unable to muster the degree of rationality, internal coherence and consistency which both approaches necessarily imply. And yet law remains an important site of feminist struggle because of the many ways it constrains and controls the lives of women" (1990, 12-13). Naffine suggests that only some men benefit from the male construction of law. This view is consistent with work done by Messerschmidt (1997) and Connell (1995) as well as the more recent writing of Carmody (2003). Notwithstanding the variability in the construction of masculinity as it applies to law, there is still strong evidence of what Connell refers to as the "patriarchal dividend."

Smart (1989, 161) argues against the ready acceptance of the "resort to law" that further empowers law and disempowers women and children. That is, she expresses concern about locating a struggle for social change within the structure of the law because of what she perceives to be its essential maleness, which immediately serves to put women and children in a "one down" position or makes them dependent on the law for change.

Comack and Balfour (2004, 118) see sexual assault trials as politically charged. They refer to their research with defence lawyers: "While lawyers see the amendments as politically motivated and thus contrary to the principles of fundamental justice, their comments suggest that, for some of them, the strategies adopted in sexual assault cases are based on a purposeful defiance of the legislative reforms."

Dobash and Dobash (1992, 172-73) point out that "changing practices involves altering not just laws and policies but also the structures, perceptions and cultural practices that are deeply embedded in the system of justice." In some jurisdictions since implementation of the child sexual assault legislation, there has been a backlash against the increase in cases of child sexual abuse coming before the courts (Olafson, Corwin, and Summit 1993). This reaction appears to have taken the form of pathologizing the child victims as a means of discrediting them (Eberle and Eberle 1986) or pathologizing their mothers, claiming that the mothers plant the ideas in the children's minds in the heat of custody disputes (Gardner 1987). Some have also claimed that charges are the result of overly zealous investigators who take advantage of children's suggestibility. Some of the latest in this series of attempts to pathologize those who have been abused is the construction of "false memory syndrome" and "parental alienation syndrome" (Whitfield 2001). Additionally, extensive media coverage of the sexual abuse of male children in cases such as Mount Cashel, the training schools run by Christian Brothers in Ontario, the Catholic Church in Canada and the United States, and other institutional settings serves to focus attention on male offenders who are not the "norm." The convicted men are clerics who have taken vows of celibacy, and their victims are male children who are, for the most part, poor. This is reminiscent of the work of Platt (1977), Sutherland (1976), and others on the focus of the child-saving movement. The focus in these cases perpetuates the belief that men who abuse children are not ordinary men and that the victims are not the "norm" but the "poor" in a "public" institution.

The emphasis on the male victim is consistent with the work of Quinsey (1986), cited earlier. The focus on what can be put into the category of "homosexual" abuse feeds the perception, held by some, of homosexuality as aberrant, and obscures the reality that the largest amount of child sexual abuse cases are heterosexual with male offenders and female child victims in familial or close relationships (Finkelhor et al. 1990; MacMillan et al. 1997; Kong et al. 2003).

Conclusion

It is obvious from this brief overview of child sexual abuse, the law, and various researchers' opinions that a number of questions need to be addressed. I ask two central questions in this book: how does the criminal justice system view and respond to victims of child sexual abuse, and what influences that view? In answering these questions, other questions need to be addressed. What is the relative importance of the victim, the offender, and the offence? Is judicial comment overly sympathetic to the accused? Are judges overly concerned with the accused's background and the effect of the sentence/charge on him? Do they downplay or trivialize the severity of the offence? Is sexual assault considered a violent act in and of itself, or is violence viewed as an additional factor? What consideration is there of the victim in the sentencing process? To what degree is the "patriarchal dividend" evident in this consideration? What kinds of mitigating and aggravating circumstances are accepted in sentencing? What role does psychiatry play in delineating these variables? What is the language of the court? I will address these questions in subsequent chapters.

While recognizing that the "resort to law" is problematic, Smart (1989, 88) reinforces the significance of a careful examination of the practices of law: "Law remains a site of struggle. While it is the case that law does not hold the key to unlock patriarchy, it provides the forum for articulating alternative visions and accounts."

In 1993, Madame Justice Bertha Wilson contended that the reality of the justice system is predicated on a reality that supports traditional masculine understandings of the world, that most police officers, lawyers, Crown attorneys, and judges are male, and that those who are not are forced to live within a system of male beliefs and behaviours. Judges have been referred to as the "last elite priestly cult."[3] Their position in the system is pivotal to bringing about change.

The following chapters attempt to deconstruct the discourse of justices of the Court of Appeal of Ontario in their decisions about cases involving child sexual abuse. The patterns uncovered illustrate that, in these cases at least, efforts to change thinking by changing laws have had very uneven results.

---

3 Comment made by Parker Bars-Dunham on *Morningside,* CBC Radio, 23 September 1993, in reference to the issue of bans on publication of testimony.

2
Asking the Questions

Finding out what happens, on a broad scale, in courts is very difficult to do in Canada (Du Mont 2003). Finding answers to the questions posed at the end of the previous chapter was quite a challenge. It quickly became obvious that it was not possible to study patterns of original trial decisions, for a variety of reasons. Although it might have been reasonable to expect that the change in laws regarding child sexual abuse in the direction of specific legislation might make the tracking of these cases relatively simple, this was not the case. In spite of the proclamation of specific *Criminal Code of Canada* sections dealing with offences against children, many charges are still brought under the broader *Criminal Code* section dealing with sexual assault cases. Hence, it is impossible to determine who the victim is, child or adult, using the charge as an indicator unless the child sexual assault legislation is used. But one cannot assume that the charges laid under that section represent all the charges for child sexual abuse. Additionally, the files relating to criminal cases were not, at the time that I collected these data, centrally controlled or recorded by the Ministry of the Attorney General in Ontario or retained in the offices of the courts in which they were heard. They were returned to individual police divisions in the communities in which the investigations were conducted. I would have had to obtain permission to undertake the research from each police division, and I would have had to select files manually from among all the sexual assault files retained in each division. DuMont (2003), Comack and Balfour (2004, 14-15), and Martin (1993) describe the problems involved in getting access to data in this kind of research.

Because of the problems in and the likely unreliability of the data collection, I had to reject an early strategy of analyzing cases in three Ontario locations in favour of an analysis of Court of Appeal of Ontario decisions regarding child sexual abuse. The advantage to this source of data is that it contains cases from across Canada's most populated province as opposed to data limited to large urban centres. The disadvantage is that the cases appealed cannot be considered representative of the larger spectrum of child sexual abuse cases that comes before the courts for sentencing in Ontario. Therefore, no generalizations about the broader picture of abuse cases can be made. One can expect, however, that an examination of cases that come before the Court of Appeal of Ontario will indicate the standards for management of these cases and provide a window onto the state of child sexual abuse sentencing since the function of the Court of Appeal is, to some extent, to set sentencing guidelines.

Role of the Court of Appeal of Ontario

Young (1988, 7-8) cites *R. v. Morissette* (1970) of the Court of Appeal of Ontario in describing the role of a provincial court of appeal: "A provincial Court of Appeal, being the final court in dealing with appeals in respect of sentences, has a duty to give some guidance to trial judges in this field. Upon the Court of Appeal rests the responsibility of stating the principles underlying the imposition of a sentence so that at least uniformity of approach to this problem may be achieved. Also, while there can be no such thing as uniform sentences, it is incumbent upon the appellate court to see that the disparity in sentences for the same or similar offences can be rationalized (at 271)."

The *Criminal Code* outlines the role of the Court of Appeal of Ontario.[1] When a trial judge or a jury finds a defendant guilty or not guilty, both the Crown and the defendant are allowed to appeal those findings to a higher court. The defendant can appeal a finding of guilt, while the Crown can appeal a not guilty verdict. When the defendant is found guilty and subsequently sentenced, that person has the right to appeal the sentence if he or she thinks that it is too harsh. The Crown, on the other hand, can appeal the sentence if it believes that it is inadequate or too lenient. When the defendant appeals, he or she has nothing to lose in the sense that the only two possible outcomes are either a dismissal of the appeal, in which case the sentence remains the same, or a granting of the appeal, in which case the sentence may be reduced. The only time that the sentence is increased is when the Crown appeals and wins.[2]

Appeals by convicted offenders can be either processed through a lawyer hired for the purpose or conducted as "prisoner" appeals, in which

1 See http://laws.justice.gc.ca.

2 For a comprehensive account of the role of appellate courts in Canada, see Greene et al. (1998).

case the offender appears at the Court of Appeal to present his or her case. Many such appeals are withdrawn, presumably because the process is complex and difficult to conduct without the help of a lawyer, particularly when the offender is incarcerated. Appeals that arise out of summary convictions are heard by divisional courts. If those decisions are appealed, then the appeal is to the provincial court of appeal. Appeals of indictable offences are made to the provincial court of appeal.

R. v. F., G. (1991) is an example of a "prisoner" appeal that was withdrawn by the offender before it reached the Court of Appeal for a hearing. It involved an offender charged with sexually abusing his son, his daughter, and his wife. The offender abandoned the appeal, but the trial documents were on file. He was convicted of sexually abusing his children over a period of nine years by engaging in repeated acts of fellatio and vaginal and anal intercourse. The offender was sentenced to six years in prison. Because he abandoned his appeal, there was no possibility of a reduction in his sentence. He was not convicted for the sexual abuse of his wife since the judge found that she lacked credibility. The Crown did not appeal the acquittal even though the judge's reasons would likely have been questioned by some had the verdict been published. The trial judge gave as his reason for the acquittal that the wife didn't notice that the children were being abused, and "she admitted that she was a dirty housekeeper and that means ... she was not particularly concerned about the welfare of her children or she would have been a better housekeeper." That there was a great deal of evidence to support her claims about her husband's assaults and her heart attack in the midst of the abuse did not appear to be important to the trial judge in his reasons for determining guilt or innocence. This case is outside the scope of the studies reported here because it does not involve a completed appeal, one that the Court of Appeal heard and ruled on. It does raise questions, though, about which factors may be involved in the Crown's willingness or ability to launch appeals, and I will address these questions later in the book. In this case, since the offender received a significant sentence for the abuse of his children, the Crown may not have thought that an expenditure of scarce resources, appealing the acquittal in the case of the wife, notwithstanding the judge's reasoning, would have resulted in a longer term of imprisonment.

Relevance of Court of Appeal Decisions as Research Material

It seems reasonable to expect that an examination of Court of Appeal decisions would indicate the view of the judiciary of the relationship between the offender and the victim in the process of sentencing. It should also indicate the court's view of what the important factors are in these cases and of how sentencing decisions are made.

The original proposal for this research involved an analysis of the relevant cases considered by the Court of Appeal of Ontario since the 1988 change in legislation dealing with child sexual abuse. I considered this transitional period important since it was intended to mark a dramatic departure in the recognition and management of child sexual abuse (Badgley 1984). Yet I could not follow these timelines since the Court of Appeal had sent files for 1988 and 1989 to the archives. As a result, the files that were available covered the time period from May 1990 to those that had been closed and filed by July 1993, when I collected the data.

Since the Court of Appeal had only recently computerized its files, many of the files were not listed on its computer records.[3] The changed section of the *Criminal Code* was also not, as noted above, a good indicator of whether or not the case related to a child victim. For these reasons, it was necessary to manually review all of the files in the Court of Appeal to determine whether or not they were relevant to this research. A check of *every* file in the appeal court system led to a total of 201 files that dealt with matters involving child sexual abuse. Twenty-three (11.4 percent) of the cases initiated by an appellant, either the convicted offender or the Crown, were abandoned before they could be heard by the Court of Appeal. This left 193 completed appeals. Of these cases, 103, or somewhat more than half, were completed cases in which the sentence was being appealed, either by the Crown or by the offender.

About the time that I completed the analysis of the data in this first study, amendments were tabled and later passed by Parliament in 1996 that changed some of the ways of processing sentencing cases and resulted in changes to the possible outcomes of sentencing hearings. As a result, I launched a second study, using the same approach as the first, to track whatever changes these amendments may have precipitated and to track the progress of the construction of issues surrounding child sexual abuse. This study dealt with cases heard from late 1998 through 1999. After analysis of the data from the second study, it became clear that the number of Crown appeals had been dramatically reduced since

3 These files have two different types of identifying numbers. Files since computerization are titled C with a number following (e.g., C1000). Files opened prior to computerization are numbered according to the year in which they were filed and the order in which they were opened (e.g., 1/90). The second number indicates the year.

1993 from almost half of the appeals of sentences to 4 percent. The results of these two studies are included in the following chapters. I present some of the highlights of the studies in the latter part of this chapter.

Data Collection and Analysis

It was important to collect information on a number of variables that may have an influence on the outcome of a case and might provide competing explanations of the most significant factors in sentencing. For that reason, even at the time of the second study, when Court of Appeal decisions were available on the Internet, it was necessary to collect more information than just the reasons for sentences. It was important to view the case files in order to get demographic information about the victims and the offenders and to view whatever reports were submitted to the court at the time of sentencing. As well, in most files were trial transcripts that provided more detail than the final appeal decision would about the actual offence.

In the statistical analysis of the data collected, the dependent variables were the sentences. I conducted separate analyses using first the sentence received at trial as the dependent variable and then the sentence received after the case had been appealed and reviewed by the Court of Appeal as the dependent variable. I chose the independent variables in these analyses for their possible relationship to sentencing outcome: number of victims; number of convictions; plea; relationship of offender to victim; victim age at abuse; victim age at trial; offender age; duration of abuse; sex of victim; socio-economic status of offender; type of abuse; record of previous convictions for sexual assault; record of previous convictions for any offence other than sexual assault; victim impact statement; judge;[4] mitigating circumstances; aggravating circumstances; pre-sentence reports; and psychiatrist/psychologist reports. The independent variables covered a wide range of factors that might influence sentencing decisions. A linear regression method of analysis was used since it was the most appropriate to the variety of variable types in this study (Norman and Streiner 1986; Norusis 1993; Cramer 1994). SPSS was used to perform both enter and step-wise methods of regression analysis on each of the data sets, the 1990-93 time period and the 1998-99 time period. I found no statistical significance in the predictive capacity of any of the variables in either data set. The

4 This reflects the observations of Hogarth (1971) that the personality of the judge is more of an indicator of sentence outcome than other factors.

absence of any statistical significance once again refocused the study. Nonetheless, the research question remained essentially the same: Which factors can be identified as influencing judicial decisions?

If none of the expected variables demonstrates any statistical significance as a predictor, then what are the influences on judicial decision making? I needed another approach to answer the research question. A 1971 study by Hogarth clearly documented the variability that existed then in terms of how judges arrive at sentences in criminal cases in general: "The most obvious fact which emerges from the findings is that there are enormous differences among magistrates in nearly every aspect of the sentencing process. Magistrates differ in their penal philosophies, in their attitudes, in the ways in which they define what the law and the social system expect of them, in how they use information, and in the sentences they impose. In a variety of ways it was demonstrated that the magistrates interpret the world selectively in ways consistent with their personal motivations and subjective ends" (385-86). Over three decades later, the variability in sentencing that Hogarth observed was evident in this study. It seems that variability in sentencing is a feature of all types of criminal cases even after appeal. What, if anything, does this variability tell us? Is it consistent with Naffine's (1990) statement that law lacks rationality, internal coherence, and consistency, or is there something else about the social construction of judicial reasoning that should be explored? An additional question thus joined the original research question: Can the variability in Court of Appeal decisions about child sexual abuse cases be accounted for? Is it possible in an examination of judicial reasoning to get some clues about factors considered important in the process of sentencing?

Young (1988, 10) outlined the problem inherent in attempting a quantitative analysis of justices' use of mitigating and aggravating circumstances: "The myriad of available factors defy a quantitative analysis and it is more usual for the court to approach the factors in an impressionistic manner. Instead of ascribing relative weight to each factor and carefully balancing the significance of each, it is far more common to approach this task by listing the factors and then extracting an appropriate disposition as if the factors were all thrown in a melting pot. The final disposition is a sum of the parts (i.e., factors) but in its final form it is impossible to identify the contribution made by the individual parts." Is it really "impossible to identify the contribution made by the individual parts," as the quantitative analysis seems to indicate, or is it possible to extract some meaning from the way in which the parts are emphasized or constructed by the judges? What does "an impressionistic manner" mean? How are the judges' impressions formed? Can we identify the world views of the judges that might influence how they socially construct the cases before them?

Berger and Luckmann (1966, 52) indicate that "social order is a human product or, more precisely, an ongoing human production." The appeal court judges' product is the outcome of the sentencing appeal. What part does the justices' social construction of child abuse play in their decisions? Are their opinions based on gendered views of offenders and victims? Since a quantitative analysis had not been helpful in understanding how decisions were made, a qualitative analysis, specifically a content analysis, was indicated. The qualitative study ultimately undertaken here sought to explore possible answers to those questions raised above. Smart's (1989, 34) question "how does gender work in law and how does law work in gender?" was a component of the operating theoretical framework in a search for themes in decision making. If the court is a site of struggle for justice in terms of child sexual abuse, how was this struggle played out in these cases? What roles did the offender, the victim, the offence, and the experts play in the courtroom? How much emphasis was placed on each? What cultural or traditional role understandings operated in the court? Mohr and Roberts (1994, 5) explain some of the ambiguity related to the use of the sexual assault laws passed in 1983: "The drafters of the 1983 sexual assault provisions did not define 'sexual assault.' It is judges who, by default, become the lawmakers as far as the definition of the offence itself is concerned." This issue was raised in Parliament when the changes in the law were made in 1983 and flagged as a possible source of problems for implementation of the act.[5] How sexual assault and sexual abuse are defined is critical to the understanding of how sentences are arrived at. The most useful way of attempting to understand how decisions are made within a particular context is by using the individual cases as units of analysis (Yin 1989, 1993; Stake 2003). In this study, context is obviously an important part of the methodological consideration. Any attempt to study variables qualitatively that quantitatively have not shown any power as statistically significant predictors must consider the framework within which the variables exist and the interaction of those and other variables within that framework.

In the course of the original data collection, demographic data and all of the trial judges' reasons for sentences were transcribed, as were the

---

5 See *House of Commons Debates* (4 August 1982).

reasons for appeal and the reasons given by the Court of Appeal for the decisions. Photocopying of large numbers of pages of files was not available. Information about expert testimony and/or reports and presentence reports was also transcribed. Therefore, it was possible to analyze the contents of all of the cases using these materials.

I conducted content analyses (Weber 1990; Krippendorf 2004) of the cases to extract their themes and to measure the frequency of occurrence of these themes and their interrelationships. I reviewed all 103 cases for the first period of research and all forty-one cases for the second period of research, and I scrutinized the reasons given by the trial judges and the Court of Appeal of Ontario for their decisions. I listed and counted the reasons and calculated the frequency of occurrence of reasons, and themes emerged in terms of the reasons most frequently used. These reasons could be divided into the categories of mitigating and aggravating circumstances. The next step in the analysis was to see how some of these circumstances were used together and how they were linked to the characteristics of the offence, the offender, and the victim. It became obvious that, while some circumstances might be listed frequently, others were listed less frequently but emphasized more. For example, in the 1990-93 data, aggravating factors were often listed first in the decisions and then countered or answered by a shorter but more emphatic discussion of mitigating circumstances. Since I was guided in the search for themes by the theoretical concern about reproduction of traditional understandings of gender in law, the judicial attention given to intercourse or its absence highlighted how the concept of type of abuse was paired by judges and justices with other factors, such as the relationship of the offender to the victim. Even though regression methods did not find type of abuse or position of trust to be statistically significant predictors of sentence length, probably because of the dramatic variability of the sentences within those conditions, in cases in which intercourse was performed by a person in the position of trust, the offence was emphasized more frequently, and the sentences tended to be longer. In non-intercourse cases, mitigating factors received more emphasis much of the time. It was clear that, although the new sexual assault laws were intended to minimize these kinds of distinctions, some judges continued to construe them as relevant. This construction is described in detail in Chapter 3.

Although it would have been interesting to analyze the cases based on the socio-economic statuses of the offenders and their victims, it was not possible to find this information reliably in the court files. It was particularly difficult to ascertain the socio-economic statuses of the victims. There was some indication of the socio-economic statuses of some, but not many, of the offenders.

I also considered each case in terms of the trial judge's and the Court of Appeal's use of mitigating and aggravating circumstances. I listed these circumstances and counted their frequency. The content analysis allowed for an assessment of the weight that they had in each case. Cases that were similar in terms of other factors – such as type of abuse, age of the victim, relationship of the offender to the victim, and duration of the abuse – could be compared in terms of the emphasis placed on mitigation and aggravation by the trial judge and in terms of whether that emphasis was shared or rejected by the Court of Appeal in each case. A complete description and interpretation of the findings is presented in Chapter 4.

The emphasis on type of abuse and on mitigating factors illustrates the strength of the concern with the offender and the absence of consideration of issues relating to the victim. Chapter 5 illustrates how the victims' experiences may be minimized and how this is a clear example of the gendering of law. Examples of such gendering are cases in which judges accepted the notion that the victim consented to sexual contact, in some cases as a mitigating factor, in spite of a clear statement in the law that consent is not possible in cases of child sexual abuse. The law may be changed, but the interpretation of it may still be based on old notions. Analysis of how some victim issues were dealt with in the 1990-93 data demonstrates the disqualification of the victim's experience as "subjective" in some cases in contrast to the consideration given to "objective" facts about the offender. The 1999 data show some evidence of change in this dynamic.

I also analyzed the themes present in the reports made to the Court of Appeal. As noted in Chapter 1, medicine's neutrality has been challenged in the same way that law's has. I examined Smart's (1989, 17) contention that law and medicine interact "to disqualify other discourses" in my analysis of the reports presented to the court by psychiatrists and psychologists on behalf of offenders, by members of these professions on behalf of victims, by victims themselves in terms of the impacts of the offences on them, and by probation officers. I used the critiques of the medicalization of child molesters identified in Chapter 1 to analyze the content of the expert input to the court. I scrutinized reports in terms of how they dealt with the offence, the offender, and the victim. Themes emerged both from the reports concerning offenders and from the way in which judges and justices interpreted these reports, which provide further evidence of an emphasis on the offender in many cases to the exclusion of consideration of the offence and its impact on the victim. The reports emphasize a "commonsensical" or stereotypical understanding of "real" sexual offenders as strangers and rationalize the criminal behaviour of non-strangers as understandable or excusable given the offender's circumstances.

Finally, the qualitative methodology sheds light on the decision-making process of the Court of Appeal and how it has evolved over the time frame of the studies. While this work is limited in its generalizability to the broad practice of judges in courts around Ontario and Canada, it does tell us something about the Court of Appeal of Ontario's approach to dealing with cases of child sexual abuse at sentencing, and offers insight into how judges work at both the trial and appeal levels. While the original intent of the studies – to determine which factors are most important to trial judges in cases of child sexual assault – could not be achieved, this analysis reveals significant information about how judges arrive at decisions and the approach that an appellate court tends to take in deciding sentencing in such cases. Given the purpose of the appellate court in guiding lower courts, these are key issues to raise.

Preliminary Observations

As mentioned earlier, the "big" questions raised here will be examined in relation to appeals of sentences handed out in lower courts and dealt with in the Court of Appeal of Ontario. However, before going into detail about these questions, we should look at some of the demographic, descriptive, contextual information available on these cases. It is interesting to know the people involved in these cases and to understand, to some extent, how they got to this point.

In the 1990-93 population, 69 percent of the appeals were initiated by the offender, while 31 percent were initiated by the Crown. This distribution is considered unusually high in terms of the percentage of Crown appeals. The offender has everything to gain by appealing and in most senses nothing to lose. As noted earlier, an appeal initiated by a convicted person will either be decided in his or her favour or dismissed. The offender does not risk receiving more time by initiating an appeal. While offenders can bring appeals without lawyers, their success may depend on whether or not they meet the requirements for legal aid and get appeal certificates. The Crown, on the other hand, has to justify the expenditure of public funds, time, and other resources on appeals of acquittals and sentences. The likelihood that the Crown will appeal is less than that of the offender, and appeals are initiated only if there is a point to be made or there is some public outcry about a particular crime or series of crimes; that is, if the public climate is such that it demands that the Crown be more active in pursuing longer sentences. In these data, the number of Crown appeals likely reflects the relative newness of the legislation and public concern with the number of child sexual abuse cases in the news.

In the 1999 data, the picture changed dramatically. The number of Crown appeals went from 31 percent to 9 percent. The actual number of Crown appeals in the 1999 data was four. This may well be related to the Supreme Court decision in *R. v. C.A.M.* (1996), described in Chapter 1, in which the court encouraged deference to the trial judge's sentencing decisions.

In the 1990-93 data, 49 percent of offender appeals were allowed, while 51 percent were dismissed. During the same time frame, the Crown succeeded in 41 percent of its appeals and failed in 59 percent. In 1999, 41 percent of offender appeals were successful, while 59 percent were dismissed. The Crown succeeded in 75 percent of its appeals and failed in 25 percent. Since the number of Crown appeals was only four in this data set, this means that the Crown won three appeals and lost one.

The vast majority of children victimized in these cases were female (84 percent in 1990-93, 75 percent in 1998-99), and the minority were male (12 percent in 1990-93, 16 percent in 1998-99). A small number of cases (4 percent in 1990-93, 9 percent in 1998-99) involved victims of

Figure 2.1

Victim age at abuse and trial, 1990-93

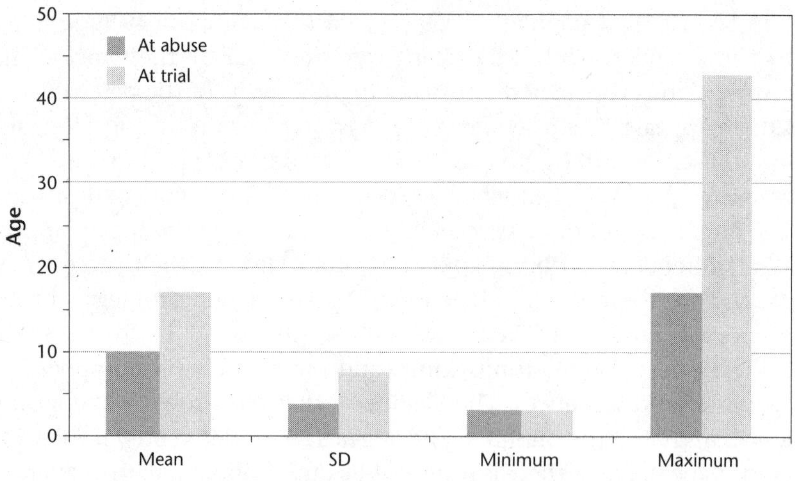

Figure 2.2

Victim age at abuse and trial, 1998-99

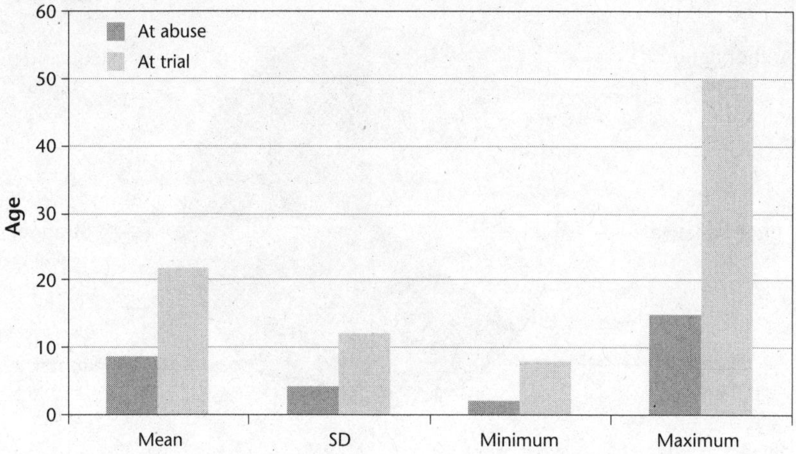

both sexes. This is consistent with Quinsey's (1986) comments, cited in Chapter 1, about the relative frequency of female victimization.

Figures 2.1 and 2.2 show the ages of the victims at abuse and at trial. The mean victim age and the standard deviations (SD) in both time periods are consistent with research done on the incidence of child sexual abuse (Badgley 1984; Finkelhor et al. 1990). The victim age at trial reflects the fact that in a number of cases the abuse was not reported by the victims until they had reached adulthood.

Figures 2.3 and 2.4 show the relationship between the victims and the offenders. The most significant difference between the two data sets is a small number of appeals dealing with sibling abuse in the 1998-99 data.

The duration of abuse was similar in both time periods. The mean period of abuse in 1990-93 was 4.1 years, while in 1998-99 it was 4.6 years. The minimum period of abuse in 1990-93 was that which occurred on one occasion only, while the maximum period was abuse over seventeen years. In 1998-99, the minimum period of abuse was one occasion, and the maximum period was 9.6 years.

Figures 2.5 and 2.6 illustrate the types of abuse in these cases. It is important to keep in mind, as will be obvious later in the book, that many of the cases involved more than one form of abuse.

The mean age of an offender at abuse in 1990-93 was 33.8 years, with a standard deviation of 9.9 years. It is thus probable that two of three offenders were from twenty-four to forty-four years of age at the

Figure 2.3

Relationship of offender to victim, 1990-93

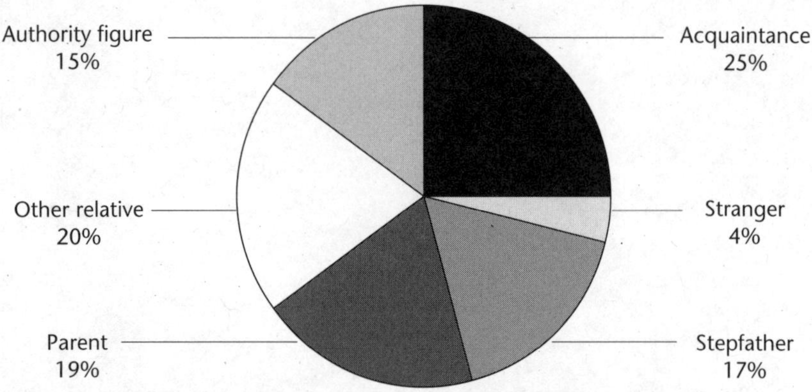

Figure 2.4

Relationship of offender to victim, 1998-99

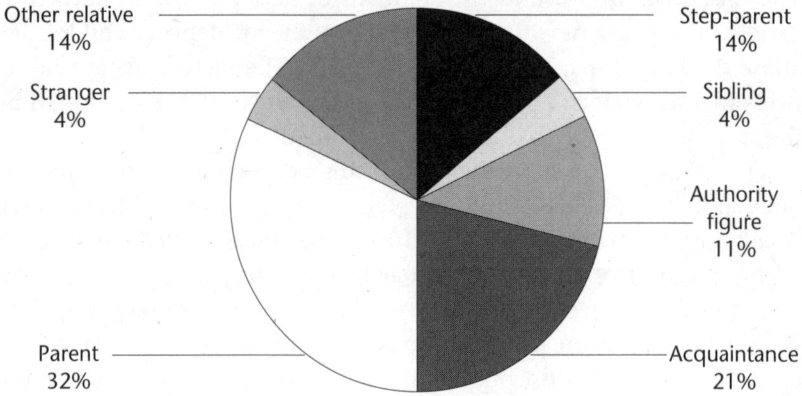

beginning of the abuse. The minimum age of an offender was seventeen years, while the maximum age was eighty-one years. The mean age of the offenders in 1999 was 45.8 years, which is older than the mean age of offenders in the early data. However, the standard deviation is

Figure 2.5

Types of abuse, 1990-93

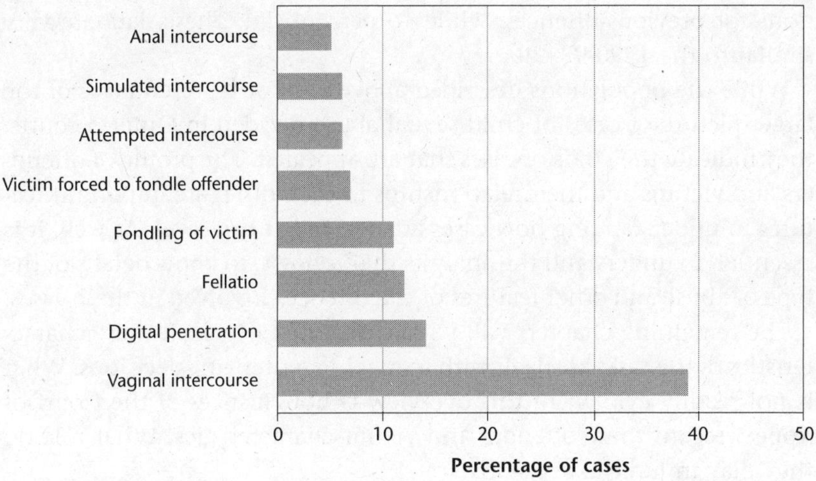

Figure 2.6

Types of abuse, 1998-99

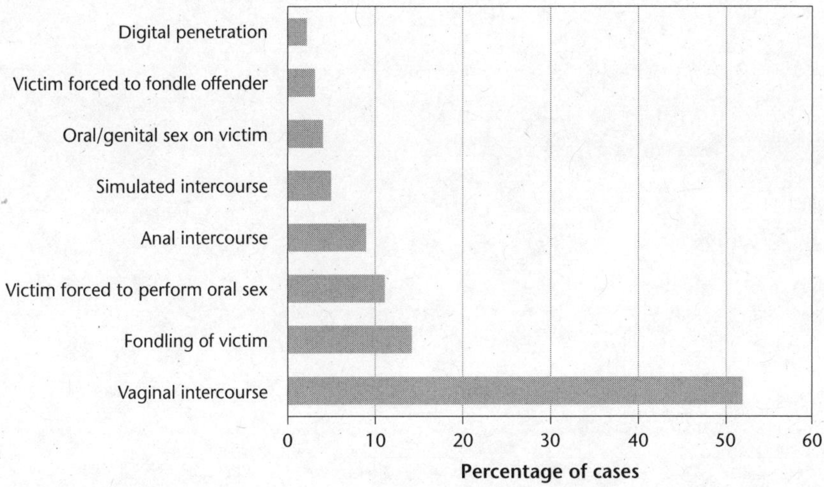

greater in this data at 14.9 years. The minimum age was twenty, while the maximum was seventy-three.

In the 1990-93 data, no previous convictions for sex offences were registered in 83 percent or four-fifths of the cases, while 17 percent or one-fifth did have previous convictions involving sexual assault. In the 1998-99 data, there was no information about previous offences in two cases. In the others, 82 percent of the offenders did not have convictions for previous offences, while 16 percent did. These data are very similar to the 1990-93 data.

While the populations described above are not representative of the larger picture of cases of child sexual abuse decided in Ontario courts, they indicate the kinds of cases that are appealed. The profile of offenders and victims and their relationships to each other are important features in understanding how cases are decided at this level. As well, it is essential, to understand the analysis that follows, to know details of the type of abuse and other features of the offences involved in these cases.

The remaining chapters will paint a picture of how all these characteristics of the cases are dealt with in making sentencing decisions. What is not readily evident in this overview is how justices of the Court of Appeal regard these offender and victim characteristics. What role do they play in judicial decisions?

3 The Essential Offence

What is child sexual abuse? Who decides? In making the decision, from whose perspective is the abuse viewed? How do judges decide which sexual acts are more or less offensive? To whom are they more or less offensive? The concerns raised in Chapter 2 about the absence of a definition of sexual assault in the law are central to the construction of this issue. As indicated in Chapter 1, Bills C-127 and C-15, and the resulting legislation, were attempts to change the emphasis in offences relating to sexually intrusive behaviour by shifting it from sex to violence. This was done by changing the offence from rape to sexual assault; however, the definition of sexual assault was left to the interpretation of the judiciary. In this chapter, we will see how the Court of Appeal of Ontario has, even with this supposed shift in emphasis, maintained the previous construct of rape as the most serious type of offensive conduct by emphasizing a distinction between penetration and non-penetration.

Type of abuse was cited by trial judges and the Court of Appeal as a mitigating factor or as an aggravating factor in both the 1990-93 study and the 1998-99 study. The judges dealt with offences by dividing them into two categories: vaginal or anal penetration, and non-penetration. That is, although penetration is not mentioned in the law, they distinguished between cases in which intercourse was part of the abuse and those in which it was not. This chapter analyzes how and why these factors are used as an explanation for sentencing decisions.

There has been little comprehensive research on the effects of abuse in terms of what type of abuse the survivor has experienced. Browne and Finkelhor (1986), considering what they refer to as the "speculation" of Groth and Birnbaum (1978) that certain variables are closely related to the impact of abuse, reviewed the literature on the trauma of sexual abuse by type and found that, although Bagley and Ramsay (1986) reported that penetration was significant in a sample of a mental health population, Briere and Runtz (1989) did not find it so in a non-mental health sample. They cite several other studies that did not demonstrate any link. Browne and Finkelhor looked as well at the literature on duration and frequency of abuse, age of victim at abuse, relationship to offender, and force/aggression, among other factors. They concluded that the most likely factors in long-term negative impacts of sexual abuse were duration, abuse by a father or stepfather or someone perceived by the victim as a father figure, and the presence of aggression. Briere and Elliott (2003, 1217), in a study of self-reported victims of child sexual abuse in the general, not a clinical, population, found that "sexual abuse at a later age, a greater number of abuse incidents, multiple abusers, victimization that involved oral, anal or vaginal penetration, and a greater level of emotional upset at the time of the abuse were equal factors in long term impact of the abuse." All the researchers conclude, in general, that so many issues about how the research has been conducted in this area make it difficult to reach valid and reliable conclusions.

Penetration

Preoccupation with vaginal or anal penetration as the extreme form of abuse is evident in most of the data since it is used as the benchmark for determining sentence. In Chapter 1, I cited Brown (1991, vi) as noting that the emphasis on penetration was a serious concern in how the new law was being interpreted: "The system continues to downgrade the seriousness of the assault if there has been no vaginal penetration." This concern about penetration was expressed even earlier by Nadin-Davis (1983) and Ruebsaat (1985) in their separate analyses of the sexual assault law proclaimed in 1983: "Given the broader scope for the exercise of judicial discretion with respect to sentencing contained in the 1983 amendments, there is a danger that many of the objectionable features of the offences will now reemerge at the sentencing stage. Examples of this might include: (1) an undue emphasis on the absence of penetration; (2) consideration of the complainant's previous sexual history in general or past sexual liaison with the accused in particular, as mitigating factors; (3) viewing the complainant's lifestyle as somehow contributing to her chances of being sexually assaulted" (Ruebsaat 1985, 94).

For many judges, and for the Court of Appeal, penetration has considerable significance. A sentencing benchmark[1] was set by the Court of Appeal of Ontario in the decision written by Blair JA, in *R. v. B.* (1990):

---

1 A more recent benchmark was established by Moldaver JA, in *R. v. D.D.* (2002).

> The decisions of provincial appellate courts establish that, except in unusual circumstances, a penitentiary sentence is called for in all cases of sexual abuse of children to whom the convicted person stands in loco parentis if the abuse involves sexual intercourse. Such sentences reflect society's denunciation of this abhorrent conduct and the breach of trust reposed on parents or guardians of children. Counsel on both sides agreed that the usual range of sentences for this type of offence is from three to five years. The length of sentences within the range of three to five years depends on a number of factors. These include the age of the victim, the duration and frequency of the sexual assaults, the criminal record of the offender, the effects on the victim and the presence or absence of collateral violence or remorse.

The benchmark sentence for assaults that include intercourse, then, involves three key elements: (1) if the assault involves intercourse, and (2) it is committed by a person in a position of trust with respect to the victim of the assault, then (3) the sentence is supposed to be three years in the penitentiary. Tables 3.1 and 3.2 demonstrate the actual pattern of sentencing at both the trial and appeal levels. Results are summarized by median, mean, and standard deviations in each condition. Obvious in these tables is that, while the medians and means in the cases of intercourse and position of trust are higher than in the other cases, the standard

Table 3.1

Trial judge sentences (in months) by type of abuse and relationship, 1990-93

Trial judge	Median	Mean	SD
Intercourse loco parentis	30.5	38.7	31.1
Intercourse non-loco parentis	23.9	33.6	21.4
No intercourse loco parentis	14	21.3	20.4
No intercourse non-loco parentis	12	18.8	19

Table 3.2

Appeal court sentences (in months) by type of abuse and relationship, 1990-93

Appeal court	Median	Mean	SD
Intercourse loco parentis	36	40.8	28.1
Intercourse non-loco parentis	23.9	27	20
No intercourse loco parentis	12	21	22.9
No intercourse non-loco parentis	12	14.4	15.4

Table 3.3

Trial sentences (in months) by type of abuse, 1999

Trial 1999	Median	Mean	SD
Intercourse loco parentis	48	44	25
Intercourse non-loco parentis	25	28	7
No intercourse loco parentis	18	38	46
No intercourse non-loco parentis	20	20	20

Table 3.4

Appeal sentences (in months) by type of abuse, 1999

Appeal 1999	Median	Mean	SD
Intercourse loco parentis	33	33	27
Intercourse non-loco parentis	25	20	18
No intercourse loco parentis	3	17	30
No intercourse non-loco parentis	14.5	9	22

deviations are so large in all cases that they reinforce the observations made earlier about the variability and unpredictability of sentencing.

In the 1999 data, the results are somewhat different, but the data continue to illustrate the same variability. Tables 3.3 and 3.4 outline similar conditions. Interestingly, the sentences are somewhat higher in the trial judges' sentences in these data. The range of sentences is lower than in the 1990-93 data and continues to show a great deal of variability from the Blair benchmark of three to five years. It is clear from these tables that, while there is considerable variability in all of the conditions, the longest mean sentences involve cases of intercourse. The variability increases in cases in which intercourse is not present. In these cases, the standard deviations are larger than the means. As well, the means and medians in cases of intercourse are higher. For Court of Appeal decisions, in cases in which intercourse is present along with a condition of "in loco parentis," the median and mean are the highest. A closer examination of the actual cases gives some indication of how this pattern developed in these data.

1990-93 Cases

As noted above, Mr. Justice Blair, in *R. v. B.*, defined the factors involved in determining sentence in cases of intercourse committed by someone in a position of trust as being "the age of the victim, the duration and frequency of the sexual assaults, the criminal record of the offender, the effects on the victim and the presence or absence of collateral violence or remorse." Table 3.5 shows all the cases in the 1990-93 data that involved intercourse where a parent or step-parent was the perpetrator. The factors described by Blair are used with the exception of the more complex factor of victim impact, which will be discussed in Chapter 5. The age column gives the age of the youngest victim at the beginning of abuse if there is more than one victim. Of the twenty-two cases listed in the table, only nine fall within the range of sentence indicated as appropriate by Blair. Even those that fall within the designated appropriate range are not explainable in terms of the factors cited above.

It is interesting to compare two of the 1990-93 cases, *R. v. McNall* (1992) and *R. v. K., D.* (1991), which are very similar except in the sentence. The first, appealed by the Crown, involved the sexual assault over a ten-year period of three girls who were daughters of the offender, and over an eight-year period of a fourth girl, a friend of the daughters. The abuse took place over a nineteen-year time period in total, when the offender was aged twenty-six to forty-six. The daughters were approximately five to fifteen years of age at the time when each was abused, and the friend was aged five to thirteen at the time of abuse. The offender digitally penetrated each victim, eventually progressing to intercourse. The victims reported considerable threats and aggression accompanying the abuse. The offender had a high school education and worked as a salesperson. His wife taught at a community college. The pre-sentence report indicated that he demonstrated no remorse and denied having had intercourse with the victims. The charges were brought by the survivors of the abuse when they were adults, and the offender went to trial when he was sixty years old. The age of the offender was included as a mitigating circumstance in the trial judge's reason for sentence. He was sentenced to a provincial term of two years less one day and three years of probation to follow because the last incident of abuse occurred in 1978 and because of the impact of the psychiatric testimony on the judge, who agreed with the psychiatrist that the offender presented no danger to society, had no previous record, and would be much better dealt with through treatment. The provincial sentence allowed him to retain contact with the psychiatrist while incarcerated and on probation. The Court of Appeal disagreed with the sentence and concluded that "this case involves sexual assault upon 4 young girls, 3 of whom were the appellant's daughters and over many years, including intercourse. The sentence imposed of two years less a day is entirely inadequate. Even taking into consideration all the mitigating circumstances set forth by the learned trial judge, we consider an

Table 3.5

Cases involving intercourse by parent or step-parent, 1990-93

Case	Relation	Duration	# Victims	Age	Violence	Remorse	Record	Original sentence	Appeal sentence
401/90	Father	14 years	1	4	no	no	no	5.5 years	5.5 years
C8074	Stepfather	13 years	1	10	no	yes	no	2 years –1 day	2 years –1 day
C10530	Father	10 years	4	5	yes	no	no	2 years –1 day	8 years
75/90	Stepfather	10 years	4	5	yes	no	no	11 years	11 years
C12226	Father	10 years	3	10	no	no	yes	2 years –1 day	3 years
464/90	Father	6 years	1	13	no	no	no	2 years –1 day	3.5 years
C12603	Father	6 years	1	8	yes	no	no	6 months	18 months
C11464	Father	6 years	1	9	yes	yes	no	6 years	4 years
C5763	Stepfather	5 years	1	11	no	no	no	4 years	4 years
C11568	Father	5 years	1	10	yes	no	no	4 years	4 years
C11389	Father	5 years	1	11	no	no	yes	2 years –1 day	2 years –1 day
C6966	Father	4 years	2	12	no	no	no	3.5 years	3.5 years
C7241	Stepfather	3 years	1	7	yes	no	no	Prob. 3 years	9 months
C8768	Stepfather	3 years	2	10	yes	yes	no	1 year + Prob.	18 months
C10854	Father	2 years	1	7	yes	no	no	5 years	5 years
633/90	Stepfather	2 years	2	3	yes	no	yes	6 years	4 years
C12071	Stepfather	1 year	1	5	no	no	no	4 years	4 years
896/90	Stepfather	8 months	2	4	yes	no	yes	7.5 years	5 years
727/90	Father	8 months	1	14	no	no	no	Prob. and CSC	18 months
C6004	Mother	7 months	2	3	no	yes	no	6 years	3 years
50/91	Stepfather	7 months	1	9	no	yes	no	3.5 years	3.5 years
432/90	Stepfather	1 month	1	15	no	no	no	5 years	5 years

Note: Original case file numbers are used here, as some of the titles for different cases (usually consisting of initials) are identical. Files opened prior to the computerization of the Court of Appeals case numbering system are numbered according to the year in which they were filed and the order in which they were opened (e.g., 1/90); files since computerization are titled C with a number following.

appropriate sentence to have been one of eight years in the penitentiary. Leave to appeal is granted and the sentence varied to one of 8 years on each count to be served concurrently."

In *R. v. K., D.,* the offender, forty-six at the time of the trial, fondled, digitally penetrated, and engaged in oral sexual practices and intercourse with four stepdaughters over a ten-year period with the oldest child, a twelve-year period with the second child, a ten-year period with the third child, and a one-year period with the fourth. Two of the children were five, one was seven, and the other was thirteen when the abuse began. These victims also reported threats and aggression. The stepfather had a PhD, lectured at a university, and ran his own research company. The mother was described as having graduate education and holding a responsible position. The trial judge listed eight factors that he considered in arriving at a sentence of eleven years.

> In this particular case, the following factors are paramount:
>
> 1 The inherent gravity of the offences.
> 2 The duration of time over which the impugned conduct lasted.
> 3 The number of victims involved. (That, of course, is in relation to the totality of the sentence imposed.)
> 4 The degree of violence and threat of violence associated with the commission of the offences.
> 5 The complete lack of remorse on the part of the accused.
> 6 The obvious thoughtful deliberation that went into the commission of most of the offences charged.
> 7 The need to reflect in any sentence imposed society's revulsion and abhorrence of such conduct.
> 8 The inevitable and, no doubt, irreparable devastation that the accused's conduct has caused to the lives of his young and innocent victims which, no doubt, will result in much, if not most, of their emotional energies being spent on merely surviving rather than living. At one point in their lives, the accused has denied them the bliss of innocence and on the other, he has changed what ought to be hope into despair.
>
> I have had careful regard to the submissions made by counsel on the question of sentencing, as I have had regard to all of the circumstances of this case. Briefly stated, the accused has callously breached that most sacred of trusts, namely that of parenthood, a breach that will leave in its wake devastating consequences that will, for a long time, maybe forever, reverberate in the lives of his victims, as well as the lives of

> those with whom they may chance to have intimate relationships. The sentence, in my opinion, must reflect that moment.

The Court of Appeal rejected the offender's appeal of the sentence: "The offences involved are of a most serious kind. The frequency and duration and the number of victims and the terrible impact of the offences on the victims are such that they call for punishment at the highest end of the range for sentences imposed for somewhat similar offences. We are of the view that the sentence was a fit one. Accordingly, leave to appeal is granted and the appeal is dismissed."

Although these offences appear to have been very similar, the trial judges' views of them were not. Two other differences are evident. One is that the sections of the *Criminal Code of Canada* under which the offenders were charged were very different. The first case involved only four charges covering the entire period of abuse – that is, one charge per victim. They were three counts of incest and one count of rape (s. 142 under the old legislation). In the second case, the offender was charged with seventeen counts of sexual assault; one count each of sexual assault with a weapon, assault, assault causing bodily harm, and sexual interference; and three counts of illicit intercourse with a stepdaughter (R.S.C. 1970, c. C-34). This was the only case in the database in which this type of charging related to the number of incidents as opposed to the number of victims. It appears that, at the original trial, in the second case, the offender had the proverbial book thrown at him. It is possible that in the first case the offences were so dated that only general charges could be brought because of the inability of witnesses to testify as to times and dates. This may not be the best explanation, however, since cases in which charges were laid at the time of the abuse often had only one or two counts dealing with a large number of incidents. Some of this can be explained with the *Kienapple*[2] principle. In the first case, the offender entered a plea of guilty, whereas in the second case the offender responded to the charges with a not guilty plea.

In the first case, the reports presented to the court were primarily about the offender. The pre-sentence report mentioned victim impact, and the victims themselves wrote statements; however, the report written by the psychiatrist was about the offender. In the second case, the

2 *Kienapple* was an important case that set the precedent preventing an accused from being convicted (or punished) for more than one offence arising from the same set of facts. See http://jurist.law.utoronto.ca/dictionary.htm.

reports were primarily about the victims and were compiled and written by psychiatrists and social workers from a children's hospital and by professional clinical staff of a well-known and highly respected child treatment agency. The reports were very detailed assessments of each child. In addition, each child wrote a compelling statement about the impact of the abuse on her. There is a strong qualitative difference in the emphasis in each case, although the type of abuse, the duration of abuse, the number of victims, and the degree of threat and aggression were similar. The original outcome was different by a period of nine years, and the outcome after appeal was different by a sentence of three years. The comments made by the Court of Appeal were also stronger in the second case in terms of its recognition of the harm done to the victims. This may have been a result of the professional reports available to the court. The eleven-year sentence in the second case was the longest in this database, and the number of charges laid was the greatest. The number and type of reports that dealt with the impacts of the abuse on the victims were also unusual.

Other cases in Table 3.5 benefit from a closer look at the reasons for sentence and the decisions of the appellate court. In *R. v. E., R.J.* (1990), the Court of Appeal thought that re-incarceration of the offender would be a hardship to him: "While a penitentiary term may have been appropriate at the time of trial, given the mitigating factors including the community service which the respondent has to date performed and the respondent's circumstances as they now exist, we would impose a reformatory sentence of 18 months." In imposing the sentence, the Court of Appeal took into consideration that the offender had already completed 500 hours of community service as part of the original sentence. In *R. v. C., S.* (1993), the appellant was the offender, not the Crown, so an increase in the sentence was not part of the discussion.

In *R. v. G., P.E.R.* (1992), a stepfather abused one child over a thirteen-year period. He received a sentence of two years less one day plus two years of probation to follow. The man abused his stepdaughter for six years until it was discovered but not reported, resolved not to do it again, and then continued the abuse for another seven years. The trial judge emphasized rehabilitation in his reasons for sentence. In this case, it appears that good reports from treatment personnel positively affected the outcome of the appeal. In *R. v. McNall,* described earlier, a treatment rationale for similar abuse of four children over a shorter period of time was not acceptable to the Court of Appeal. The difference in that case may have been, in part at least, that the offender was still serving his sentence at the time of the appeal, while in this case the offender had been released. The reluctance of justices of the Court of Appeal to re-incarcerate was also a factor in *R. v. P., R.B.* (1992).

In *R. v. C., M.E.* (1993), the offender was sentenced to six months of imprisonment (with a recommendation for immediate release on the Temporary Absence Program) and eighteen months of probation. The victim impact statement outlined the impairment to the young woman's personal development, her inability to form close relationships with males, the loss of childhood and innocence, and the damage to relationships with other family members, particularly her mother. The young woman experienced suicidal ideation and had undergone group and individual counselling. In his reasons for the sentence, the trial judge emphasized the offender's economic situation and the witnesses who testified about his "good character." The judge also noted his willingness to attend a sexual behaviours clinic with his wife. The Crown appealed the sentence, citing examples such as "during the act of intercourse, the respondent continued, despite the victim's plea to stop, given the pain he was causing her," and "the respondent's utter disregard for the victim, treating the assaults, especially those in the bathroom, as a joke, laughing at her when she tried to escape." Rehabilitation again seemed to be the focus of the appeal court decision. No mention was made of the victim impact or of the violence to which the Crown referred, and although the sentence was increased the recommendation for immediate release on a temporary absence permit was reiterated, with no explanation why it was appropriate. The message seemed to be that the offender was attempting to rehabilitate and that this effort was important to the decision of the court. The sentence was certainly not in the range given by Mr. Justice Blair even though the abuse occurred over a significant period of time, involved "collateral violence," and resulted in considerable impact on the victim.

In *R. v. I., R.* (1992), a Crown appeal, the justices of the Court of Appeal considered factors other than the offence in their decision:

> In our view, the sentence failed to reflect the gravity of the offences in the 8 counts of sexual assault which involved two young female complainants over a period of time and genital touching by an offender who was in a position of trust, in loco parentis, vis a vis the children. We consider however the respondent's plea of guilty, and the remorse exhibited and the serious consequences to him in terms of loss of family, loss of employment and general disgrace in a small community. The appeal is allowed, sentence varied to be 12 months on counts 1, 4,

> 5, 6, 7, 8, and six months on counts 2 and 3 to be served consecutively to the sentence of 12 months ... The probation order shall stand.

Originally, the offender was sentenced on all the above counts concurrently, which means that he would serve the sentences for the offences at the same time, ultimately serving out the longest. The Court of Appeal changed the individual sentences to make some of them consecutive to the others; that is, some were changed so that they were served after the others instead of at the same time. The sentences of six months were added onto the sentences of twelve months, resulting in a sentence of eighteen months of incarceration.

1998-99 Cases

In contrast to the 1990-93 data, all but two of the cases in Table 3.6 met the benchmark sentence of three years set by Mr. Justice Blair. The first case that did not, *R. v. D., P.* (1999), involved a father who abused his daughter over a period of four years, beginning when she was six years old, by exposing his genitals to her, masturbating in front of her, fondling her and digitally penetrating her, performing cunnilingus, forcing her to perform fellatio, and simulating and performing intercourse on her. The intercourse was described as "incomplete" and was apparently performed at the end of the long period of other abuse. The offender was charged with sexual interference and invitation to sexual touching. The child disclosed the abuse at age ten. The offender was thirty-six to forty years old during the time of abuse.

In his rationale for sentencing, the trial judge gave as his reasons that the offender had no previous offences and had been financially responsible during his common-law relationship. He had been in his present job for over ten years and had been given increasing responsibility over time. The judge indicated that the offender came from a dysfunctional family and that he abused alcohol. There was some information that he had been sexually abused as a child and that his family and friends continued to support him and could provide a structure for his monitoring in terms of public safety and rehabilitation. He entered a guilty plea early in the proceedings and began counselling soon after disclosure. He accepted responsibility and indicated willingness to assist his daughter financially or in any other way to recover. According to the judge, he no longer represented a danger to the family or the community, "providing he continues and makes progress with his counseling and substance abuse programs." The trial judge identified the issues as "general deterrence and denunciation with respect to the particular facts of the case and a determination of a sentence that is proportionate to the gravity of [his] actions." The judge accepted the argument of the defence that the case did "not fall into the category of cases relied upon by the Crown asking for penitentiary, and that your activities with your daughter did not involve a level of conduct as represented in those cases cited, namely, repetitive intercourse." The judge interpreted the benchmark as being cases that "generally involve sexual activity that included a greater degree and frequency of intercourse or sexual conduct." He went on to say to the offender:

> [you] never used physical force as a threat or device to obtain your personal gratification, but I also recognize that the psychological force of a trusted parent on a young child is so powerful, especially where the age of the child and the circumstances and the relationship between father and daughter are such that the child lacks any reasonable opportunity to repel or resist that force. The acts speak for themselves. The complainant eventually disclosed the matter to her mother last December, 1997, when she thought she may be pregnant from having sexual intercourse with her father ... Weighing all the mitigating and aggravating circumstances, directing my mind to the provisions of the *Criminal Code* that relate to sentencing, and those that there were more particularly in issue in this case, denunciation and general deterrent, but the others as well, including your rehabilitation, your remorsefulness, specific deterrent and protection of the community, in view of all the circumstances I am imposing a sentence of two years less one day, plus three years probation.

The trial judge seemed to believe that intercourse in this case was the primary point in the decision. He did not dwell on the potentially intrusive effects of forced fellatio, which according to Briere and Elliott (2003), as noted earlier, are at least as potentially harmful as intercourse. As well, this judge thought that there needed to be a repetition of the intercourse for the penitentiary benchmark to be invoked. He seemed to favour the provincial sentence because it allowed him to put the offender on probation to follow the sentence and thereby give him the opportunity to continue treatment under supervision in the community. This was the theme in the trial judge's sentence in *R. v. McNall,* cited earlier. The trial judge also did not mention the information in the presentence report pointing out that the offender had been sexually involved with his sisters when they were children. As well, the psychologist's report available to the judge did not mention this previously undisclosed information. This case was appealed by the offender, not by the Crown, so there was no question of increasing the sentence.

In the other 1998-99 case that did not meet the three-year benchmark, *R. v. A., H.* (1998), but in which the judge did impose a penitentiary sentence, no reasons for the sentence were available that would shed light on the trial judge's thinking in the case. It involved charges under the pre-1983 *Criminal Code;* they were incest, gross indecency, and indecent assault. The victim was five years old when the abuse began and thirteen in 1981 when she told her mother about it. In 1985, she reported it to the police. "Much as the investigating officer considered the complainant to be a reliable and believable witness, after consulting with Crown counsel, it was felt, for reasons which proved to be unsound, that it would be difficult to secure a conviction against the appellant. Accordingly, a decision was made not to prosecute and this was brought to the attention of the complainant and the appellant." The victim persisted in asking for charges to be laid, and they finally were in 1993. There is very little information about the offence in the file and minimal information about the offender. There were reports about victim impact from a physician who had examined her as a child and from victim/survivor services indicating that she had been involved in therapeutic programs since the abuse. Again, this case was appealed by the offender and not by the Crown.

In the case involving the longest sentence, *R.v. R., H.* (1998), which also involved the longest period of abuse, the offender received a five-year term for the offence of incest, which involved vaginal and anal intercourse with five victims and a sentence of three years added for a charge of indecent assault under the old legislation. The judge's reasons for the sentence included deterrence to the offender and deterrence to the public as well as a concern about repetition of the behaviour, so protection of the public was a consideration.

There were other cases in the 1999 data in which the offender was not a parent but was in a position of trust and the abuse consisted of intercourse. In *R. v. N., W.R.* (1999), an offender was convicted of three counts of sexual touching, two counts of sexual exploitation, one count of obstructing justice, and three counts of failing to comply for hugging and kissing that evolved to mutual fondling, then to oral sex, and then to "numerous encounters where they engaged in sexual intercourse." The offences took place over an eighteen-month period and involved a man who was forty-four at the time when the offences began and a victim who was twelve. The offender was the victim's neighbour and

Table 3.6

Cases involving father/stepfather intercourse, 1999

Case	Relation	Duration	# Victims	Age	Violence	Remorse	Record	Original sentence	Appeal sentence
C31319	Father	4 years	1	6	no	yes	no	2 years –1 day	2 years –1 day
C22766	Stepfather	2 years	1	10	no	?	yes	3 years	3 years
C22761	Father/ grandfather	28 years	5	13	no	no	no	8 years	8 years
C23088	Father	8 years	1	5	no	no	no	2.5 years	2.5 years
C24588	Father	2 years	1	4	no	no	no	5 years	5 years
C24344	Father	14 years	3	5	no	yes	no	5 years	5 years
C25432	Father	13 years	1	4	no	no	no	4.5 years	4.5 years
C28966	Stepfather	1.25 years	1	5	no	no	yes not sex	4 years	4 years
C27047	Father/ stepfather	18 years	3	12	no	no	no	6 years	6 years

Note: Original case file numbers are used here, as some of the titles for different cases (usually consisting of initials) are identical.

was identified by the sentencing judge as being in a position of trust. The offender appealed his sentence and contested the conclusion that he was in a position of trust. In his reasons for sentencing, the judge cited what he perceived as mitigating circumstances: that his family was supportive, that he had a gentle, engaging personality, and that he had experienced deterioration following the death of his son. The judge went on to say that "the court is not confident that it understands the accused's motivations, past and future, towards [the victim]. Obviously, the facts speak for themselves. Only jail kept Mr. N away from [the victim]. He says that he understands the immorality of his relationship with one so young. There are, however, indications that Mr. N lacks insight into the extent of his wrongdoing. He has undertaken, personally and through counsel in open court, to stay away from her. The question remains, is [he] so troubled by life's circumstances that he cannot, of his own volition, do so?"

The judge cited the probation and psychiatric reports, which stated that the offender needed counselling and that he lacked direction and represented a risk to reoffend with this victim. The offender was in jail for twelve and a half months because he violated the terms of his bail, which indicated that he must stay away from the victim. The judge noted that being in jail had been difficult for the offender , as the notoriety of the trial had been. Even though the judge recognized that violation of the terms of release was an aggravating factor and pointed to the need for specific deterrence, he appears to have taken the time served awaiting trial as a credit in terms of calculation of the sentence, which might have made sense under other circumstances; in this case, however, it seems to have been counterintuitive. The judge apparently thought that the man needed treatment. The probation and psychiatric reports, however, were not very optimistic. The probation report listed his gambling addiction, his mismanagement of money, his self-destructive behaviour, and the fact that "he has lived the life of a teenager" without any sense of direction for the previous four years. The psychiatric report compiled during a thirty-day, court-ordered assessment stated that "the offender says he feels resentful, ashamed and guilty about his actions but does not regret them." It quotes him as saying that he thinks he was a good influence on the victim because "he was able to show her what it is like to be loved." The report concluded with the comment that he could be a continuing risk to reoffend with the present victim.

The offender appealed his sentence, claiming that he was not in a position of trust and that he should have been given a conditional sentence. The Court of Appeal rejected both arguments:

> In our view, there was ample support, in the circumstances, disclosed by the evidence, regarding the evolution of their relationship, the complainant's vulnerability and weaknesses and the significant differences in their ages, for the trial judge's finding that the appellant stood in a position of trust to the complainant ... Given the circumstances of the offences of which the appellant was convicted, the term of incarceration imposed was not beyond the appropriate range. The trial judge specifically considered the possibility of a conditional sentence and rejected it, principally for reasons of denunciation and specific deterrence. In this, we find, he made no error in principle.

Since the offender appealed his sentence, the fact that it did not meet the benchmark was not the focus of the Court of Appeal. That would have been the case only had the Crown appealed. The fact that all the cases from the 1999 data listed in Table 3.6 came to the Court of Appeal via the offenders makes one wonder whether or not there were cases that did not meet the benchmark but were not appealed by the Crown for other reasons.

In summary, while the appeal court appeared to clearly state that intercourse in these cases was unacceptable and should result in at least a three-year sentence, cases with similar circumstances, or what Mr. Justice Blair referred to in *R. v. B.* as "all things being equal," did not have similar outcomes in the 1990-93 data. In the 1999 data, only two cases involving fathers were below the benchmark, while others involving people in positions of trust who were not identified as parents were below the benchmark.

The cases outside the range did not emphasize the offence but seemed to include other considerations focused on the offender. In the cases cited above, these considerations included rehabilitation, the "good character" of the offender, his loss of employment, or the hardship that he might suffer from re-incarceration or incarceration after some time has passed since the conviction. These considerations, which take the emphasis off the offence and put it on the offender, offer some hints about the variability in sentencing. They are consistent with early criticisms of the law cited previously, that judicial comment is "overly concerned with the accused's background and the effect of the charge/sentence on the accused" (Brown 1991, xiii). The fact that the appeal court recognized penetration as the most serious type of sexual assault and distinguished it in this way may tend, in combination with other offender-related mitigating factors, to minimize other kinds of sexual assault that may have been just as traumatic or intrusive for the victim.

Non-Penetration

As demonstrated in the tables earlier in this chapter, even given great variability in all sentences, there appears to be a difference in the sentencing outcomes of the Court of Appeal if the offence did not involve intercourse. They demonstrate that the absence of penetration results in a view of the abuse as less serious. Two features emerge. One is that the offence appears to be minimized because it is not intercourse, and the other is that factors other than the offence are more likely to be emphasized. Of the cases illustrated in the 1990-93 table, seven, or 33 percent, were appeals brought by the Crown. Only one of those appeals succeeded. In those cases in which the appeals failed, the reasons given by the justices of the Court of Appeal included their belief that the offence was not the most serious.

For example, in the 1990-93 data, in *R. v. T., J.* (1992), a principal of a school was convicted of sexually assaulting ten victims ranging in age from seven to fourteen at the beginning of the abuse. The abuse ranged from one time for one victim and periods of one, two, and three years for the others. The offender was sentenced to a period of eighteen months of incarceration. The victim impact statements cited what would be recognized as post-traumatic stress symptoms resulting from sexual abuse as well as problems that seem to stem from community support for the offender rather than the victims. The Crown appealed the sentence on the bases that (1) it amounted to an error in principle in that it failed to adequately reflect the aggravating factors of breach of trust, the vulnerability of the victims, and the number and nature of the offences themselves and that (2) it failed to adequately embody the principle of general deterrence. The Court of Appeal refused to increase the sentence for the following reasons:

> We can never minimize the severity of sexual assault upon young children when the assaults were inflicted by a person in a position of trust here. The assaults ... were not severely invasive and the punishment quite apart from the imprisonment including the loss of position, profession, reputation has been devastating. The sentence imposed while perhaps at the low end of the range is substantial and indicates to the accused and others the distaste, indeed horror, with which such conduct is

viewed. Moreover, the accused has served his sentence and has relocated and reorganized his life and the court is always loath to re-incarcerate. Leave to appeal is granted but the appeal is dismissed.

The Court of Appeal may not have viewed the offences as being "invasive," but the victims clearly did. The number of victims and the period of time over which the offender behaved in an abusive way toward students in his care were not mentioned. The court also did not seem to give notice to the evidence contained in reports to the court about the loss of reputation and shame in the community that the *victims* experienced and the additional price they had to pay in terms of controversy in their community for taking the offender to court. The decision by the Court of Appeal would likely have heightened this loss of reputation and reinforced the view that "good character" is a factor in excusing or explaining this type of illegal behaviour. The emphasis was shifted from the offence to the offender. The offence was minimized, while the losses of the offender were highlighted.

There is evidence of similar thinking by the court in another 1990-93 case, *R. v. T., A.* (1991) concerning an appeal brought by an offender. The man was convicted of indecent assault, under the old legislation, on his niece over an eight-year period during which he was ages twenty-three to thirty-two and the victim was ages four to twelve. The offender regularly fondled the girl's vagina and breasts and exposed himself to her. The writer of the pre-sentence report indicated that the offender tended to minimize his problems and the seriousness of the offence even though he entered a guilty plea and did not see any need to receive treatment. The trial judge sentenced him to two years less a day, stating that "this was a young child, and the incidents went on for a long, considerable period of time. What we do not know is the long term effects it will have on the complainant, who is now a mature person. I have read the pre-sentence report. The accused has had a good home upbringing. He has had no great financial difficulties during his lifetime. He has a good work record, and he takes his lust out on a child. Our society will not tolerate it, and he will be sentenced to two years less one day."

The trial judge seemed to be saying that this offender had the advantages of financial security and work but still committed these acts. The tone of the decision appears to be that the offender should have known better. When he appealed the sentence, the Court of Appeal reduced it for the following reasons: "We do not wish our disposition in this case to in any way imply condonation of the offence of sexual abuse of a young child. Such an offence is serious and will generally justify a sentence of significant incarceration. In this case, however, we are all of the view that the sentence was too severe. The appellant pleaded guilty, was a first offender and the sexual assaults consisted only of touching and fondling and on one occasion exposing himself to the complainant." Unfortunately, the tone of the decision implied insensitivity to the impact of years of abuse on the child. The minimizing of the behaviour as "only touching and fondling" and the absence of any notice of the duration of the abuse overlooked the intrusiveness of such sexually abusive behaviour on the victim. As Summit (1988, 41) says, "it is adult skepticism that blinds us to all but the most blatant sexual assaults." The relative powerlessness of a child who has to endure the emotional and physical force of an adult relative's sexual advances over an eight-year period was not conveyed in the reasoning of the court. The fact that the abuse was carried out over a period of time as a pattern of activity was not mentioned. Perhaps it is easier to rationalize sexual assault if it does not involve intercourse.

The de-emphasis on the offence and the emphasis on the offender indicate a different approach by the court from that in cases of intercourse performed by a parent. These two examples of cases with men in positions of trust are consistent with the reasons given in the other cases of abuse committed by men in positions of trust when that abuse was not intercourse. They are indicative of how the court constructs the case around offender issues rather than offence or victim issues.

A final 1991 example, *R. v. D., J.M.*, demonstrates how the court's construction of what is sexual in abuse is defined by penetration. A stepfather was convicted of two counts of gross indecency under the old legislation and one count of common assault, and sentenced to three years of imprisonment on the gross indecency charges and three months of imprisonment on the common assault charge. The offences involved the offender, ages thirty-eight to forty, forcing the stepdaughter, ages nine to eleven, to masturbate him and then clean the semen off his (the offender's) body. During the thirty-month period of abuse, the offender beat his stepdaughter with a belt and used the beatings and the threats of beatings to facilitate the sexual abuse.

In his reasons for the sentence, the trial judge cited the victim impact statement, which indicated that the victim expressed fear of the offender and of men in general. She was afraid to tell her mother about the abuse because of the threats. She had persistent nightmares and felt that the offender had driven her sister away and ruined her dating years. She had feelings of guilt and of being different because her mother always blamed herself. The trial judge also cited the pre-sentence report, in which the offender was quoted as calling the victim a "liar," as an indication that the remorse that he claimed to feel for the abuse was not genuine.

The Court of Appeal granted the offender's appeal of the sentence:

> The stepdaughter's mother and all her children left the appellant when the offences were discovered and since then they have lived separate from him. The prosecution was not commenced until approximately ten years after the offences were committed when they were first disclosed to law enforcement authorities.
>
> The appellant's acts were disgusting and repugnant but they did not involve penetration or touching of the stepdaughter in a sexual manner. A victim impact statement showed that the stepdaughter was still seriously affected by the offences. She has nightmares, is mistrustful of men, finds difficulty in relating to people of her own age and "can't explain some of the terrible feelings and fears" she has experienced.
>
> A penitentiary sentence was called for in this case but, in our opinion, in all the circumstances, it would be more consistent with authority to reduce it to two years. Accordingly leave to appeal is granted, the appeal allowed and the two concurrent sentences for gross indecency are reduced to two years. The concurrent sentence of three months for common assault will stand.

The Court of Appeal was again making a distinction between intercourse and other forms of abuse, a distinction that seems to be insensitive at best to the reality of the victim's experience. When the justices say that the abuse did not involve touching the girl "in a sexual manner," they minimize the offender's behaviour and responsibility by overlooking the fact that she was coerced into touching the stepfather. She was beaten to ensure that she would masturbate him, and then forced with threats of further beating to clean his body. This seems to comprise a significant, sadistic, *sexual* intrusion on the child. The absence of violence is often mentioned as a mitigating factor in sentencing in these data (22 percent by trial judges and 7 percent by the Court of Appeal), raising the issue that Marshall (1985, 220) addressed in stating that courts do not recognize the inherent violence present in sexual assaults. In this case, explicit violence and threats of violence were ignored by the Court of Appeal.

In the 1999 data, there are similar cases. The appeals were brought by the offenders, not by the Crown. In the first case, *R. v. B., J.S.* (1998), the offender, the stepfather of the victim, received a sentence of two years less one day. Over a period of ten years, the offender weekly fondled the vagina and sucked the breasts of his stepdaughter, who was from four to fourteen years old at the time of abuse, and forced her to perform fellatio on him. He accompanied the abuse with verbal insults of "slut" and "whore" and occasionally with death threats. The judge's reasons for sentencing were that, "although the offender at one point threatened to kill the victim and on another occasion, to do harm to [the] mother if she should reveal what was happening, I note that the sexual acts were not accompanied by overt violence (aside from the inherent violence of the acts themselves) ... and that there were no allegations of sexual or anal intercourse." The judge also cited psychiatric reports and observed that the offender had no previous criminal record except driving while impaired, and that he was university educated, owned his own business, and was currently in a good relationship. He further observed that the offender had no problems at the moment with substances and had the support of family and friends. The judge gave a lot of weight to the offender's friends' letters of support and dismissed the Crown's depiction of the man as domineering and controlling. He also cited the victim impact statement but said that a large part of her trauma was due to her not being believed: "There is a bright side to the picture, however. A large part of her trauma hinged on her not being believed by anyone. Since the conviction, her mother testified that her self-esteem has shot up, her home life has improved and that generally she has taken her life in hand. Moreover, while she is still alienated from her brother, the trial has brought [her] and her mother closer." The judge went on to give his final reasoning in arriving at the sentence:

> The cardinal sentencing principle here must be general deterrence. The court must reflect society's abhorrence and denunciation of this type of conduct which involved both a young child and an adult in a position of trust. On the other hand given the absence of pedophilic or psychiatric disorder, the good conduct of the offender (apart from the one conviction of impaired driving) since the last of these assaults in 1982, the improbability of repetition and absence of risk to the community, the strong family, business, church and community ties the offender enjoys, the prior relatively unblemished record and his remorse, I do not find that this is an appropriate case for the penitentiary.

In each of these cases, the illegal behaviour is minimized because it fails to meet the intercourse standard. While the sentences are variable, a pattern emerges in which those cases that involve intercourse are more likely to receive a penitentiary sentence, but only if the Court of Appeal emphasizes the offence in its deliberations. Other considerations enter into the decision-making process. These factors include efforts taken toward rehabilitation, the hardship of re-incarceration, a guilty plea, loss of family, disgrace in the community, loss of employment, first offence, and exemplary citizenship. In cases in which such factors are considered and the offence is not intercourse, there is much more variability in the sentencing. This is clear from the analysis in this chapter of the cases involving intercourse performed by a father or stepfather. The language of the judgments indicates the priorities of the court. There is a stronger emphasis on the offender than on the offence in non-intercourse offences and intercourse offences committed by someone who is not in a position of trust. The impacts on the victims are minimized or not mentioned. While these cases illustrate the discrepancy between offenders who breach trust by engaging in intercourse and those who breach trust by engaging in fondling or other behaviours, they raise issues about how the offender is viewed by the court.

One of the Crown's appeals was a case that did not involve penetration. *R. v. Stuckless* (1998) was a highly publicized case concerning the abuse of forty-four male victims over a period of approximately twenty years. Some victims were abused once or twice and others over periods of more than a year. The trial judge sentenced the offender to two years less one day and three years of probation, primarily for rehabilitation. According to the Court of Appeal, the trial judge "identified the gravamen of the charges as consisting of repeated acts of 'fondling, fellatio and masturbation upon and with children whose participation had been obtained by breaches of a position of trust or authority.' This is undoubtedly true, but this technical characterization fails to capture the full nature and scope of the offences." The Court of Appeal went on to say that the trial judge "appears to have disregarded the need for a denunciatory sentence reflecting S's 'moral culpability' and society's outrage." Interestingly, the court spoke to the issue of sentencing in cases that do not involve penetration:

> The absence of penetration does not automatically relegate the sexual abuse of children to the "lower range" of sexual offences. There is no question that "additional force," "collateral crime" and penetration are aggravating factors. But their *absence* does not thereby transform them into mitigating circumstances, nor neutralize the other aggravating factors found in this case: the abuse of trust, the number of victims, the

> frequency of the assaults and their devastating impact on the lives of the victims. These offences were, individually and collectively, unconscionable. Any characterization which purports to diminish their magnitude is unacceptable. I am unable to find a single reported appellate decision in recent years which does not view the sexual abuse of children as extremely serious, whether or not there is penetration. In saying there was no violence "*apart from* the coercion implicit in the relationship between the parties" [emphasis added] or "beyond what was implicit in the interference with the physical integrity of the complainant," [the judge] misappreciated how serious these offences were. Sexual abuse is an act of violence. When committed against children, the violence is both physical and profoundly psychological. It is coercive and exploitative conduct, and represents the use of compulsion against someone who is defenceless.

This was an important decision that may, in fact, set another benchmark; however, as is evident in these data, many cases seemingly do not meet the sentencing standards set out in this case and by Blair. We are aware of these cases not because they are appealed by the Crown but because they are appealed by the offender. The cases that do come before the Court of Appeal, when the appellant is the offender, do not lend themselves to the possibility of comment on inadequate sentencing. It is possible that the Crown appealed *R. v. Stuckless* because of the enormous amount of publicity the case received in the media. Most cases of child sexual abuse go through the courts relatively quietly. How many cases have there been in which we remain unaware of the victims' experiences because they were not reported?

Finally, in sentencing an offender to four years for a series of sexual assaults, one trial judge in the 1990-93 study questioned the emphasis on penetration:

> So now we have before me a 78 year old man with no criminal record who, 25 years ago, coldly and calculatingly, over an extended period of time, ravaged his three granddaughters ... [I]n this case it may be that these events took place 25 years ago; but for the victims, it is as if they took place yesterday ... There was no intercourse and our Court of Appeal does seem to make a distinction in that the penalties to be imposed should be higher, all things being equal, where intercourse occurs as opposed to when it does not. I must say I am not too sure why. It may be that that is some age old male attitude that the worst thing that can happen in cases like this is intercourse. It may be that there is some

> evidence to back that up ... I must say, however, that in this case, as I look at the impact on these three ladies, I find it hard to conclude that intercourse could have made it worse. ... Much has been said about the age of the accused. He certainly is the oldest man that I will be sending to jail or have so far. It may be that age should work in his favour and that I should either not send him to jail or make the time that he has to spend there somewhat less because he is old; he is not well. Well, I say to you counsel, that for purposes of this sentencing, if he dies there, so be it.
>
> I cannot remember having heard or seen such tragic evidence of impact. These ladies have suffered for 25 years. I will make their statements to me exhibits. There are words about flashbacks, insomnia, sexual dysfunction, no self-esteem, drug abuse, histories of counseling and therapy; all in all, a litany of unhappiness and despair ... This entire family is split. The defence has filed letters describing Mr. W as a perfect gentleman, and an honourable man, as a good man. Well those people are mistaken; he's not, and I don't treat him like that.
>
> Mr. W was the head of his family. He was in a position of power and trust. He abused that trust. He abused that power. I denounce him for that. My sentence reflects that denunciation. (*R. v. W., C.C.* [1991])

The Court of Appeal dismissed the offender's appeal of his sentence without comment. For this trial judge, the significance of the impact on the victims was derived from their statements and not dependent on the concept of penetration for consideration. He demonstrated his rejection of what he perceived to be the traditional view when he talked about the "age old male attitude that the worst thing that can happen in cases like this is intercourse." It is not clear whether or not the Court of Appeal shared his rejection of that traditional view since it did not explain why it agreed with the sentence.

Conclusion

Mr. Justice Blair of the Court of Appeal of Ontario set a standard in *R. v. B.* for cases involving intercourse that is recognized and cited in both trial judges' decisions and decisions written by the Court of Appeal but not necessarily followed. Blair identified intercourse as the most serious form of sexual assault that can be perpetrated on a child victim. This standard was set in spite of an attempt by Parliament to move away from a rape standard in sexual assault laws. It is a good indication of how application of the law differs from intent of the law and represents a patriarchal interpretation that, as noted earlier, was predicted by some

(Nadin-Davis 1983; Ruebsaat 1985; Brown 1991). In the sense that penetration remains an important consideration, feminist critiques of the law as gendered have merit. MacKinnon's (1983, 644) critique that "the law sees and treats women the same way that men see and treat women" is clearly applicable here. If penetration is the standard in terms of harm, then it represents a gendered way of assessing harm. In so doing, it allows for the harms experienced by child victims of sexual assault to be minimized if they do not meet this gendered standard. These are commonsense explanations (Boudreau, Sennott, and Wilson 1986) of harm that are not informed by discussion on the actual offence in its fullest context. This is consistent with Smart's (1989, 45) interpretation of Adler (1987): "'common sense' about female sexuality has a way of invalidating legal reforms which seem to go against the conventional wisdom." The emphasis on penetration is a gendered approach to child sexual abuse; it is "some age old male attitude."

In these data, the notion of penetration is paired with the concept of "in loco parentis" in order to legitimize the imposition of a penitentiary sentence. The mean sentences in cases that involve penetration and an abuser in a position of trust with respect to the victim are higher than sentences that do not involve penetration and a position of trust. Increasingly, the Court of Appeal does appear to uphold and/or impose longer sentences on men in positions of trust with regard to their victims as long as they are fathers or stepfathers. This accountability is paired, however, with intercourse in defining what the most serious cases of abuse are. It would appear, then, to some extent at least, that the intent of the 1988 law to emphasize breach of trust is considered as a critical factor in sentencing. However, when intercourse is no longer part of the equation, the relationship does not seem to be all that relevant to the decision. It appears, rather, that the offence in non-intercourse cases is often considered less serious, and the lack of appreciation of its seriousness in all but a few cases negates any interest in the notion of breach of trust even when the duration of abuse has been significantly long. The message seems to be "what trust has been breached when little harm has been done?" However, as noted in the previous chapter, neither type of abuse nor relationship of the offender to the victim was statistically significant in predicting the sentence that the offender received in both the 1990-93 and the 1998-99 data. In this chapter, we have seen in more detail why that may be the case.

In Chapter 1, Hornick and Bolitho (1992, xiv) were quoted as identifying one of the goals of the 1988 legislation as bringing the sentences in cases of child sexual abuse in line with the severity of the offence.

One question that emerges from these data is: What constitutes severity? Should intercourse be the standard? Other features, as noted in the trial judge's comments above, surely merit more consideration. Duration of abuse should be a major consideration (Briere and Elliott 2003), but it does not seem to be in cases that do not involve intercourse.

This analysis leads to further questions about how variability is constructed. What kinds of offender issues are considered by the court that would account for variability in sentencing? Do they represent further understandings of gendered notions of sexuality? Where does the victim fit into the picture? Can a pattern of predictable decision making be arrived at? In the next chapter, I will analyze the Court of Appeal's use of mitigating and aggravating circumstances to examine its thinking.

4
The Understandable Offender

Popular perceptions of men who sexually abuse children portray these men as visibly deviant or demonic. The media present them as being "different." What happens when a "normal"-looking man comes before the court having been convicted of the sexual abuse of a child? How do we explain his behaviour given that he looks like us? Judges may tend to lose their focus on what the offender did in their attempt to understand who the offender is. In this chapter, I will examine how concepts such as the character and work record of the offender are used in mitigation. In Chapter 5, I will examine other circumstances cited as mitigating or aggravating that deal directly with the victim. And in Chapter 6, I will analyze rehabilitation, the most frequent mitigative circumstance cited by justices of the Court of Appeal of Ontario in the 1990-93 data, in conjunction with the court's use of expert reports.

In Chapter 1, the theme emerged of a change in the laws regarding the sexual abuse of women and children without a concomitant change in other structures of the judicial system. Marshall (1985), Mitra (1987), and Brown (1991) were critical of the interpretation or application of the law in the sentencing process. They viewed the activity of judges in sentencing as reflecting and supporting patriarchal notions of the dominance of males and gendered concepts of male/female/child roles in the family. In this chapter, we will look at how judges use mitigating and aggravating circumstances within the framework of this gendered view. An examination of these circumstances demonstrates that how they are considered may account for the framework in which sentencing variability takes place.

Black's Law Dictionary (Garner and Black 1999, 236) defines a mitigating circumstance as "a fact or situation that does not justify or excuse a wrongful act or offence but that reduces the degree of culpability and thus may reduce the damages (in a civil case) or the punishment," or as "a fact or situation that does not bear on the question of a defendant's guilt that is considered by the court in imposing punishment and esp. in lessening the severity of the sentence." The same dictionary defines an aggravating circumstance as "a fact or situation that increases the degree of liability or culpability for a tortious or criminal act" (ibid.). This is a fitting subject for analysis using feminist critiques of the law. Mitchell (1985, 96) says in regard to child sexual abuse that "we have only ever heard one side of the story." Does an examination of the use of mitigating and aggravating circumstances in the Court of Appeal of Ontario demonstrate that we are now hearing sides, the victim's and the offender's? Is the version of reality presented in considering sentences for men who have committed child sexual assault more balanced than Mitchell's observation would have us believe?

In gender-neutral language, interestingly, Ruby (1994, 110) outlines the rationale taught to lawyers that provides them with an understanding of the consideration of mitigating circumstances: "The Court is always willing to listen to the reasons which impelled a prisoner to commit a crime in the hope that the circumstances may disclose that the prisoner is not one who is committed to crime as a way of life, but rather the pressures of the immediate human situation led to the criminal activity. This factor has more weight, of course, when it can be shown that the situational exigencies have ceased or have some likelihood of abating." There is a certain logic in Ruby's explanation if the reasons for commission of the crime have some relationship to the crime. For example, recent cases of mercy killing have dealt with the mitigating factor of the killer's altruistic wish to relieve the suffering of the terminally ill person. Other examples might include cases of fraud or theft where the person committing the crime was stealing food or money in order to feed a family. In these cases, the otherwise good character or work record, as well as the motivation to commit the offence, might be relevant in mitigation of the offence.

In cases that involve sexual abuse, though, it is difficult to imagine any altruistic motive, although offenders have been reported as offering such motives in justification of their behaviour (Segal and Stermac 1990). As well, anyone who committed crimes over the period of time during which many of the cases under discussion here were tried (i.e., a mean period of 4.1 years in the 1990-93 data or 4.5 years in the 1999 data) likely would not get much credit in terms of mitigating circumstances. Four years of burglaries or bank robberies would be difficult to rationalize. Why is it that four-plus years of child sexual abuse seem, at least in these data, easier to explain?

Ruby (1994, 210) cites a 1969 court decision that spells out limits to the use of "good character": "Good character may be a mitigating circumstance in some kinds of crimes, e.g., an isolated case of criminal negligence or an unpremeditated assault in a fit of anger. But, in my opinion, this is not so, where the offence is a series of acts, planned and carried out over a lengthy period. The person of good character, who can appreciate to the full how wrong what he is doing is, seems to me to be just as culpable as a person of poor character who appreciates less clearly the wrongness of his acts." According to this standard, good character would not be a mitigating circumstance in many of the cases in these data.

Walker (1985, 43) has indicated that few legal texts give as much attention to aggravating circumstances as they do to mitigating factors: "Sentencers are supposed to take as their starting point the sentence appropriate to the 'most serious type of case' and work downwards, as it were, by allowing for mitigating factors. This does not mean that there is no such thing as aggravation. First the notion of the most serious type of case involves criteria of seriousness which are in effect aggravating considerations, whatever they are called. The mere absence of such features is sufficient, without positive mitigating features, to reduce the sentence. Second, mitigating features are often said to be canceled by unpleasant features of the crime."

The obvious question here is who decides what the criteria of seriousness are? Is penetration the only way in which seriousness is or can be constructed? Is the duration of abuse a factor in the seriousness of the offence? In cases of sexual assault of children, does the victim impact statement dictate the degree of seriousness, or is the concept decided in some other way by someone not connected to the reality of the victim's experience? As the Court of Appeal noted in *R. v. Stuckless* (1998) described in the previous chapter, speaking about aggravating circumstances such as penetration, in what appears to be disagreement with Walker (1985), the absence of aggravating circumstances does not equal a mitigating circumstance.

A careful examination of the sentencing practices in these data from the beginning and the end of the 1990s illustrates that the factors involved are somewhat more complex and detailed than those observed by Mitra (1987) and elaborated earlier; nonetheless, some demonstrate evidence of the issues raised in feminist critiques such as Mitchell's (1985). How mitigating circumstances are used and explained can also be viewed critically in terms of the work of Scully and Marolla (1984) and Scully (1990), who outline the process by which people who violate societal norms by committing the crime of rape present or reframe the behaviour in such a way that it is acceptable or socially normal. They contend that such representation or reframing is based on our cultural views of women: "The sexual objectification of women must be understood as an important factor contributing to an environment that trivializes, neutralizes and perhaps ... facilitates rape" (Scully and Marolla 1984, 542). Their analysis is consistent with the feminist critiques of sexual assault in which the law is seen to be gendered and women's and children's existence is usually understood in reference to men. They also use the work of C. Wright Mills to explain how deviants neutralize their deviance through what Mills refers to as a "vocabulary of motive" (1940, 904). They cite the work of Scott and Lyman (1968), who make useful distinctions in these attempts to neutralize deviant behaviour between excuses, justifications, and accounts: "Excuses admit the act was bad or inappropriate but deny full responsibility, often through appeals to accident, or biological drive or through scapegoating. In contrast, justifications accept responsibility for the act but deny that it was wrong – that is, they show in this situation the act was appropriate. Accounts are socially approved vocabularies that neutralize an act or its consequences and are always a manifestation of a negotiation of identity" (Scully and Marolla 1984, 530). The concept of neutralization and rationalization is consistent with the work of Cressey (1960) and Sutherland (1961), who examined the explanations of "white-collar criminals" or otherwise upstanding citizens who commit offences that they consider to be technically illegal but justifiable, partly because of who they are (middle- or upper-class males) and largely because the illegal behaviours are understood as "part of doing business." Sykes and Matza (1957) develop the notion further in an examination of the justification behaviours of a wider range of juvenile wrongdoers. This kind of rationalization is similar to that noted in the literature on convicted child molesters, which indicates that they tend to support their behaviour by espousing the beliefs that its effects on the children are not negative and that the child was a willing and appropriate participant in the sexual behaviour (Abel, Becker, and Cunningham-Rathner 1984; Finkelhor 1984; Abel, Mittleman, and Becker 1985).

An example of an offender's perception of the concepts of mitigation and altruism was cited in the previous chapter, *R. v. N., W.R.,* in the discussion about the forty-four-year-old offender who believed that he was a good influence on the twelve-year-old victim because "he was able to show her what it is like to be loved." In analyzing these data, it is necessary to ask, to what extent do judges accept the excuses and justifications of men who have sexually abused children?

Overview of Mitigating and Aggravating Factors

In the cases from 1990 to 1993, the factor most frequently cited by trial judges in mitigation of the sentence was work record (33 percent). The factor most frequently cited by the Court of Appeal was receiving treatment (22 percent). Table 4.1 outlines all the mitigating circumstances cited by trial judges and the Court of Appeal of Ontario.

In the 1999 data, there were fewer cases and fewer mitigating circumstances (see Table 4.2). The mitigating circumstances in these data demonstrated some of the same emphases as in the 1990-93 data, but the tone was different. There was less emphasis on the "male role" of the offender and more emphasis on individual considerations. The concept

Table 4.1

Mitigating circumstances, 1990-93

Trial	*N* = 103	Appeal	*N* = 103
Work record	24	Receiving treatment	10
No previous related offence	24	No previous offence	8
Positive report	23	Hardship of re-incarceration	7
Good character/reputation	21	Positive report	6
Guilty plea	17	Previous good character	6
No violence	16	Age of offender	5
Involved in rehabilitation	12	Delay in processing appeal	5
Age of accused	10	Guilty plea	4
Remorse	10	Pre-trial custody	4
Type of abuse (no penetration)	8	Minimal/no impact on victim	4
Stress/family disturbance	7	Mental health/health of offender	4
Substance abuse	7	No force/violence	3
Personal problems	7	Employed	3
Shame to family	6	On or close to parole	3
Active volunteer/church member	6	Type of abuse (no intercourse)	3
Health of accused	5	Offences dated	2
No risk to reoffend	4	Victim cooperated/consented	2
Pedophile	4	Recent marriage	2
Sole support of family	4	Judge erred re guilty plea	2
Good education	3	Not a pedophile	1
New relationship/recent marriage	3	Duration of abuse	1
Consent/victim willing	3	Sole support of family	1
Offence not planned	2	Should have had a TAP	1
Not a pedophile	2	Offender unaware of STD	1
Offence dated	2		
Previously abused	2		
Pays child support	2		
No substance abuse	1		
No physical harm to victim	1		

of good character, overtly stated, did not appear in either the trial judges' or the Court of Appeal's reasons for sentences. The idea of the good public citizen, working man, volunteer, and breadwinner did not have as large a presence as it did in the 1990-93 data. The cases in which it is mentioned represent situations in which the offender was the only source of income for the family and in which the victim impact statements supported the idea that incarceration would cause them further damage. There was still emphasis on employment and community support, but the shift to psychological attributes of the offender is worth noting. On appeal, harkening back to Walker's (1985) comments cited earlier, the fact that the illegal behaviour was not intercourse was considered mitigating, as was the absence of a criminal record and the perceived absence of future risk to reoffend.

Table 4.3 outlines the aggravating circumstances cited by the trial judges and the Court of Appeal in the 1990-93 data, while Table 4.4 presents these circumstances for the 1999 data. Some factors were cited as both mitigating and aggravating. Substance abuse was cited as a mitigating circumstance, while alcohol abuse was cited as an aggravating circumstance by trial judges. Age of the offender was cited as both mitigating and aggravating by both the trial judge and the Court of Appeal. Pedophilia was cited as a mitigating circumstance by some trial judges and as an aggravating circumstance by both the trial judges and the

Table 4.2

Mitigating circumstances, 1999

Trial	*N* = 41	Appeal	*N* = 41
Support of family and friends	12	Type of abuse	3
Situational crisis/health problems	12	No criminal record	3
No previous offence	11	No risk to reoffend	2
Employed	11	Pre-trial custody	2
From a dysfunctional family	8	Gainfully employed	2
Counselling	7	Sought treatment	2
Guilty plea	6	Compliance with bail conditions	1
No danger/risk to reoffend	6	Out of character	1
No violence	6	Primary source of family income	1
Alcohol abuse	5	Wife dependent on him	1
Accepts responsibility	4	Previous treatment	1
Remorse	4	Historic abuse	1
Financially responsible to family	3	Support of family and friends	1
Childhood sexual abuse	3	Age of offender	1
Type of abuse	3	Health problems	1
No alcohol abuse	1	No position of trust	1

appeal court. The absence of pedophilia was considered mitigating by some trial judges and the Court of Appeal and aggravating by some of the trial judges. While this may seem confusing, what is clear is that there is considerable difference in the application of mitigating and aggravating factors. This may be an illustration of Naffine's (1990) critique that law lacks internal coherence. Young's (1988, 10) words come to mind again: "The myriad of available factors defy a quantitative analysis and it is more usual for the court to approach the factors in an impressionistic manner." Young was referring to how the factors cited add up to the final sentence, but it is also obvious in studying these data that the factors themselves are part of a judicial impression of what constitutes child sexual abuse. When there is no clear understanding of the role of intoxicants or a diagnosis of pedophilia among judges, no clear message can be sent in their decisions. It is difficult to be precise about the reasoning behind the use of mitigating and aggravating circumstances when there is so much variability in understanding and applying them.

Table 4.3

Aggravating circumstances, 1990-93

Trial	*N* = 103	Appeal	*N* = 103
Position of trust	44	Position of trust	18
Victim impact	37	Duration of abuse	11
Nature of abuse (penetration)	27	Intercourse	7
Age of victim	25	Age of victim	7
Duration of abuse	21	Victim impact	7
No remorse	20	Relationship to victim	4
Negative report	14	Previous sex offences	4
No treatment	12	Number of victims	4
Age of offender	9	Age of offender	3
Planned	8	Pedophile	2
Previous offence	7	Nature of offence (penetration)	2
Previous sexual offences	5	Force/violence	2
Impact on family	5	Previous criminal record	2
Victim had to testify	5	No remorse	2
Presents risk	5	No insight into harm done	2
Psych reports on victim	5	Planning	1
Alcohol abuse	4	Offender experienced	1
Pregnancy/abortion	3		
Victim unconscious	3		
Homosexuality	3		
Pedophile	2		
Not a pedophile	1		
No guilty plea	1		

Table 4.4

Aggravating circumstances, 1999

Trial	N = 41	Appeal	N = 41
Victim impact	40	Position of trust	9
Duration/frequency	23	Duration/frequency	6
Position of trust	22	Type of abuse	6
Age of victim	14	Seriousness of offence	4
No remorse	13	Relationship	4
Type of abuse	10	Age of victim	3
Planning/predation	10	Victim impact	3
Criminal record	9	Criminal record	2
Risk to reoffend	7	Treatment unsuccessful	2
Report	7	Premeditation	2
Lacks insight	6	Absence of remorse	1
Denial/no responsibility	6	Continued threats	1
Vulnerability of victim	6	Risk to reoffend	1
Pedophile	5	Vulnerable victim	1
Age of offender	5	Physical violence	1
Violation of terms of release	4	Pedophile	1
Threats	4	Circumstances of offender	1
Escalation of assaults	3		
Number of offences	3		
Not a pedophile	1		

Position of trust stands out in the data from both time periods as important to both the trial judges and the Court of Appeal. Interestingly, pedophilia shows up in contradictory terms again, though only in one case. In another case, *R. v. Stuckless,* Abella JA, wrote that "pedophilia is an explanation, not a defence. Society is entitled to protection no less from pedophiles than those who sexually abuse children without this tendency." A qualitative look at the language of the courts and how they construct the circumstances of the offence and the offender gives a clearer picture of what is considered to be relevant in this decision making.

Factors in Context

Given that sentence variability is difficult to understand when mitigating and aggravating circumstances are examined broadly, it is more useful to look at how they are used in the context of the judicial decisions in specific cases. In fact, legal interpretation as based on the gendered roles of men and women can be seen in an examination of mitigating and aggravating factors in the context of case decisions. In the 1990-93 data, use of mitigating factors overshadowed use of aggravating factors and seemed at times, as noted in the previous chapter, to supersede discussion of the offence. This is consistent with Mitchell's (1985) contention that only one side of the story is told.

Of the cases in which mitigating factors were cited, the vast majority also contained some mention of aggravating factors; however, in many the aggravating factors were downplayed. Examining the language of the decisions, it becomes obvious that many of the factors operate in combination rather than in isolation to form the substance of the judicial decision.

The following categories of factors emerge from an analysis of the judges' reasons for their decisions. In the Court of Appeal decisions, mitigating circumstances were usually grouped together. The two main groupings can be considered to relate to the offender's "public" persona and delays in the processing of the case and/or the fact that the offender had already paid the original penalty. Woven through these categories was the concept of rehabilitation, the mitigating factor most frequently mentioned by the justices of the Court of Appeal. I will consider rehabilitation in greater detail in Chapter 6.

Good Character, Reputation, Work Record 1990-93

The concept of "out of character" in the 1990-93 data is in keeping with what Burgess (1985) perceives to be the definitions of masculinity and expectations about the male role that lie at the heart of sexual offences. Comack and Balfour (2004, 143) cite Mandel (1991, 144) when they discuss how the law treats high-status offenders: "The courts recognize it as a legitimate part of the sentencing function to determine the severity of the sentence on the basis not only of the nature of the offence, but also the nature of the offender, not as an offender but as a *social being*. Part of this has to do with the criminal record but a good part of it has as well to do with the extent to which the offender fulfills his or her role in the productive apparatus."

The factors relating to work and character are predicated on notions of what constitutes a "good" man. If a man's public behaviour is acceptable, then his private or domestic behaviour can be excused to some extent. None of these "public" characteristics has anything to do with the actual offence. How, then, are they relevant?

In one notable case, *R. v. M., G.* (1991) in these data, the Court of Appeal appeared to be asking the same question. A fifty-two-year-old father (from thirty-three to forty at abuse) was convicted of twelve counts of indecent assault for fondling the vaginas, digitally penetrating, and performing cunnilingus on two daughters ages eleven to eighteen and twelve to seventeen years at abuse. The daughters were thirty and twenty-nine years of age respectively at trial. The offender was given a suspended sentence and one year of probation by the trial judge, who gave as his reasons that vulnerable victims were exploited, there was a breach of parental trust, there were two victims, and the number of offences amounted to systemic misconduct. In mitigation, the judge cited the nature of the offences, which were not intercourse, the relatively minimal victim impact, and the age of the offender, who was a successful and respected businessman in the community. As well, the judge considered (as indicated in the psychiatric assessment of the offender) that the breakdown in the sexual relationship with his wife was a partial cause of the offences. The judge also said that the offender did not use threats with the victims and that he completely disclosed in 1980 and sought treatment (after the daughters told their mother about the abuse). Finally, the trial judge said that the offender "fully and generously" supported his wife and children until 1988 and that there was no application of specific deterrence in this case and no need for rehabilitation. The judge did not believe that the principle of general deterrence applied in cases of child sexual abuse of natural children.

The Crown appealed the sentence, contending that it did not reflect the gravity of the offender's behaviour. The Court of Appeal allowed the appeal and increased the sentence to twelve months of incarceration with no probation, stating that the trial judge's emphasis on mitigating factors had been misplaced but acknowledging that the offender had attended counselling, that he had lost status in the community, and that considerable time had elapsed between the sentence and the appeal. Challenging the trial judge's use of mitigating factors, the Court of Appeal stated:

> I agree that the respondent acknowledged and apologized for his assaults, but only after his older daughter disclosed them to her mother. His "fully and generously" complying with his legal obligation to pay financial support to his wife and children after the disclosure resulted in their separation is, it seems to me, a neutral factor, as is his age in this case ... Nor is it clear to me why the breakdown of "the sexual part" of the relationship between the respondent and his wife, for whatever reason, is in any way relevant to his having abused his daughters. It suggests that the daughters were understandable substitutes in the same home, or that the wife was in some way morally culpable for the father assaulting their daughters, both completely untenable suggestions.

The Court of Appeal recognized and rejected as "untenable" the trial judge's use of the myths of masculinity, which Dominelli (1991, 31) believes are accepted by some men and are used by sex offenders to minimize and rationalize their abuse of women and children. Some of these beliefs are that

- men by nature need a lot of sex;
- men cannot abstain from sex for long;
- men must get sex from somewhere;
- women are mere sex objects;
- women lure men into sex; and
- women are responsible for how far men go sexually.

Comack and Balfour (2004, 111) have a similar list of myths in their analysis of how law deals with sexual assault, and they claim that, "drawn from a wider patriarchal culture, these rape myths have played a significant role in Canadian jurisprudence."

The trial judge obviously accepted the idea that the offender's inability to find a sexual outlet in his wife made turning to his daughters for sex understandable. He also accepted the notion that the offender's financial support of his wife and children somehow excused his actions. Performance of this traditionally expected male role was constructed by the judge as indicative of the offender's "goodness" as a man. Although the offender was acknowledged to have engaged in what "amounted to systemic misconduct," another important consideration was his success as a businessman. He was a "good" public man. Clearly, the Court of Appeal did not accept this construction of the offender as mitigating. Appeals to traditionally accepted constructions were rejected by the higher court as irrelevant to the offence. As noted in the previous chapter, the distinction is made consistent with the standard of penetration by a person in a position of trust. Interestingly, although the appeal court rejected the myths of masculinity and of protection of the traditional role, this was a case that did not involve intercourse. Sometimes the language of the court still recognizes factors that are irrelevant to the behaviour in any positive way and, in fact, should indicate that the offender, if anything, ought to have known better:

> There were strong mitigating factors in this case. The accused is presently forty-nine years of age and is the sole support for his present wife and child. His present marriage is a successful one. He has no criminal record. A favourable psychiatric report says he has no paedophiliac or

> incestuous interest at this time ... We have evidence of rehabilitation which is striking ... He formed his own company ... which employs approximately twenty-five workers who are active mainly on weekends. At the time of trial he was also employed ... as a career counselor. He was active in organizations dealing with the rehabilitation of alcoholics. While we recognize that this is a serious case of child abuse, we are of the opinion that the nature of the sexual assaults by the appellant do not justify going beyond the normal range of sentence for this type of offence. While it was proper for the trial judge to emphasize the victim impact statement, in our opinion, he did not give sufficient consideration to the mitigating factors referred to above. (*R. v. W., W.* [1992])

The language of the Court of Appeal says much about what is important to it. Most of the factors relate to issues that are very consistent with the accepted standards of success in the male role. Even the reference to rehabilitation in this example does not include ideas about the offender's better understanding of appropriate parenting; rather, the focus is on the fact that the offender formed his own company. He received a significant sentence, even after the appeal, but the court gives the message through its language that the factors noted excuse the man from total responsibility for his actions. The court might have reduced the sentence by applying the usual "benchmark" and relating it to the offence; however, by referring to the offender's public life as an employer and an employee, it introduces issues related to appropriate role performance with traditional divisions of labour based on gender rather than deals with his performance as a father. Would a woman who abused her child for six years be considered less responsible because she had a responsible job during that time or because she had formed her own company and employed a number of people?

Another example from the 1990-93 data that illustrates more concern for work record and family status is the case of an offender who held a managerial position in a computer company and whose father was noted in the record as being a physician. The judge cited as mitigating circumstances the positive report by a psychiatrist about the offender; the support that the offender had from his family; the offender's medical problems, which followed laying of the charges; and a report from the offender's employer, who indicated that some employees of the firm might lose their jobs if the offender were to be incarcerated. In the judge's words:

> There was not the depravity of the type noted in other cases in respect to fellatio or sodomy or anything of that nature. A distinction must be

> made in respect to pedophilia which is a differently motivated child sexual assault involving an accused who has a compulsion as opposed to individuals who are child sexual assaulters absent a compulsion. I have educated and cautioned myself in respect to the use to be made of victim impact statements. The case of *R. v. Clubb* (O.C.A. 20 O.A.C. p. 157) indicates that a judge is not to be moved by his own emotion; that opinion is confirmed in *Regina and Owens* (1986), 33 CCC 3rd 275 at p. 285 ... Public deterrence is partially satisfied by the publicity, shame and loss of status of the offender. He is a person of general good character with the exception of this aberration and has the support of his family and his community. (*R. v. E., P.* [1991])

In this case, the judge made it clear that the abuse was not penetration. The offences involved the fondling of four boys between the ages of ten and fourteen. Three of the boys were fondled on one occasion each, and the fourth, who was the "Little Brother" to the offender's role of "Big Brother," was fondled over a four-month period. The offender's sentence was for ninety days to be served intermittently on weekends, primarily because of his "good character."

The Crown appealed the sentence on the grounds that it did not reflect the gravity of the offence and failed to reflect society's denunciation of the accused's conduct, given the serious breach of trust involved. The Court of Appeal dismissed the appeal: "In the light of the very favourable prognosis given by Dr. X, and of the interference with the respondent's treatment programme that a different custodial sentence would cause, we think that although this type of offence calls for a denunciatory sentence, the 90 day sentence, although at the low end of the range, does not, in the circumstances, detract from the denunciation inherent in this custodial sentence." It seems, however, to detract from the denunciation in that the effect of the abuse on the children was not seriously considered, nor was the position of trust. The language of the decision made by the trial judge is excusatory, and the appeal court accepts that excusing or minimizing of the actual behaviour of the offender. Here, as in other cases, the mitigating circumstances are combined with concern about rehabilitation. The court does not seem to consider, since it does not mention, what the offence may have meant to the child victims. One of them, at least, was obviously in a position of need, being in the Big Brothers program, and he trusted, along with his mother and the Big Brothers organization, that the offender's purpose in contact with the boy was to provide him with a positive relationship with a male adult. The court accepts that the offender has a "mild, transient and curable" problem (Scully and Marolla 1984, 540) while also identifying him as being "motivated" to change and, therefore, not someone who should have to accept a significant level of legal consequence. Emphasis on the offender's family status, his valuable employment, the consequences to the offender of disclosure of the abuse, and the diagnosis of compulsion ignores the reality of the offence and its impact on the victims. Emphasis on good character and characterization of the offences – which occurred over a four-month period – as an aberration once again construct the offender as a good "public" man. He is a good person because his employer needs him. The emphasis in the sentencing is on possible loss of business for the employer and on stress on the offender as a result of having been caught abusing children. This emphasis has nothing to do with the offence. It certainly has nothing to do with the victims.

In cases in which the Court of Appeal has used concepts related to good character, it appears to be operating from the idea of what a typical sex offender "looks like" and accepting the stereotype of the clearly perverted or "sick" offender as described by Herman (1990) and others. If an offender does not fit the stereotype of the stranger offender and is not diagnosed as being a pedophile (the majority of the offenders in these cases are not), then the court tends to minimize criminality by citing all the factors that make the offender a "normal" man (Scully and Marolla 1984, 540). The court's decisions are consistent with the findings of Taylor (2004) in Australia and Mitra (1987) in Britain. Both researchers found that the judges in their studies used patriarchal belief systems to assess appeals related to offenders who had committed sexual assaults on children. It is clear in the 1990-93 data that many judges found it difficult to accept that men who otherwise appear to be normal could have committed sexual assaults against children. How "expert" testimonies and reports contributed to their perceptions will be discussed in Chapter 6.

The Court of Appeal rejected the excuses of offenders most frequently in cases involving intercourse performed by a person "in loco parentis." In others, it tended to accept the "justifications and accounts" as described by Scully and Marolla (1984, 530) that they were otherwise "normal" men who had made mistakes.

Hardship of Re-Incarceration or Delay in Processing Appeal

These mitigating factors appeared only in the 1990-93 data. This may be an effect of the small number of Crown appeals (four) in the 1999 data. The Court of Appeal of Ontario indicated in 16 percent of the 103 cases that an increase in the offender's sentence at appeal would constitute a hardship. This concern sometimes co-existed with another issue noted by the court: delays in processing appeals in 11 percent of the 103 cases. The Court of Appeal dealt with the issue of re-incarceration or increase in an already served or partially served community disposition in fourteen cases in these data. In two cases involving this subject, the court was split in making the decision. In some cases, offenders' sentences were extended, while in others they were not. In *R. v. D., J.G.* (1993) and *R. v. M., S.J.* (1993), the amount of time between sentence and appeal was approximately two years. *R. v. D., J.G.*, an appeal by the Crown, involved intercourse over a twenty-three-year period:

> The respondent pleaded guilty to 2 counts of rape and 8 counts of Indecent Assault. The offences were committed on 8 nieces of the respondent and commenced when some of the victims were only 4 or 5 years of age. General deterrence and societal denunciation require a custodial sentence in this kind of case. The respondent is 63 years of age. He suffers from depression. There has been considerable delay by the Crown in processing this appeal. Taking these factors into consideration we believe that a fit sentence would be 2 years less a day. If it were not for the factors mentioned we would have imposed a penitentiary term. Leave to appeal is granted. The appeal is upheld, the suspended sentence is set aside and there will be a sentence of imprisonment of 2 years less 1 day. The probation order will stand. A warrant may be issued if the Crown requests it.

This case falls below the benchmark set by Blair. The mitigating circumstances include the age and depression of the offender and the delay by the Crown in processing the appeal. These factors appear to be more important than the twenty-three years of abuse, including intercourse, of eight victims. However, the sentence was increased.

R. v. M., S.J., another Crown appeal, involved offences other than intercourse. A stepfather was convicted for the second time of sexually assaulting his stepdaughter. After the first conviction, the offender was sentenced to ninety days and two years of probation. For the second offence, he was given a sentence of thirty days of incarceration. The delay in processing the appeal and the hardship involved in re-incarceration were critical factors for the Court of Appeal:

> The respondent was convicted for a second time of sexual assault upon his step daughter. The sentence of 30 days imprisonment was totally

> inadequate. However, he was convicted on February 26, 1991 and the Crown Attorney has just now come before this court for hearing. We are not satisfied as to the adequacy of the explanation given by the Crown for the delay. It in no way appears to have been the fault of the respondent. For this reason alone we are not prepared to increase the sentence because it would mean re-incarcerating the appellant long after he has served his sentence and re-established himself in the community. Accordingly, leave to appeal is granted but the appeal is dismissed.

Use of the concepts of delay and hardship follows lines similar to other mitigating circumstances. These two cases illustrate the difference. In all the cases in which there was no increase and the reason was delay by the Crown or hardship of re-incarceration, the offences were not intercourse. The length of time between trial and appeal is not as relevant in cases of intercourse as it is when the offence does not involve intercourse. Seven of the ten cases in the 1990-93 data, which were successfully appealed by the Crown and in which the sentence was increased, involved intercourse. *R. v. L., R.A.* (1993) was not intercourse but involved seven years of significantly planned and frequently aggressive sexual acts. In *R. v. M., G.,* cited earlier, the offender was presented as a good man because he "fully and generously supported" his wife and children; however, the justices of the appeal court rejected this presentation.

R. v. L., A.P. (1991) and *R. v. K., M.* (1993) were two Crown appeals in which a dissenting opinion was given. Both cases involved non-intercourse offences over a period of time. In the former, the sentence was increased, while in the latter it was not. In that case, an uncle was convicted of abusing his two nephews over a period of twelve years. The abuse was not disclosed until another twelve years had passed. The trial judge sentenced the offender to six months of incarceration, and the majority of the appeal court upheld that sentence. In *R. v. L., A.P.,* the majority of the appeal court thought that the sentence should be increased, while a minority opinion was registered in opposition to the increase. The majority appeared to be concerned with the impact of the offence on the victim:

> Leave to appeal is granted. Sentence is increased to 9 months. The period of probation to stand ... While the interest of the respondent is a legitimate concern in sentencing, in my respectful view the trial judge did not discuss the respondent's prior conviction for the sexual assault of another young girl nor the fact that he was still on probation when he committed the offence in question nor did he allude to the traumatic

> effect the offence had on the victim and her family. There was no evidence that the respondent would lose his job if he went to jail.
>
> In a case such as this, involving sexual molestation of a young child by a person occupying a position of trust, a significant period of incarceration is generally called for. The sentence in this case did not reflect the gravity of the offence and a lengthy reformatory sentence would have been more appropriate. However, having regard to the fact that the respondent has served his 90 day intermittent sentence, and that his return to custody will impose additional hardship, I would increase his sentence to 9 months, only.

The dissenting justice emphasized the hardship on the offender in his reasons for not wanting the sentence increased:

> I agree with the summary of the circumstances which has just been made by ... I am also in agreement with him that the sentence imposed at the time it was imposed was too low and that a more substantial sentence ought to have been imposed by the trial judge. I agree with Mr. Justice Griffiths as to why a higher sentence ought to have been imposed. My sole reason for not being able to agree with the disposition proposed by him is that it seems to me that re-incarceration after the respondent has served the complete custodial portion of his sentence would constitute a hardship greatly in excess of that which he would have suffered had he been sentenced to an appropriate custodial period at the time of his trial. A similar problem was faced by this court in *R. v. Inwood* (989) 48 C.C.C. (3d) 173 ... The term which the respondent has served was not an insignificant one. It is my view that the hardship of re-incarceration would not only be greatly out of proportion to the hardship a proper sentence imposed at trial would have caused him, but also out of proportion to the deterrent effect which a sentence of nine months would now have.

Concern with victim impact, demonstrated in this case, is unusual and will be discussed in the next chapter. In some cases, usually involving intercourse, the Court of Appeal recognized that re-incarceration might cause a hardship but increased the sentence nonetheless. This approach is consistent with findings in Chapter 3 that, in these data, penetration is the main factor considered by the Court of Appeal. It is also consistent with the court's willingness to entertain other mitigating variables, discussed earlier in this chapter, when penetration is not part of the offence. Duration of abuse and position of trust appear to be secondary to penetration and can be downplayed when penetration is not present. This issue does not appear in the 1999 data simply because there were only four appeals initiated by the Crown.

Good Character, Reputation, Work Record 1999

Keeping in mind the fact that in the 1999 data there were very few Crown appeals, the climate seems to have changed considerably. The language of the courts is much more denunciatory and focused on the behaviour of the offenders. For example, in *R. v. B., C.I.* (1999), an offender who was the father of his victims appealed after the trial judge sentenced him to six years in the penitentiary for sexually abusing his four daughters by forcing them to have intercourse with him and with their brother over a twenty-one-year period. The victims were all adults in their late twenties or early to mid-thirties at the time of the trial. The judge gave as his reasons for the sentence that the offender, "to satisfy his own personal pleasure, systematically, knowingly and persistently abused his four daughters for a large part of their childhood and young adolescent years thereby robbing them of something no one can give them back, their childhood, and causing them a lifetime of misery. Since escaping from the clutches of their father, at least three of the four abused daughters have undergone extreme trauma in attempting to rebuild their lives from the ruins caused by their father's abuse. They will continue for the foreseeable future to deal with these emotional wounds." In response to the defence counsel's request for leniency, the judge argued that

> such a request might find favour with the court if B showed genuine remorse or compassion for his daughters ... Such remorse as there is, is superficial ... A father's duty to his children is to protect them. He is entrusted with this obligation. B violated that trust and used his children to satisfy his own sexual desires ... B tells everyone who will listen that he is a Christian, God fearing man whose fault is that he fell victim to Satan. I see scant evidence that he feared God at the time he was sexually abusing his daughters. B inserted file handles into his daughters' vaginas and by doing so he sought to teach them to be good sex partners. He stopped short of having intercourse with some of his daughters, as he failed to achieve an erection because he said he was terrified. He testified that because he could not achieve an erection he utilized the handle of a file. He said that because his wife was not as responsive sexually to him as she should have been, he wanted to check out his daughters' responsiveness ... Every person is subject to temptation. Every person has a choice. B had a choice. He chose wrong.

The Court of Appeal said little about his appeal other than to note that he had been released and to state that "in any case we see no merit in the sentence appeal; appeal dismissed."

In *R. v. G., A.* (1998), the trial judge took a witness for the defence to task for minimizing the responsibility of the offender, who was sentenced to five months and three years of probation to follow for fondling his niece's vagina on three occasions over a fifteen-month period. After commenting that the offender's behaviour was not an isolated occurrence and citing the victim impact statement and her testimony, as well as the offender's continued denial, the judge explained that conditional sentences should be reserved for offenders who demonstrate remorse and have taken steps toward reconciliation and rehabilitation at the time of sentencing. He then spoke to the testimony of a physician giving character evidence:

> Whenever I hear people such as Dr. O. offer character evidence for someone who's been convicted of a crime of this nature accompanied by words that he tells me – such as "He tells me he didn't do it and I believe him. I don't believe he could've committed such an offence." It makes the support that's being offered by Dr. O. in this case conditional. It gives the accused a feeling that "He wouldn't forgive me if he knew what I really did." I think that the kind of support that a person who has fallen into committing a criminal offence who is otherwise of good character and reputation would be better if his supporters would say to him, "Notwithstanding that you failed on this occasion, that you did this bad thing, we still love you. We still support you. We still want to help you." That kind of support would be a better framework within which to go forward than support saying, "oh, we know that you're not the kind of person that would ever do any such sort of thing" because it makes the victim [sic] feel that if he does admit his wrongdoing he would lose that support.

The judge did not speak to a similar character reference provided by the offender's priest.

Nonetheless, the appeal court granted the offender's appeal and reduced his sentence to a conditional one of five months as opposed to five months of incarceration, saying that "the conduct did not escalate beyond fondling." The court went on to say that

> rehabilitation does not appear to be a pressing concern since the appellant has not engaged in similar conduct since approximately 1987. His

> lack of any other criminal record strongly suggests that he will not re-offend and therefore does not pose any danger to the community. He has complied with all bail orders since he was charged with this offence. In addition, the offence was completely out of character. The appellant has the support of his family, friends and others who knew him and he is a productive member of his community. He is gainfully employed and the primary source of income for his family. This is an appropriate case for a conditional sentence. In these circumstances, a conditional sentence is consistent with the fundamental purpose and principles of sentencing.

The probation officer in this case, describing the offender's circumstances, said that his family did not believe that the man had committed these offences and said that "as long as he denies the offence, he is not a candidate for treatment." Although the trend in the 1999 data is to reject the defence of "out of character," particularly in cases involving intercourse, in this fondling case the appeal court did invoke the same ideas about "out of character" and "gainfully employed" that existed in the 1990-93 data. One has to wonder how this message was interpreted by both the victim and the offender. It is particularly striking that the Court of Appeal gave credibility to the fact that the offender had the support of people in his community since both the trial judge and the probation officer spoke strongly about what they saw as qualifications to that support.

On the other hand, in *R. v. W., E.* (1998), a trial judge imposed a conditional sentence on a man accused of having had intercourse with his half-sisters over a period of four years when they were between seven and eleven years old from 1970 to 1974 when his mother had left him in charge of them. He was between seventeen and twenty-two years old at the time of the offences. The sentencing judge imposed a conditional sentence, stating that the offences were historical and that the offender was in a dysfunctional family and not disciplined as a child. He noted that there had been no further reported offences and that the offender was steadily employed and in a stable relationship, abusing neither alcohol nor drugs. "I accept that you feel an empathy for the hurt to your sisters, although I do note that there is no admission of the offence by way of remorse or rehabilitation." The judge indicated that the offender was "put in a position of authority by your stepmother and you abused that position." He gave the offender credit for time served of fifty days pre-trial. The judge noted that it was the "only time in your life you have been in jail." He allowed three months for that time. He imposed a condition that the offender pay $1,000 to each of the complainants for counselling. On appeal by the Crown, the appeal court stated:

> We agree with the Crown that a conditional sentence was manifestly unfit. These were horrible crimes in which W. engaged in repeated acts of sexual intercourse with his two half sisters, while he was entrusted by his mother to baby-sit them. These acts of intercourse took place over a four-year period when the two complainants were both young girls. The victim impact statements eloquently attest to the enormous damage, both physical and psychological, suffered by these women because of W.'s acts. In our view these offences called for a very substantial penitentiary term. We accept the Crown's submission that a fit sentence is five years. In imposing this sentence we have taken into account the following mitigating considerations: W. spent 50 days in pretrial custody, for which the trial judge gave him three months credit; apart from these offences W. does not have a criminal record; since these offences have occurred he has made efforts to rehabilitate himself; he has maintained steady employment and generally has led a good life. But for these mitigating considerations, an even longer penitentiary term would have been warranted.

This case was treated differently from the one detailed before it presumably because of the duration of the abuse and the fact that intercourse took place. Other similar facts – such as length of time since the offence, community support, position of trust, absence of remorse, supposed absence of a need for treatment, and good character/work record – are treated differently. One might ask whether these two factors made the critical difference.

Conclusion

The emphasis in sentencing in the 1990-93 data was primarily on the character of the offender and not on the harm of the offence. Sentencing language that began as denunciatory of the offence often ended with excusing the offender to a significant extent. These excuses are consistent with Scully and Marolla's (1984) work on the neutralization of responsibility. The concerns expressed by Mitra (1987) and Taylor (2004) are relevant here, as are the concerns raised by Marshall (1985), Brown (1991), METRAC (1992), and Comack and Balfour (2004). The patriarchal view of child sexual assault can be seen in the frequent evidence of concern with the offender as someone of previous good character, with a good work record and/or education, who for some reason (stress, alcoholism, compulsion, victim complicity) became "temporarily insane" (Ptacek 1988, 152) and committed offences usually believed to be committed by perverts. This view is consistent with the emphasis on penetration in sentencing, noted in the previous chapter, that appears to negate the intent of the legislation to give more credibility to other forms of sexual assault. The pattern that emerged is an interpretation of the law at the time of sentencing that appears to undermine or minimize the effect of the law.

Analyses of the 1990-93 data demonstrated that the previous "good character" or "work record" of a convicted offender was a strong influence on the judges' thinking in terms of sentence. This emphasis demonstrated a tendency to downgrade cases of non-penetration, even those in which the offender was in a position of trust, consistent with what was discussed in the previous chapter. Emphasis on good character ignored the often long-term abuse that this "good" person had perpetrated. The convicted offender was assessed at the sentencing hearing not for what he did, often over a long period of time to a child in a domestic or private relationship, but for what he did in his public or work life. This emphasis on work life has little or no relationship to the offence at issue. It is a demonstration of how social institutions, such as the courts, can act to maintain a traditional view of men's worth, which is largely related to work.

In the 1999 data, which consist primarily of offender appeals, the picture is somewhat different. There was a much stronger emphasis on the offence itself and on its impact on the victim, and more consistency in sentencing when the offence involved intercourse even though there was no statistical significance to these factors as predictors in a quantitative analysis. The focus on the "good man" was gone for the most part, and the judge's commentary in the majority of the cases both at trial and at appeal demonstrated this change in focus. Unknown is how representative this change is of cases of child sexual abuse sentencing in general. Crown resources were significantly cut back in the mid- to late 1990s in Ontario. Perhaps cases containing an emphasis on the offender as a credit to his male role were appealed in 1990-93 but not in 1998-99.

As noted earlier, appellate courts have been instructed by the Supreme Court in *R. v. Proulx* not to interfere with a trial judge's decision unless the sentence is demonstrably unfit. This must have had a chilling effect on the willingness of Crown counsel to appeal cases, as evidenced by the difference in the number of Crown appeals in the 1990-93 data versus the 1998-99 data. As well, in Chapter 1, I observed that there are cases in which the sentence is based on a joint submission to the judge from the Crown and the defence. In these cases, the Crown has agreed to a certain sentencing time frame and is not going to appeal its own agreement. Some of these cases may be seen as inadequate by those on the victim's side of the court, but there is no recourse through appeal because of the Crown's agreement at sentencing. This relative powerlessness of victims and their advocates will be examined in some detail in the next chapter.

5
The Invisible Victim

MacKinnon (1989, 180) says that "the injury of the act of rape lies in the meaning of the act to the victim, but the standard for its criminality lies in the meaning of the act to the assailant." This distinction between injury and criminality is an important one in the cases considered here. The harm done to the victim seems, on the surface at least, to be a substantial consideration for the courts. As we saw in Chapter 3, in these data the harm considered most significant was that attendant on the act of intercourse. The acts were more likely to be clearly denounced as criminal when they met that standard. The harm as defined by the victim impact statements was most clearly noted in those cases. Other invasive, coercive acts were not viewed as seriously, regardless of the period during which they were inflicted on the victim. In cases that did not involve intercourse, emphasis was placed, when possible, on the offender's good character or public persona. Harm to the victim, as presented in victim impact statements, was not a serious consideration, though there was some change from the 1990-93 data to the 1998-99 data. As Finkelhor (1984, 199) has observed, "the impact of an event on childhood itself is treated as less important. It is only 'childhood,' a stage which, after all, everyone outgrows." Finkelhor refers to this as "adult ethnocentrism." This concept is evident in how victim impact is dealt with by the courts in these studies, and has been demonstrated in some of the discussion on other factors in previous chapters.

In 1988, the *Criminal Code of Canada* was changed to allow for victims to provide written statements, or in some cases testimony, about impact. The amendment outlined the place of the victim's statement in the court process: "For the purpose of determining the sentence to be imposed on an offender or whether the offender should be discharged pursuant to section 136 in respect of any offence, the court may consider a statement, prepared in accordance with subsection (1.2), of a victim of the offence describing the harm done to, or loss suffered by, the victim arising from the commission of the offence" (s. 755[1.1]). In 1996, proclamation of Bill C-41 resulted in a change in the law requiring that victim impact statements be considered by judges in the sentencing process. In 1999, the *Criminal Code* was amended to require sentencing judges to ask whether the victim has been advised of the right to give a statement, orally or in writing. Section 722 of the *Criminal Code* outlines the law.

Ruby (1999, 558) contends that "no one can doubt that the victim impact statement creates more severe sentences by confronting the court with the effect of the crime upon the victim. Judges ought not to lose touch with this aspect of a crime." Complainants do not have any special status in law by reason of being the persons named in the indictment. They have no status in criminal proceedings other than as witnesses for the Crown. There has been a good deal of discussion and some research on the use of victim impact statements. The conclusions contradict Ruby: "Despite the high hopes of victim's rights advocates and the pessimism of opponents of victim participation, victim input in court processing has failed to transform the court outcomes and routines in the ways prophesied by either the critics or supporters of the reform" (Erez and Laster 1999, 531). Some of the most significant findings of research on victim impact statements in Canada are their low rate and variability in many jurisdictions (Young 2001). Roberts and Edgar (2002), in a study of Ontario judges' attitudes and experiences with victim impact statements, report that the statements were submitted in only a small number of court cases.

Erez and Laster (1999) and Erez and Rogers (1999) have written about the results of research conducted on the attitudes and beliefs of legal professionals about victim impact statements. They conclude that "practitioners routinely objectify, and thereby minimize, the injuries sustained by victims, and impose an implicit 'reasonable victim' test to evaluate VIS" (Erez and Laster 1999, 530). This is evident in the material that follows in this chapter, particularly in the 1990-93 data.

In addition to the variability in whether or not victim impact statements are present at sentencing, how victim impact is conveyed to the courts is quite variable. Table 5.1 shows the percentage of cases in which victim impact statements were made either through professional reports or through statements written by the victims themselves. Those written by the victims were often handwritten on lined paper or on forms supplied by the police. The handwriting was often difficult to read, and the text was poorly written and characterized by frequent

Table 5.1

Victim impact statements

	1990-93	1999
Self-statement	33	61
Professional input	17	7
No statement	50	32

mistakes in spelling and grammar. The professional clinical reports were always typed, well written, and well presented. It is interesting to note the large number of cases in 1990-93 (50 percent) in which no statement about victim impact was available. By 1999, this had changed: 32 percent of the cases had no statement from the victim, while 61 percent did.

The professionally written impact statements found in the 1990-93 data detail the short-term and long-term effects demonstrated by survivors of abuse. Their observations are consistent with those documented by most of the researchers who wrote in this area at the time (Summit 1983; Browne and Finkelhor 1986; Conte and Schuerman 1987; Finkelhor and Lewis 1988). Most framed their explanations in terms of post-traumatic stress disorder or Finkelhor and Lewis' (1988) "Traumagenic Dynamics." This is consistent with what Erez and Laster (1999, 538) report as the objectification of the victim: "Victim harm was objectified, and a new legal standard of the 'reasonable victim' was invoked to minimize the effect of victim impact." They go on to say that "adhering to an ideal of objectivity allowed judges, for example, to discount many victims' accounts of crime impact as merely subjective and, therefore, irrelevant. Objectivity was also the yardstick by which other occupational groups involved in the preparation or presentation of victim harm statements were also judged."

Cole (2003) conducted a study of Ontario Crown attorneys' perceptions of the use of victim impact statements. He indicated that the majority of the Crowns surveyed recommend to victims that they submit a victim impact statement, but that contacting victims and encouraging them to submit reports are problematic: "The current reality of the case workload in the Canadian justice system is that there is a huge backlog in the system. In an effort to reduce this backlog, a variety of different mechanisms is used to speed up courtroom proceedings and reduce caseloads. These include practices such as plea bargaining and the use of pre-sentence reports. It is possible that the pressure to resolve cases rapidly may undermine the victim impact regime" (36). Prosecutors were asked if they thought that, given more time, they would encourage more victims to submit statements. Of those surveyed, 38.2 percent said definitely yes, 29.4 percent said probably yes, and 32.4 percent said probably not. No one said definitely not.

Victim Impact, 1990-93

In the 1990-93 data, before the 1996 amendments, judges cited *R. v. Clubb* (1984) and *Regina and Owens* (1986) to state that a "judge is not to be moved by his own emotion" when referring to victim impact statements. Judges failed to caution themselves in a similar way when they dealt with offender issues. They did not seem to be aware of their own values vis-à-vis traditional notions of masculinity and aggressive male sexuality and often negated or minimized victim impact. In two cases in the 1990-93 data, *R. v. L., A.P.* (1991) and *R. v. F., V.* (1992), one judge, while talking about his need to be objective in considering victim impact, talked about a psychiatrist's report as being objective even though the material contained in it was based solely on his impressions of an offender's self-report. The judge commented that he knew the report was credible because, in the one case, his wife had gone to high school with the psychiatrist and, in the other, the founder of the psychiatric clinic was a personal friend. The judge went on to make a very confused argument about the offender's status as a pedophile.

In the 1990-93 data, victim impact was cited as an aggravating circumstance by trial judges (41 percent) and by the Court of Appeal (18 percent). The impression here is that the impact on the victim was an important consideration in sentencing. However, consistent with the findings described in Chapter 3, victim impact was usually seriously considered only in cases where penetration occurred. *R. v. W., W.* (1992), referred to briefly in the previous chapter, illustrates that, even in some cases where intercourse has occurred, there is a "yes, but" quality to consideration of victim impact. In that case, a young girl, abused over a period of six years by her father, who was convicted of incest, wrote in her statement to the court that she had developed a strong fear of knives, of men, and of the dark. She had developed anorexia nervosa and bulemia and had been hospitalized many times for long periods as a result. She had made three serious suicide attempts and had become addicted to drugs and alcohol. She stated that her mother no longer wanted contact with her because she was afraid that she would seduce the mother's new husband. Finally, she related a recurring fear that her father would find her and kill her.

The trial judge based his six-year sentence on the harm done to the victim. When the offender appealed, the Court of Appeal reduced the sentence to four years on the following grounds after describing the trial judge's reasons for the sentence: "He was strongly influenced by a victim impact statement which sets out vividly the effect of this conduct on the young victim and the recurring problems which she still has as an adult. On the other hand there were strong mitigating factors in this case. The accused is presently forty-nine years of age and is the sole support for his present wife and child. His present marriage is a successful one. He has no criminal record. A favourable psychiatric report says he has no paedophiliac or incestuous interest at this time." The Court of Appeal left the offender with a four-year sentence, not an insignificant period of time. However, it sent a message that certain offender characteristics overrode the trial judge's concern about victim impact. Concern about his age (forty-nine) and the fact that he was "the sole support of his present wife," and mention that his "present marriage is a successful one," were "yes, but" qualifiers of victim impact. As noted earlier, in these data, victim impact is most likely to be taken seriously in cases involving intercourse. Where other behaviour has taken place, there is an even greater tendency either to say "yes, but" or to ignore victim impact altogether.

R. v. R., P. (1991) is illustrative of this point. In one of the most unusual cases of victim impact, the sentencing judge considered an abusive situation in which a thirty-two-year-old offender sexually assaulted a six-year-old child, who subsequently contracted herpes. The trial judge became caught up to some extent in the issue of penetration: "I must examine the manner in which the offence was committed. In this case, there were a series of events, possibly four in number over a two month period of time. It is uncertain the extent of the genital contact, but the inference is irresistible that there was obviously some form of genital contact. The question of full penetration, complete intercourse, has been considered. There is evidence that the hymen of the child was not broken. The severity of the intrusion is perhaps uncertain." In this case, the offender was not sentenced relative to the actual harm done because he testified that he did not know he had the virus until the child's infection with it became known. Erez and Rogers (1999, 217) point out that although information on victim impact is supposed to ensure proportionally increased sentencing, other considerations are taken into account: "Culpability has a limiting effect on punishment when the harm inflicted by the offender was unforeseen." Nevertheless, it is difficult to understand the concern about the child's hymen being broken when the consequences of contracting the herpes virus for a six-year-old girl are so obviously serious. This case illustrates preoccupation with an interpretation of reality that depends on gendered notions: actual damage to the child is viewed from the perspective of what did not take place rather than what did. This is similar to the case described in Chapter 1 in which Madame Justice Verreault sentenced a father for not having had vaginal intercourse with his daughter, thereby saving her virginity, rather than for having had anal intercourse with her, thereby causing her pain, humiliation, and lasting trauma. Discussion on what the offender did or did not intend to do is privileged and made more important than the obvious damage done to the child. A life-long condition such as herpes certainly increases the possibility of serious long-term effects of the abuse on the victim, since there would be a constant reminder of its occurrence. Characterization of the severity of the intrusion as being connected to whether or not the hymen was broken is evidence of an emphasis on physical damage relative to the idea of a female's value as being connected to her virginity. This emphasis obstructs a proper view of the emotional and other damage.

Offender culpability was minimized and excused. The judge went on to explain his other reasons for arriving at the sentence:

> The criminality of the conduct of the accused is in my opinion the most important factor in the determination of the appropriate sentence. The consequences of his wrongful act cannot be ignored, but it is my view that the criminality of the conduct is the overriding consideration in determining the sentence. In this case, the consequence of his wrongful act, apart from the psychological damage which is not in any way to be minimized, was the infliction of the herpes virus. I am satisfied on all the evidence that the accused did not know at the time and could not have known that he was a carrier of the herpes II virus ... In this case the accused has undergone a course of treatment and analysis and has had extensive psychiatric consultation. The results of those examinations have been put before me. The results say that he exhibits a course of pedophilic tendencies and that there is reason to recommend a particular course of treatment for him. Those pedophilic tendencies can be treated and counseling can be undertaken which will be directed to preventing the same or similar type of offences in the future. Those pedophilic tendencies must of course be taken into consideration in addressing the issue of protection of the public.

> At the same time the presence of pedophilic tendencies is considered and has been considered by the courts of appeal as a reason for imposing a sentence which is less harsh than a sentence that would be imposed on somebody who committed this kind of offence without that psychological impediment or psychological weakness.
>
> ... I am satisfied from the recitation of those events, that there is a clear indication of remorse for having committed the offence. I am satisfied that the accused is genuinely receptive to direction and counseling with respect to his pedophilic tendencies. I am satisfied that he is one who will respond to continued treatment for that disease, emotional upset.
>
> I observe in passing that the psychiatric report makes reference to examples of what the psychiatrist referred to as cognitive defects, and which the psychiatrist identifies as symptomatic of the psychological weakness that the accused has. I interpret that in the same manner as is done by the psychiatrist and I do not interpret it as any indication of want of remorse on the part of the accused.

Clearly, the judge did not understand the psychiatric report, which explained that the offender rationalized his behaviour by stating that he was sexually frustrated because his wife was pregnant and that he found the six-year-old child to be seductive. The phallometric testing conducted by the sexologist indicated that he did not show a preference for children in his sexual responses; rather, he demonstrated a preference for adult women.

The Crown appealed the sentence on the grounds that it did not reflect the gravity of the offence and did not consider the impact of the offences on the child victim. The Court of Appeal dismissed the request: "The offences were serious and had particularly severe and tragic consequences for the young victim. The trial judge properly took those consequences into consideration, but he also properly considered that these consequences were not reasonably foreseeable to the Respondent at the time he committed the offences. The trial judge in careful and detailed reasons considered all of the relevant factors both aggravating and mitigating, and in our view the sentence he imposed was within the appropriate range."

This theme of absence of responsibility of the offender for the outcome of the abuse is troubling. If an adult sexually assaults a child, should he not be held responsible for the effects of that assault on the child, regardless of what they are and whether he could have predicted them at the time of the assault? Are we not all, as adolescents and adults, inundated regularly with messages about safe sex and sexually transmitted diseases? Is it unreasonable to hold an adult responsible for passing on such a disease in the course of sexual assault? The trial judge indicated that his job was to "deal with the offender who has committed the offence and done the damage." Unfortunately, the judge's emphasis was not on the damage but on the offender as "sick" and remorseful as opposed to accountable. As Conrad and Schneider (1985, 27) have observed, this label "may shift the attribution of responsibility": "Sinful and criminal deviants are responsible for their behaviour; sick deviants are not." Moreover, "medical diagnosis affects people's behaviour, attitudes they take toward themselves, and attitudes others take toward them" (31) .

In a 1992 case, appealed by the Crown, a trial judge dismissed the extensive victim impact statements by saying that they were "not facts upon which I can rely or should rely":

> [The accused was] not in loco parentis except for a very short time but was in a position of influence as an uncle. It would appear from the report from the [clinic] that the accused is definitely a homosexual but aside from these occurrences before the court there is nothing to suggest that he is a pedophile ... Based on the evidence available Mr. F. does not feel that the accused needs to attend a sex offender program but possibly he might benefit from psycho-therapy aimed at helping him come to terms with his homosexual orientation ... The victim impact statements have been filed and make tragic reading. I am sure that all are sincere in wanting to blame a great many of the past and present difficulties on these occurrences and this is only natural especially this day and age of no fault living ... I am sure there is and has been serious repercussions from these offences. Can't we say this about all criminal activity? We ... should not lose track that the civil courts are available and maybe should play a part and we must also say that nothing this Court does will change the impact on the victims themselves. The accused is at present forty-eight years of age for the first time convicted of offences which took place some twenty years ago. He is not a pedophile but is an admitted homosexual, a fact that he has considerable difficulty coming to terms with. Alcohol and drugs are not a problem. He shows genuine remorse and is not resentful or hostile and has actively sought medical help. He has a good reputation in the community and he has been steadily employed with a good job for twenty years ... What would normally be a penitentiary term will be reduced to a period of six months incarceration. (*R. v. K., M.* [1993])

The Crown cited victim impact in contending that the sentence did not reflect the gravity of the offences. The Court of Appeal dismissed the appeal, with one justice dissenting: "This was a very serious offence. The majority however while appreciating that the sentence is of the low [end] of the range see no advantage in re-incarcerating the accused for an offence that occurred 20 years ago. Tarnopolsky dissenting would have increased the sentence to two years less a day for purpose of general deterrence and considering the nature of the sexual assaults and the circumstances surrounding their occurrence and the time over which they occurred. Leave to appeal is granted but the appeal is dismissed." The court's message to the victims was not clear in its denunciation of the offender's behaviour. The trial judge gave the offender credit for not being resentful or hostile toward his nephews for bringing charges against him. This judge focused on what a reasonable guy and good worker the offender was rather than on the offence and its effects. The Court of Appeal did not challenge the trial judge's dismissal of the victim impact statements. The majority further contributed to their minimization by emphasizing the fact that the offences happened twenty years earlier. The passage of time was irrelevant to the obvious continuing presence of the damage done.

In contrast to this split decision is another one in the 1990-93 data. In this Crown appeal, two justices of the Court of Appeal emphasized the harm done to the victim by the abuse committed by an offender who had already been incarcerated for a similar offence. The numerous factors listed by the trial judge in mitigation were rejected, and the emphasis was on the harm done to the child. This case involved a forty-four-year-old man who was a family friend. He babysat the three-year-old, whom he fondled, digitally penetrated, and caused to touch his penis. After discussing the psychiatric report, and commenting that the founder of the mental health centre from which the report originated was a personal friend of his and that therefore he knew the centre did excellent work, the trial judge gave his reasoning as follows:

> The court cannot permit itself to let emotion overrule logic. For a person who is "normal" to sexually molest a little girl is one thing, and for a person who is a confirmed and diagnosed paedophiliac is another. Since persons having behavioural patterns involving assaulting children respond to certain drugs, it would be my respectful submission that the behaviour is not caused by depravity or by falling from grace or normal behaviour as a normal person would understand those terms,

> but is quite possibly the result of some chemical imbalance in the human body or some such psychological situation. I think there are various medical theories. Medical research, to date, has not given us the final answer. But it is clear that you cannot apply moral precepts to persons under medical disability (i.e. insanity). From what we have seen of these cases, some day they will be able to control genes or change body chemistry by some other medical process and eliminate this particular offence. We are here dealing with a paedophiliac, as per expert opinion. You do not effect a cure by any period of incarceration ... A judge has to be governed by logic, not by emotion, and not by opinion, if that opinion is not an informed opinion. I have the opinion of trained experts ... and that is the opinion I must look to." (*R. v. L., A.P.*)

The judge did not mention the victim or the many victim impact statements. The Court of Appeal, however, did: "As a result of the assault, the child suffered a significant change in her behaviour and personality. In particular the child began to suffer from increased anxiety, constant agitation and swift mood swings. Although previously a happy, affectionate and loving child she began to act out of character by displaying fits of aggression, rudeness and defiance ... [The trial judge did not] allude to the traumatic effect the offence had on the victim and her family." The Court of Appeal's full decision is about three pages long. Cited at length are reports, written by experts, about the impact of the offence on the victim. This is the longest appeal decision in the 1990-93 data; the dissenting justice disagreed solely on the ground that re-incarceration would likely cause the offender hardship. The majority decision was also unusual because of the emphasis on the abuse in the absence of intercourse. The comprehensive professional reports referred to by the majority may have been a factor in the decision.

Consent of the Victim

This issue appeared only in the 1990-93 data. In the following discussion of consent as a mitigating circumstance, construction of the child victim as consenting and of the offender as vulnerable to temptation demonstrates how the classic notions of victim blaming and offender as victim were sometimes present in the court process during this time period.

The issue of consent, or willingness to participate in the abuse, was used as a mitigating circumstance in 4 percent of the cases by both the original trial judge and the Court of Appeal. Although this does not seem like a large number, by its very presence it represents a serious issue. In a Crown appeal, the fifty-four-year-old father of a sixteen-year-old Children's Aid Society ward was convicted of two counts of sexual assault under section 271 for fondling her and performing simulated intercourse on her while she was home on a weekend pass from a group home. She had been made a ward of the CAS at age twelve after having been abused by unidentified third parties. Reports indicated that the victim suffered from sleep disturbance and had dreams that her father was trying to kill her. She also felt the loss of her relationship with her mother, who had taken the father's side in this situation and remained supportive of the father. The judge imposed a sentence of four months of incarceration plus two years of probation. His reasons for the sentence were as follows:

> In assessing sentence here I have to ask "is this man a danger to society? Is he likely to re-offend?" I would like to have had more facts. The Children's Aid did remove this young victim from her home on a previous occasion. She had been a ward for a number of years and was it to deal with her problem or to prevent further offences? I have really no facts that would help me. Also I have to consider *who is the victim here?* Certainly the mother has been the common best friend shall I say for both, the victim and the accused. One has to wonder what the effect would have been if the mother had ... believed the victim ... *If she had dealt with it as a family matter the results might have been quite different* ... Both the accused and the victim indicated ... they had [the] mother's consent for her to go to the room to be with the accused. And quite properly so, it was their home and they were a family unit, and the mother was there. Certainly [she] didn't expect any problem. I have had the benefit of hearing from the victim, seeing the victim on the stand. She is no longer a little child. She is a young lady who has had the benefit of counseling over a period of years. I find as a fact that she went to the accused's room and engaged in play fighting with him both days which I find *triggered the sexual assaults.* There are special circumstances here in considering the accused for I find that he is of limited ability. He has needs for guidance just as the victim has shown to need guidance. The victim here as reported in the victim impact statement is ... very upset, hurt and isolated as a result of this. She indicates that she is also very angry with her mother for not believing her, but I reiterate it was not her mother that she turned to as a confidant. It might have been helpful to the court to have had a professional assessment of the accused, his ability, his mental age. I reiterate

> that on the facts I do not consider that he is a danger to society, I find that his needs are for the simple basics of life. He requires his wife's support, similar to that of the victim. The accused had not been brought up in a loving protective home where he learned to accept responsibility. He did not force himself on her as indicated. I find that the play fighting triggered an assault and he offered her money to get her consent. She admitted that she did consent because she wanted the money, and that is why. After the events she became very confused and hurt, and she was told that she could not tell anyone or she would not be able to come home and would have to go to jail. *They both knew it was very wrong and it has to be dealt with on the facts* (*R. v. L., H.* [1991]; emphasis added).

The judge went on to say that the *offender* had endured a trial and that a penitentiary sentence would be devastating to both him and his family.

The Crown appealed the sentence on the grounds that it failed to reflect the gravity of the offences and did not adequately reflect the principles of general and specific deterrence and protection of the public. The Court of Appeal dismissed the appeal for the following reasons: "The sentence imposed is at the extreme low end of the range for such offences. Having regard, however, for the age of the offender, the fact that he has no prior conviction for offences of this kind and the report that he is unlikely to offend again and having particular regard to the fact that he has served his sentence and a period of approximately one year has elapsed since serving his sentence, we are of the view that we should not now interfere with the sentence. Accordingly, leave to appeal is granted and the appeal is dismissed." The Court of Appeal did not challenge the less than subtle blaming of the victim in the trial judge's reasons for the sentence. Nor did it pick up on the implication that somehow the mother was responsible as well for what had happened, unlike the rejection of that position made in *R. v. M., G.* (1991), cited earlier. When the judge says "I have to consider who is the victim here?" and when he speculates about the mother allowing the father and the daughter to be in a room alone together, he implies responsibility for the assault. He also implies that the mother should have kept the abuse within the family. By saying that the "play fighting ... triggered the sexual assaults," the judge does not acknowledge the father's culpability for assaulting his daughter; he is saying, rather, that the daughter prompted the assaults by going to her father's room and engaging in play fighting with him. Because she has had counselling, he assumes that she is more sophisticated or mature than the average child. He does not understand it as an indication of her vulnerability. Is a child who goes into a parent's bedroom responsible for being sexually assaulted there? Is a child who engages in play fighting with her father responsible for triggering his sexual interest in her?

The second rationale used by the trial judge is that the daughter consented in exchange for money. If consent was a genuine issue in this case, then how was the offender convicted? Why does the notion of consent in child sexual assault arise at sentencing? The *Criminal Code* clearly outlines the viability of the concept of consent for the purpose of sexual assault in section 271.1(1):

> (2) No consent is obtained, for the purposes of sections 271, 272 and 273, where:
> (a) the agreement is expressed by the words or conduct of a person other than the complainant;
> (b) the complainant is incapable of consenting to the activity;
> (c) the accused induces the complainant to engage in the activity by abusing a position of trust, power or authority;
> (d) the complainant expresses, by words or conduct, a lack of agreement to engage in the activity; or
> (e) the complainant, having consented to engage in sexual activity, expresses, by words or conduct, a lack of agreement to continue to engage in the activity.

Although the victim's consent is not a viable defence for the offender who pleads not guilty at trial, it appears to be a viable defence in mitigation of sentence which, in effect, tells the offender that, although he is technically guilty and will go to jail, he really isn't at fault or responsible. The judge appears to be operating out of some belief that the offender is not responsible for his behaviour and that the women around him are. Certainly this judge is not familiar with the distinction made by Smart (1989, 34) between submission and consent. Smart discusses the disqualification of women's reality in the process of a rape trial: "The rape trial may not celebrate random rape, but it does celebrate the deep-seated notions of natural male sexual need and female sexual capriciousness." (Smart, 1989, 34)

West (1987, 82) echoes these sentiments: "Far from being actionable at law women's 'gender specific injuries' are dismissed as trivial (sexual harassment on the street), consensual (for example, marital rape) or 'participatory, subconsciously wanted, or self-induced' (for example, father/daughter incest)." West appears to capture the essence of the trial judge's thinking. Construction of the victim as participatory and of the abuse as self-induced is dismissive of the harm inherent in the crimes, blaming of the victim, and excusing of the offender. Unfortunately, this judge was not alone in his view of sexual assault.

In another case, the Court of Appeal introduced the concept of consent as mitigating. A thirty-three-year-old offender was convicted of six counts of sexual exploitation and sentenced to two years less one day for seducing and having intercourse with a fourteen-year-old girl who was his employee in a pizza business. The offender pleaded not guilty and appealed both the conviction and the sentence. The trial judge, stating that the offender showed no remorse for his abuse of the girl, explained the sentence:

> Here then, is mature man, hung with all [the] trappings of the good life, a loving wife, a fine family, a successful business, a reputation in the community for charity and probity, who acts without conscience in the gratification of his sexual desires; who acts without constraint in his conduct towards an innocent immature female; who in his position of authority takes advantage of a young person who has not yet found the means or the strength to defend herself ... No term of incarceration must be of such length as to risk the destruction of his marriage and his close relationship with his three daughters. These two elements are paramount in my mind in deciding to reduce the period of incarceration from that of a term in penitentiary, to that of a term in an Ontario Reformatory. (*R. v. G., T.* [1992])

In its decision, the Court of Appeal allowed the offender's appeal of his sentence by reducing it to fifteen months of imprisonment:

> On the appeal against sentence, the maximum punishment for the offence is imprisonment for five years. The intercourse, as we have noted, was consensual. The Crown concedes that there was no actual exploitation of the employer/employee relationship by the appellant. Further, there was no evidence of trauma or psychological damage to the complainant. The appellant was a person of previous good character and appears to have enjoyed an excellent reputation in the community. Although there are elements of the commission of the offence which are troubling, such as the act of intercourse in the parent's home, we believe that, having regard to the maximum sentence for the offence and the sentences in somewhat similar cases to which we have been referred by the Crown, a 15 month sentence would be appropriate.

It is not clear how the Crown could concede that an employer in his thirties did not exploit the employer-employee relationship with a fourteen-year-old employee when he seduced her except that he did not explicitly threaten her with loss of employment to get her to comply. Instead, he used his position of power and trust to engage in a course of sexual seduction that resulted in intercourse. The Court of Appeal found that the intercourse was consensual. The definition of sexual exploitation in the *Criminal Code* in section 153(1) does not specifically mention consent, but the entire category of sexual offences against children, of which this one is a part, precludes the use of consent as a defence (Rodriques and Ouellet 1993). The offence of sexual exploitation is premised on the relationship of authority of the offender and/or dependency of the victim. To use the notion that the behaviour was consensual and to claim that the employer-employee relationship was not directly exploited seem to contradict the purpose of the section of the *Criminal Code* under which he was convicted of six offences. The Court of Appeal went further in mentioning that one of the troubling aspects of the offence was that the offender engaged in sexual intercourse with the girl in her parents' home. This seems to echo the concept of children (and their sexuality) as the property of their parents, and the most offensive part of the behaviour seemed to be the location in which it took place since it could be construed as even more intrusive and offensive to the parents. The essence of the exploitation of the fourteen-year-old girl by a thirty-three-year-old man was overlooked. The facts that he "enjoyed an excellent reputation in the community" and was of previous good character were used in mitigation of what he did, not as an indication that he should have known better in the first place.

1998-99 Data

In the 1999 data, there is a higher percentage of victim impact statements, the majority of which were written by the victims themselves. As in the 1990-93 data, the self-statements were often poorly written on photocopied forms, which contrast starkly with the glossy reports that lawyers and professional expert witnesses usually submit to the court. As noted earlier, of the three cases of Crown appeals, two dealt with the imposition of conditional sentences, while one concerned the imposition of a provincial sentence. Proportionality, or the degree to which the sentence fit the crime, was one of the primary factors in bringing the appeals forward. Victim impact was an important feature in identifying proportionality.

In *R. v. M., J.* (1998), a sixty-five-year-old man was convicted of sexual touching, forced fellatio, and simulated intercourse in relation to his two step-grandchildren over a three-year period, from 1991 to 1994, and to his niece over a one-month period in 1991. He had been sentenced earlier for similar behaviour with different victims during the same time period. The sentence on this occasion was a twelve-month conditional sentence with three years of probation. The victim impact statements from this case were as follows:

> Victim # 1: typed onto the usual form. She said that her faith in men was shattered and that she felt unworthy of love. She always felt as if something bad was about to happen. "This whole ordeal, including the potential outcome of his trial, ha[s] only strengthened my belief that I mean nothing ... He will never receives [sic] what he deserves and this is just one more thing we have to come to terms with and move on from. I have to ask now why I bothered. Why did we? The most important thing that I have to deal with is the fact that I do not feel safe ... What if this happens again? How do I prevent a situation from occurring again when I have no control?"
>
> Victim # 2: handwritten on the usual form. Her handwriting was very child like as she explained that her grades were going down because she couldn't concentrate. She said that she was very uncomfortable with men and boys and spent most of her time alone. She has lost all faith in people and spends most of her time crying.
>
> Victim # 3: handwritten on the usual form. She said that she felt stupid and angry at the offender. "Embaressed [sic] of the fact that I did not do anything." She said that she "is upset, mad, scared and never feels safe anywhere." She said that she feels like an outcast and no one understands.

The trial judge did not mention the victim impact statements when he gave his reasons for the sentence:

> These are offences which had already been committed by the accused but had not been disclosed at the time of the imposition of the earlier sentence; prison sentence had already been served by the time he got to court on these charges; offender is complying with the conditions of a probation order imposed by sentencing judge in 1995 and is

> participating actively in group counselling for sexual offenders. There is a psychological assessment which was filed as part of the defence brief, and which indicates that the accused now represents a low risk for re-offending.
>
> The prosecutor in this case has argued strenuously that the nature of the offences for which the accused is to be sentenced, that is the repeated sexual abuse of young persons in respect to whom the accused stood in a position of trust, requires that a mid-range reformatory jail sentence be imposed ...
>
> The difficulty I am faced with is to determine whether at this time in light of the events which have transpired since the accused committed the offences for which I must sentence him, it is now appropriate that he serve a sentence of imprisonment in jail or in the community.
>
> I find myself in the rare situation, more frequently encountered by courts of appeal, where events have transpired during an intervening period of time which require that a different sentence be imposed than that which might originally have been appropriate.
>
> On the evidence presented to me, I am satisfied that the accused does not at this time pose a danger to the community in the light of the prison term he has already served and the rehabilitative steps he has already taken and continues to take.

When the Crown appealed the sentence, the Court of Appeal also did not mention victim impact in its decision: "This is a most unusual case. On its facts, we are not prepared to say that the trial judge did err in principal [sic]. However, assuming that is so, we are never the less of the opinion that it would not be in the interests of justice to interfere. The Crown [is] quite right in bringing this case to this court. The appeal is dismissed."

In the other conditional sentencing case, *R. v. B., J.* (1998), the offender was the thirty-one-year-old uncle of a twelve-year-old victim forced to have intercourse over a one-week period. The victim impact statement was written on the usual form. The handwriting and grammar were reasonably good. The victim described how the abuse incidents tore her family apart: "The guilt and blame that I have lived with [are] never ending. I feel enormous blame for not telling anyone right away for fear of hurting the family. I was to [sic] ashamed to stand up for my rights and I believe this continued in my life where people take advantage of me. It is something evil and sickening to deal with and the fact that he will not admit it makes me feel even more hurt and angry." She went on to say that the offender took her virginity and caused her physical pain and humiliation. She said that she became promiscuous as a result of the abuse and allowed men to use her sexually, while she has never been able to have pleasure from sex.

In sentencing the offender to a conditional sentence of two years less one day, the trial judge observed that he was a successful man respected by his neighbours and his friends and that his family was split by the revelation of these incidents. The judge said that the offender's good reputation was not unusual since sexual incidents are often hidden, but nonetheless he found the community support for the offender mitigating. He gave him credit for agreeing to take counselling, even though he denied the charges, and for the fact that the incidents took place nearly twenty-five years previously. The offender was also credited for leading a successful and productive life since that time. The judge stated that the victim impact statement was tragic but that the purpose of the sentence was not vengeance: "Often those who have been hurt by a crime will naturally seek vengeance." He pointed out that the "sting of these proceedings on these charges has touched him severely" and that he was satisfied that specific deterrence had been accomplished in this case. The judge also commented on the concession that the offender would take counselling as an important part of his rehabilitation and that, although there was victim impact, it was a first offence.

When the Crown appealed the sentence, the Court of Appeal did not mention victim impact in its decision to overturn the conditional sentence:

> An unusual feature of this case is that while the offences were committed over twenty years ago, the respondent since that time engaged in threatening conduct towards the complainant in an attempt to continue to suppress the complaint. This included attempts to see the complainant and years later calling the complainant at work and telling her to "keep her mouth shut." As well, the respondent uttered a death threat to his ex-wife, a person he knew to be a Crown witness, after the charges were laid. In his otherwise very complete reasons for sentencing, the trial judge made no reference to this conduct. This evidence was crucial in determining whether the respondent represented a risk to the community and whether a conditional sentence properly reflected the principles of specific and general deterrence. In our view the trial judge erred in principle in imposing a conditional sentence in the circumstances. Bearing in mind that the respondent has already completed the two hundred hours of community service during the seven months he has been serving the conditional sentence, we would grant leave to

> appeal, allow the appeal and vary the conditional sentence of two years less one day to fifteen months.

In contrast, victim impact was introduced as one of the factors to consider in another appeal case, *R. v. Stuckless* (1998). A fifty-year-old man was convicted for a variety of sexual acts, including fellatio and mutual masturbation as well as having boys perform sexual acts with others while he watched. There were forty victims, and seventeen victim impact reports were presented to the court. Most of them were handwritten on the usual forms. Most of the victims spoke about the long-term damage of the abuse. Some described suicide attempts, and one, writing about one of the victims, described his successful suicide, attributed to his abuse at the hands of this offender.

In raising the sentence from two years less one day to five years after the Crown appealed it, the Court of Appeal addressed the failure of the trial judge to properly consider victim impact as one of many factors including planning and a position of trust. The appeal court outlined his reasons for the sentence: "The sentencing judge observed that S's pattern was initially to establish a 'relationship of trust and confidence with his target,' or to take advantage of an already established position of trust by virtue of his being a teacher's assistant or hockey coach. He then, as [the trial judge] stated, 'consistently and without apparent hesitation, violated the trust reposed in him.'" His conduct was further described as follows:

> His conduct was purposeful, his approach predatory. He had but one goal in mind. The boys were merely means to an end, the sexual gratification of S. The crimes of S. were an integral part of an overall scheme of defilement. They were not situational, momentary lapses of judgment when reason was temporarily dethroned. They were, rather, carefully orchestrated, deliberate and predatory. For nearly twenty (20) years, S. systematically abused two (2) dozen vulnerable persons. He cultivated, only to violate, their trust. For nearly two (2) decades, S. routinely targeted and cultivated more than two (2) dozen naive, often disadvantaged, boys to satisfy his own sexual fantasies and desires. Equally routinely, he violated a position of authority and a trust that he had so assiduously created and sedulously fostered. He was indifferent to his victims, unaware and uncaring of the effects, immediate and long term, on those whom he had victimized. His approach was purposeful, predatory and single-minded.

The Court of Appeal pointed out the problems in the trial judge's assessment of these behaviours as being at the "lower end" in terms of seriousness in speaking to victim impact:

> [The trial judge] recognized that the offences left a "profound and enduring impression" on the victims, but he nonetheless emphasized that S. "neither caused nor threatened actual bodily harm" or force, "apart from the coercion which is implicit in conduct which takes place in the context of any relationship where there is a power imbalance." He concluded, therefore, that while these offences would warrant a substantial term of imprisonment, they would not attract the maximum punishment of 10 years sought by the Crown. In his view, "the crimes of S. are nearer to the lower end of the spectrum."

Finally, in pointing out that the trial judge had made an error in sentencing the offender to a provincial sentence, and in increasing the sentence to five years, the Court of Appeal concluded that there were several important factors, including but not limited to victim impact. These errors resulted in a reduced emphasis on the many aggravating factors in this case: the premeditation, the number of victims and years of victimization, the history of failed treatment and denial of responsibility by S., the abuse of trust and confidence of vulnerable boys, the profound impacts on the victims, and the fragility of rehabilitative prospects over time.

Mention of victim impact is notable in some other cases. In *R. v. G., J.* (1998), a fifty-eight-year-old man was sentenced to two and a half years for the sexual touching of an eight-year-old victim, again using section 271 of the *Criminal Code* in addition to section 151 (sexual interference). In giving his reasons for the sentence, the judge cited the offender's criminal record, which dated back to 1958 and included four convictions for sexual assault, one for assault causing bodily harm, and one for contributing to juvenile delinquency:

> To say that he has not inflicted on this victim the hurt of more specific sexual assault or extended sexual assault than occurred here is blowing in the wind because I have read the impact statements filed, not just by the victim but by her mother who expresses to me and to the court and to the public the horrible effect upon the eight year old victim and her family ... It's useless and less than helpful to me to hear that well there wasn't oral sex here but the circumstances show that there

> was an invitation to oral sex and if young K. had not been determined there would have been, obviously, oral sex. So it's no help to say that well it's not as bad as what occurred back in 1987 or 1979 ... The crime, in my view, is serious and can't easily be analyzed on the basis of the level of its impact on society ... To say that Mr. G. has suffered as a result of this charge, and being incarcerated awaiting trial, then through the trial, is almost an insult to the victims because it's absolutely clear that in sentencing proceedings we can't just focus on the accused. [We] need to address the concerns of the community; even with treatment he has committed this offence ... What hope is there? What confidence is there that he would not commit further offences before too long?

Finally, the trial judge emphasized the need for the offender to receive treatment.

There were two victim impact statements. One was completed by a staff member in a child witness program and reported that the victim felt mad and scared and that she did not want to tell the police what happened and to use words such as *penis* and *vagina.* She was also reported as saying that "eight year olds should not have to go to court – they're too young." Yet she was glad to go to court so that Mr. G. could not hurt anyone else. The second report was typed by the victim's mother, who said that her daughter's faith in the world had been shaken by this crime and that she (the mother) had intense feelings of rage and guilt because she had not been able to protect her child. She said that the child's daily routines had to change to adjust to her fear and her sleep problems as well as a variety of physical symptoms. As well, the child had to change schools after the criminal charges became known.

In granting the offender's sentence appeal, and reducing his sentence to time served, followed by a probation term of two years, the Court of Appeal spoke to the limits of considering victim impact:

> As to sentence, we are of the view that the sentence is grossly excessive and requires our intervention, notwithstanding the appellant's record for similar offences. The trial judge was motivated to impose this sentence primarily for the purposes of treatment. However, in s. 718.1 of the *Criminal Code,* Parliament has laid down as the fundamental principle of sentencing that the sentence be proportionate to the gravity of the offence and the degree of responsibility of the offender. While an offence involving sexual touching of a young child is always serious, not all offences are of equal gravity within the meaning of s. 718.1. The

> appellant was not in a position of trust. The touching was brief, on the top of the complainant's underwear, and had few of the more serious aggravating features often associated with this kind of conduct. We acknowledge the serious consequences upon the complainant's family, but that does not justify a sentence out of the appropriate range. As well, the degree of responsibility did not warrant this length of sentence. The appellant immediately desisted from the conduct. He has sought treatment in the past. The objectives of treatment and protection of the public are best met by the imposition of appropriate terms of probation and the order made under s. 161 of the *Criminal Code.*

When the sentence was reduced to time served, the offender had served twelve months on these charges. The statement that not all offences are of equal seriousness warrants closer examination. Are the offences only the behaviour of the offender, or do they include the consequences of that behaviour for the victim? Sexual touching is not intercourse. Does that automatically make it a less serious offence? By whose calculation? How are the courts to weigh the impacts of various forms of abuse? What happens when victims of similar forms of abuse report different impacts?

Finally, in *R. v. B.S.* (1998), a forty-two-year-old stepfather was convicted of sexual assault for offences over a three-month period involving masturbating in front of his fifteen-year-old stepdaughter, talking sexually to her, digitally penetrating her, and getting her to pose nude. He was sentenced to eighteen months in jail, with two years of probation to follow. In her victim impact statement, the fifteen-year-old said that she was "crushed inside to see how it has effected [sic] my mother" and that "the fear of seeing him again is unexplainable." In outlining her reasons for the sentence, the judge said that the offender had spared his stepdaughter from having to testify by pleading guilty, that he had no criminal record, and that there were positive professional reports about his attempts at rehabilitation since the offences were discovered. The judge also pointed out that the abuse did not stop until the victim reported it and that the offender's conduct had escalated from sexual talk to masturbating in front of her to digital penetration. The trial judge cited victim impact and the victim's demeanour in court and her irretrievable loss of innocence. She concluded that this egregious breach of trust needed to be denounced.

The Court of Appeal reduced the offender's sentence to eight months of incarceration:

> We agree with the trial judge that the conduct of the appellant towards his step-daughter was most reprehensible and it amounted to a serious breach of trust. Under these circumstances, we are not persuaded that the trial judge erred in refusing to impose a conditional sentence.
>
> That said, we note that apart from the two incidents of sexual touching, the misconduct in question essentially amounted to sexual exploitation. In view of that, we believe that the trial judge over-emphasized the principles of general deterrence and denunciation in arriving at the 18 month sentence she imposed. Moreover, although the trial judge referred to the significant mitigating factors favouring the appellant, we are not persuaded that she gave sufficient weight to them.

The Court of Appeal may have been influenced by the professional reports presented at the sentencing hearing. The next chapter deals with that influence.

Conclusion

Mitchell's (1985) question about whose side of the story we hear in cases of child sexual abuse is still relevant. In these data, it appears to depend on who is listening. The variability noted earlier about sentencing exists as well in how the victim impact statements are heard and what use is made of them.

MacKinnon's (1989, 180) observation quoted at the beginning of the chapter – "the injury of the act of rape lies in the meaning of the act to the victim, but the standard for its criminality lies in the meaning of the act to the assailant" – appears to be borne out in the data. Victims' views of the offences are not the dominant consideration in the sentencing proceedings. Their experiences of the crimes committed against them are subjugated to a different order of understanding of the behaviour. Different judges hear them differently, and most judges hear other voices speaking more loudly to the issues in front of the court. Although victim impact has been given a clearer place in the *Criminal Code of Canada,* in the majority of cases in which victim impact was mentioned, there was a "yes, but" quality to the judicial notice. Attention was usually turned to those offender issues that judges seem to construct as more relevant to their decisions. The victims' invisibility conjures up an image of a small child lost to the sight of the judge in front of an imposing bench. It is tempting to attribute the child's relative lack of presence to the smallness of childhood, but some of these victims, as noted in Chapter 2, were adults at the time of trial. Their invisibility goes beyond their small size. Indeed, their stature appears to be small because of how it is constructed relative to that of the male defendant.

The next chapter deals with how the stature of the defendant is portrayed by the clinicians who present reports about them to the court. Some of these reports mirror traditional misconceptions about child sexual abuse and thus have an impact on the victim's visibility or relevance in the process.

6
The Elevated Expert

One of the more interesting and revealing findings in my research is how judicial decision makers depend on "experts" to help them understand the offenders and, by extension, the offences. Particularly interesting and concerning in the 1990-93 data was how little attention was paid to the victim's input unless it was presented through the voice of an "expert." Conrad and Schneider (1992) go beyond Gusfield's (1992) challenge to the neutrality of medical opinion and examine what they call the medicalization of deviance in an effort to analyze the interaction between the social construction of behaviour and the medical definition of it. They define the notion of medicalization and their view of its importance as follows: "Medicalization is primarily a definitional phenomenon – that is, one of how a problem is collectively defined, by whom, and with what consequences ... Our view of the medicalization thesis is that it is essentially about culture, focusing on the creation and use of categories and how this process constitutes, shores up, or challenges existing notions of reality. We need to examine carefully the nature of medical knowledge/power: where and how it is deployed; and who is deploying it ... The emphasis of the medicalization thesis remains on the production of definitions, their use, and the consequences of that use" (Conrad and Schneider 1992, 278).

In this chapter, I will examine the production of medical definition as it applies to the data gathered. What influence do medical/psychiatric and psychological reports have on the sentencing process? What is the construction of the offender in these reports? What role do other reports play? Table 6.1 shows which reports are submitted to the court in these data, giving both the profession of the writer and the number of reports in each category. In 1990-93, there were no reports in 9 of the 103 cases studied.

Table 6.1

Reports submitted to court on sentencing

Type of report	Total number 1990-93	1998-99
Medical/psychiatric/psychological	48	15
Pre-sentence	83	36
Clergy	5	8
Both psych and pre-sentence	40	10
Victim impact statement	36	25
Professional report on victim impact	14	6

The greatest number of reports written in both data sets were pre-sentence reports. They are written by probation officers at the request of the judge to provide the judge with information about the previous history and current life context of the offender. The *Criminal Code of Canada* (s. 721[3]) outlines what information the pre-sentence report should contain:

> Unless otherwise specified by the court, the report must, wherever possible, contain information on the following matters:
>
> (a) the offender's age, maturity, character, behaviour, attitude and willingness to make amends;
>
> (b) subject to subsection 119(2) of the *Youth Criminal Justice Act,* the history of previous dispositions under the *Young Offenders Act,* chapter Y-1 of the Revised Statutes of Canada, 1985, the history of previous sentences under the *Youth Criminal Justice Act,* and of previous findings of guilt under this Act and any other Act of Parliament;
>
> (c) the history of any alternative measures used to deal with the offender, and the offender's response to those measures; and
>
> (d) any matter required, by any regulation made under subsection (2), to be included in the report.
>
> 4) The report must also contain information on any other matter required by the court, after hearing argument from the prosecutor and the offender, to be included in the report, subject to any contrary regulation made under subsection (2).
>
> 5) The clerk of the court shall provide a copy of the report, as soon as practicable after filing, to the offender or counsel for the offender, as directed by the court, and to the prosecutor.

The probation officer, then, writes the report at the request of the trial judge after the offender has either been convicted or entered a plea of guilty. Given that the judge has asked for the report, which likely accounts for the numerous reports written by probation officers compared to those written by others, one would expect it to be mentioned in the trial judge's reasons for the sentence.

Reports written by experts are most often solicited and paid for by the offender. Table 6.1 shows that some are also solicited by the Crown. Some are reports written by child service agencies, which would not require payment, and some are written by self-employed professionals who are presumably paid by the Crown or by the victims.

In the time between the 1990-93 and the 1998-99 data, changes were made to the rules governing "expert" testimony. One of the cases in the 1990-93 data was *R. v. Mohan* (1992). The offender, a pediatrician, was convicted of sexually assaulting four young female patients. He appealed his conviction, while the Crown appealed his sentence of nine months plus two years of probation. Some of the reasons he gave for appealing his conviction were the following:

> 1) the judge erred in ruling inadmissable the evidence of a psychiatrist with respect to the particular characteristics of the offence which rendered its perpetrator a member of an unusual and aberrant group; 2) that the judge erred in ruling inadmissible the evidence of a psychiatrist that the offences were unlikely to have been committed by the same person having regard to the fact that one of the offences was likely to have been committed by a member of an aberrant group which the perpetrator of the other offences would not have been a member; 3) the judge erred in failing to admit evidence that the Appellant having been assessed by a psychiatrist, was not a member of either of the unusual groups of aberrant personalities who would have committed the offences alleged.

His argument was that the trial judge had not allowed a psychiatrist to testify that he was not a typical sex offender. The psychiatrist who testified did not conduct any of the standard assessment tests that might have been used in a forensic psychiatric clinic to help him arrive at his diagnosis. In instructing the jury, the trial judge stated:

> The evidence of Dr H. is not sufficient, I believe, to establish that doctors who commit sexual assaults on patients are in a significantly more limited group in psychiatric terms than are other members of society.

> There is no scientific data available to warrant that conclusion. A sample of three offenders is not a sufficient basis for such a conclusion. Even the allegations of the fourth complainant referred to in Count seven are not so unusual, as sex offences go, to warrant a conclusion that the perpetrator must have belonged to a sufficiently narrow class.
>
> These days it is trite to say that a large number of men from all walks of life commit sexual offences on young women. While all may have some type of character disorder, I doubt that expert evidence regarding the normality of any given accused would be of assistance to a trier of fact absent some[thing] more distinguishing with[in] the wide spectrum of sexual assault.

The Court of Appeal ruled that the trial judge did not understand the psychiatrist's testimony and that he should have left it to the jury to decide whether they accepted it or not. The appeal court set aside the verdict and ordered a new trial. The Crown appealed this decision to the Supreme Court of Canada. In 1994, the Supreme Court allowed the appeal, set aside the judgment of the Court of Appeal, restored the convictions, and sent the case back to the Court of Appeal for disposition of the sentence appeal. The Court of Appeal for Ontario subsequently rejected the Crown's appeal and left the sentence at nine months plus two years of probation.

In making its ruling, the Supreme Court set out four criteria by which courts should assess expert evidence: relevance, necessity in assisting the trier of fact, absence of any exclusionary rule, and a properly qualified expert. In defining the concept of relevance, the Supreme Court gave the following questions as a test:

1. Is the evidence likely to assist the jury in its fact-finding mission, or is it likely to confuse and confound the jury?
2. Is the jury likely to be overwhelmed by the "mystic infallibility" of the evidence, or will the jury be able to keep an open mind and objectively assess the worth of the evidence?

The Supreme Court defines necessity in assisting the trier of fact, stating that "an expert's opinion is admissible to furnish the Court with scientific information which is likely to be outside the experience and knowledge of a judge or jury. If on the proven facts a judge or jury can form their own conclusions without help, then the opinion of the expert is unnecessary." Its definition of absence of any exclusionary rule is "compliance with criteria (a), (b) and (d) will not ensure the admissibility of expert evidence if it falls afoul of an exclusionary rule of evidence separate and apart from the opinion rule itself." And finally, in regard to the properly qualified expert, the Supreme Court says that "the evidence must be given by a witness who is shown to have acquired special or peculiar knowledge through study or experience in respect of the matters on which he or she undertakes to testify."

The experts in my two studies were most commonly psychiatrists and psychologists. The professions represented in these "expert" reports are generally accepted as qualified to offer opinion to the courts and as such fulfill the role described by Conrad and Schneider (1992, 244) as gatekeepers: "Medicine acts not only as an independent agent of social control, but frequently medical collaboration with other authorities serves social control functions. Such collaboration includes roles as information provider, gatekeeper, institutional agent, and technician. The medical profession is the official designator of the 'sick role.' This imbues the physician with the authority to define particular kinds of deviance as illness and exempt the patient from certain role obligations. These are general gatekeeping and social control tasks. In some instances the physician functions as a specific gatekeeper for special exemptions from conventional norms." This notion appears to be supported by the use of reports in judicial justification of sentencing decisions.

Table 6.2 shows the frequency with which various types of reports were cited by the trial judge at the original sentencing hearing and/or the Court of Appeal in their reviews of sentencing decisions. In 1990-93, trial judges cited the professionally written reports about the victim most frequently. These reports were second lowest in frequency in terms of their availability to the court. Next they cited the professionally written reports about the offender. Victims' self-reports were third in frequency of citation, and pre-sentence reports, the most frequently occurring reports, were actually the least frequently cited.

Table 6.2

Reports cited in sentencing

	Cited by			
	Trial judge		Court of Appeal	
Type of report	1990-93	1998-99	1993	1998-99
Medical/psychiatric/psychological	30	14	8	4
Pre-sentence	20	10	3	0
Written by professional about victim	13	4	10	0
Victim self-report	12	25	3	6

Interestingly, in the 1999 data, possibly as a result of the changes in the *Criminal Code,* the most frequently cited reports were the victims' own reports about impacts of the crimes on them. They were also the most frequently cited reports by the Court of Appeal, though this court did not cite any reports with great frequency. The second most frequently cited reports at the original trial were those written by professionals about the offenders. These were the only other reports mentioned by the Court of Appeal. The probation reports were cited by the trial judge in ten of forty-one cases, and reports written by professionals about the victims were cited least frequently. To look at these reports from another perspective, however, there were only six written by professionals in this time period, and four of them were cited, while there were fourteen reports in 1990-93, thirteen cited by the trial judge, and ten of those cited by the Court of Appeal. In percentage terms, given the actual number of cases in each data set, the differences are less than 1 percent in terms of frequency of production of reports. In terms of citing of reports, changes to the law to mandate consideration of victim impact statements may have resulted in victim impact being considered more generally by judges with less of a perceived need to resort to external or "expert" reports for justification of their concern about victim harm. As Erez and Laster (1999) pointed out, judges have come to accept an objectified version of victim harm that may speak to the degree to which victim impact has become "medicalized," with the result that judges may believe they know what a "typical" victim experiences without any help from "experts." We move now to an examination of what is said in the various types of reports and how trial and appeal courts make use of them.

Medical/Psychiatric/Psychological Reports

Conrad and Schneider (1992, 246) point out the social implications for the medicalization of deviance: "By defining deviant behaviour as an illness or a result of illness, one is absolved of responsibility for one's behavior. It diminishes or *removes blame* from the individual for deviant actions." They further note that "defining behavior as a medical problem removes or profoundly diminishes responsibility from the individual. Although affixing responsibility is always complex, medicalization produces confusion and ambiguity about who is responsible. Responsibility is separated from social action; it is located in the nether world of biophysiology or psyche" (248). We tend to look for causes of and solutions to complex social problems in the individual rather than in the social system (250). This absolving of responsibility or diminishing or removing of blame is very similar to the description of excuses, accounts, and justifications by Scully and Marolla (1984) in the previous chapter. Their definition of accounts is particularly relevant to this chapter: "Accounts are socially approved vocabularies that neutralize an act or its consequences and are always a manifestation of a negotiation of identity" (530). An analysis of the reports presented to the courts about offenders illustrates the views expressed by both sets of authors. There is considerable confusion and ambiguity in the judicial comments as judges attempt to balance the view of the offenders expressed in many of the reports and the harm done to the victims as documented by both the victims and the professionals who have assessed the damage to them. Table 6.3 shows the major themes evident in the reports. Not surprisingly, given that professional reports are socially constructed and reflect the current beliefs and knowledge of the professions, there are differences between the reports to the court in the 1990-93 data and those in the 1999 data.

1990-93

In 1990-93, the most common theme in these psychiatrically and psychologically oriented reports is about the pathology of the offender. This is not surprising because of the approach to assessment of these professions, which share an emphasis on the individual. This is consistent with critiques in earlier analyses of issues in the study of child sexual

Table 6.3

Psychiatric/psychological/medical reports

Observation/recommendation	# in 1990-93	# in 1998-99
Pathologizes individual	25	7
No risk to reoffend	11	10
Recommends prov sentence	11	0
Not a typical sex offender	9	0
Says do not incarcerate	9	3
Diagnosis as a pedophile	8	2
Accepts offender's self-report	4	3
Recommends incarceration	4	1
Blames alcohol	3	2
Deals with male socialization	3	0
Discusses victim impact	3	3
Considers offender a risk	3	5
Blames victim	2	0
Blames victim's mother	2	1
Deals with actual behaviour	0	2

abuse (Gil 1971, 1975; Gelles 1973, 1975; Pelton 1978). Some of Pelton's thoughts appear to be relevant today: the inclination to seek psychological solutions to social problems, to view social problems as solely due to individual "diseases" and deficits, is by now so ingrained in the thought processes of many of our helping professionals and social scientists, as well as those of the public, that it will be a long time before it is entirely dislodged (Pelton 1978, 12-13). Analysis of these data illustrates that, although twenty-two years have passed between the first cases and the publication of these comments, not much appears to have changed. As noted in the review of the literature in Chapter 1, much of the research on people who commit sexual offences against children focuses on a search for biological and personality explanations.

It is clear from Table 6.3 that no physician, psychiatrist, or psychologist who wrote reports for the court in the earliest data made any mention of the actual assault. This is contrary to recommendations made by Becker and Quinsey (1993) and Mair (1993), who indicated at that time, from their examination of the assessment literature, that the actual offence behaviour should be an important part of any assessment of such offenders: "Regardless of whether the purpose of the assessment involves treatment or risk issues, clinicians are well advised to obtain as much detail about the alleged molestation(s) as possible. This can be accomplished by requesting police reports and victim statements and, where possible, directly interviewing the victim(s)" (Becker and Quinsey 1993, 170). In three of the cases, the clinician accepted the offender's self-report of the abuse. That is, the clinician's sole source of information about the offence was the offender. Becker and Quinsey (1993, 170) are critical of this practice: "Interviews of the offender are similar to other clinical interviews except the validity of the information provided by the offender is more likely to be suspect. Frequently, the alleged child molesters distort information, falsely deny that the alleged offence occurred, and report difficulty in recalling events surrounding the offence." In spite of the caution that these authors express, clinicians in these data were willing to make judgments about an offender's risk based solely on the offender's input. In *R. v. K., M.* (1993), a psychiatrist concluded, based on the offender's self-report, that the offender was essentially a "nice guy" who had resolved his age-inappropriate sexual attraction and was now a homosexual with a preference for adult males. In his reasons for the sentence, the trial judge cited the psychiatrist's opinion in his decision to sentence the offender to six months in jail: "It would appear from the report from the [psychiatric hospital] that the accused is definitely a homosexual but aside from these occurrences before the court there is nothing to suggest that he is a pedophile ... Based on the evidence available Mr F does not feel that the accused needs to attend a sex offender program but possibly he might benefit from psycho-therapy aimed at helping him come to terms with his homosexual orientation." While the judge was not willing to consider the victim impact statements as statements of fact, he was willing to accept the psychiatrist's opinion, which was based on the offender's self-report, as fact.

It is also evident from Table 6.3 that clinicians do not include input about the victim in their assessment of the offender. The impact on the victim was mentioned in only three of the cases. In only one of these cases were the victims contacted for information.

In six cases, the professional actually blamed the victim or the victim's mother for the assault. For example, in *R. v. M., G.* (1991), a father's affectionate playfulness, such as tickling his children and kissing them openly, moved on occasion beyond the usual limits, yet his touching and kissing were not considered premeditated molestation, and the psychiatrist presented no evidence of protest or indignation or psychotrauma among the children. The psychiatrist did not deal with the cunnilingus and digital penetration, which could easily be distinguished from tickling and considered premeditated. In fact, the psychiatrist went on to blame the offender's wife for the abuse by contending that she had "castrated and controlled [her husband] and sexually frustrated him." The psychiatrist also said that, "despite her father's financial help and affection, [the victim] and her older sister listed the charges which were laid." He reported that the offender had a high IQ and demonstrated no psychopathology. His contact with the victims and the information that he received from them were not mentioned in the report in terms of the harm done. His interview with them appeared to be for the purpose of finding excuses for their father's actions, and his conclusions about them did not reflect any notice of harm done to them. Rather, his report reflected a certain incredulity that they would actually charge their father with abuse after all he had done for them.

In another case, *R. v. G., D.* (1990), the assessing psychiatrist indicated that the offender did not fit the DSM III category of pedophilia. In explaining the offender's behaviour, he discussed the family situation: "D. has known this child and her younger brother and mother for about 3 1/2 years. During this time, they lived together as a family. There was the usual sexual relationship between the adults for most of the time, but it gradually deteriorated as the young girl created more and more trouble within the family." This reference is a less than subtle deflection of blame onto the child victim, whom the psychiatrist labelled a troublemaker. He continued by saying that

> D. continuously analyzed his relationship with his ex-wife. She had left a marriage of 10 years from which she had the 2 children (a boy age 6 and a girl, now age 10). He told me that the girl was socially and emotionally disturbed. He and his wife had attended various counselors regarding the problem behaviour of the child. The child's problem behaviour came between his wife and himself. D. reported that there was no resolution to the problem. He and his wife were no longer having a conjugal relationship. D. has learned from this experience that he had a sensible and systematic parental upbringing. He realized that his own childhood home was a much better place than the one he was involved in with his common-law wife and her 2 children.

Nowhere did the psychiatrist explain how the problems with the child or the absence of a conjugal relationship with the wife was linked to a sexual assault on the child. There appears to be an assumption that the reader can fill in the gaps and reason that the responsibility for this assault did not lie with the offender. In another report to the lawyer, the psychiatrist wrote that

> his difficulties started when he was age 14 ½ years. A seventeen year old girl introduced him to sexual intercourse at that time. This relationship lasted about one year. At age sixteen he met another girl where the relationship was based mostly on sexual activity. Later he met a married young woman who sought him out for sexual favors. Three years ago he met a woman and her children with whom he has been living. The sexual relationship with her deteriorated partly because of the emotional disturbance of the oldest daughter. In each case the relationships broke up when the sexual needs of the women were not met. Mr D. is now sexually inhibited and faces life with a confused idea of how to relate to women.

The implication here seems to be that women have failed this offender and that he has offended because of his contacts with women in the past, which have left him scarred.

In explaining the six-month sentence with twelve months of probation, the judge appeared to attempt to balance the offence, the offender's position of trust vis-à-vis the victim, and the offender's attempts at rehabilitation. He did not seem to accept the psychiatric report with much enthusiasm. The Court of Appeal rejected the judge's reasoning, particularly with reference to the issue of treatment: "This is a first offence and there appears to be no indication, on the basis of the new evidence, that he has any continuing illness like pedophilia. Accordingly, leave to appeal is granted and the appeal is allowed to the extent of varying the sentence of incarceration to one of 90 days intermittent. The probation order will stand and will apply during the times when the appellant is not in confinement under the intermittent sentence imposed hereby." The trial judge's emphasis on victim impact and his skepticism about the offender's remorse were overruled by the Court of Appeal. Its focus on an absence of pedophilia is a further indication of acceptance of the medicalization of child sexual abuse, which the appeal court interpreted as meaning that the offender did not meet the DSM III criteria to be labelled a sex offender. The court did not, in this instance, challenge the clinician's attempts to transfer responsibility onto others. It did note the fact that the clinician did not assess this offender to be suffering from "any continuing illness like pedophilia."

As noted earlier, pedophilia was cited as both an aggravating and a mitigating circumstance by trial judges, as was the absence of pedophilia. This signals some confusion among judges about what a diagnosis of pedophilia means. There is no indication in these cases that the Court of Appeal at the time had any better understanding. Although, as indicated in Chapter 1, there is no such thing as a typical profile of a child molester, there was a psychiatric diagnosis of pedophilia in the DSM III at the time, which was applied by psychiatrists in eight of these cases. In nine of the cases, the clinician gave the opinion that the offender was not a typical sex offender, which appeared to mean that he did not fit the criteria for pedophilia according to the DSM III. As noted in Chapter 1, psychologist and researcher Ron Langevin pointed out that the majority of men who sexually offend against children are not pedophiles but are "conventional heterosexuals who offend for other, psychological reasons" (1993, 70); "a child may be molested for reasons other than sexual preference" (74). It is obvious in these data that the judges were not clear about the relevance of these distinctions. As noted earlier, defining behaviour as a medical problem removes or profoundly diminishes responsibility of the individual. Although affixing responsibility is always complex, medicalization produces confusion and ambiguity about who is responsible (Conrad and Schneider 1992, 248).

Sentences are handed out based on assumptions about what a typical sex offender is and on what a pedophile is without any real understanding of the issues or any knowledge of Langevin's and others' similar research findings. If judges depend on the psychologists and psychiatrists who come before them or who submit reports to them to give them the most accurate and up-to-date information about offenders, then it appears from these data that they are unlikely to get it. Unfortunately, most of the clinicians who appeared in these 1990-93 data presented an impression of the typical sex offender, yet only rarely was the person whom they were writing about one of them. They appeared to rely on their own interpretations of the offenders' behaviour and did not refer to or rely on recent research to form the opinions they presented to the judges. In only one case did a psychiatrist try to explain to the judge that a conviction for a sexual offence was the best indicator of a problem:

> Mr X, of course, does not see himself as having any difficulty in the area of sexual adjustment and I know from the other information provided that he did have sexual preference testing ... These testing results are of limited value only in the present circumstances because of the significant number of false negative results which can be obtained, and are more likely to be obtained, in an individual who is highly motivated to appear normal. Were Mr. X to be convicted in relation to one or more of the charges against him, I think he should be encouraged to re-examine his situation in this regard since that alone would be fairly strong presumptive evidence that a problem does exist in this area. (*R. v. T., J.* [1992])

This psychiatrist identified for the court that the real issue was the behaviour, not the diagnosis. If someone has been convicted of sexually abusing a child, particularly over a period of time, then this is evidence of a problem. A diagnosis of pedophilia or its absence is really irrelevant. Skinner and Blashfield (1982, 730) attempted to address this issue: "Traditional diagnostic schemas, such as DSM III, are based to a great extent on consensual agreement among experienced clinicians that the category 'makes sense.' Discrete types are popular because they facilitate communication." While it may make sense to identify those men who primarily offend against strangers or non-family members as pedophiles, this distinction or classification obfuscates the reality noted above and earlier that the vast majority of men who offend against children are not "pedophiles." That is, they do not identify themselves, either through self-report or phallometric testing, as having a sexual attraction to children that excludes attraction to adults.

Even in cases in which the diagnosis of pedophilia was applied, there was variation in how the clinicians giving information to the courts interpreted it. In *R. v. L., A.P.* (1991), also outlined in the previous chapter, the trial judge expressed a clear view of what he interpreted pedophilia to be, and he was prepared to excuse the offender because of how the psychiatrist had framed his behaviour: "We are here dealing with a paedophiliac, as per expert opinion. You do not effect a cure by any period of incarceration."

In Chapter 4, I presented two cases that involved two offenders with high socio-economic status. In both cases, the assessing psychiatrists diagnosed the offenders as pedophiles. However, the pedophilia was downplayed, and other factors were emphasized in the assessment. In *R. v. E., P.* (1991), the psychiatrist presented the offender's history in some detail and noted that the offender had grown up in an affluent area of the city, was the son of a physician, and had attended private school. He related the offender's past experience of sexual abuse by a neighbour and by older boys in the private school. He reported positively that the offender had been a coach of boys' sports teams and a Big Brother, even though in this latter capacity the offender had abused his position of trust and sexually assaulted the victims. He described the possible benefits of group therapy and reported that phallometric testing indicated pedophilia, which the psychiatrist minimized by saying that "Mr X has been able to acknowledge that he is a pedophile and this is confirmed by laboratory testing here. Although I agree with him that he does have a 'way to go' in his treatment I would also say that he has been unusually cooperative and well motivated." The psychiatrist went on to explain that, although the offender could not be cured, the programs that the psychiatrist's hospital offered could help him to control his impulses: "One reason why many pedophiles do reoffend is that they do not want to change and sustained motivation to do so, coupled with an ability to function heterosexually and an ability to show empathy, are encouraging features." The psychiatrist recommended a disposition that would allow the offender to continue with the program at the hospital, which meant, of course, that the offender should not be incarcerated.

There was also a report from the offender's physician, which indicated that he had been treating the offender for irritable bowel as a result of the stress of this court process and noted that "there is no doubt that the stress of a prison sentence with its added consequences, namely the very real possibility that should this happen, he would not be able to support his wife and thus face the possibility of losing their home, as she would be unable financially to manage it on her own. This would result in very severe punishment not just for Mr X but for his innocent wife and child as well."

There were also two victim impact statements. One, handwritten and difficult to read, indicated that the victim felt weird after what happened. There was another from the victim's mother in poor spelling, handwritten, often illegible; it indicated that her son had been in individual counselling for two years as a result of the abuse and that it hadn't helped. She also stated that no group counselling was currently available. She said that her son was now failing in school and was socially withdrawn. She also indicated that her physician had prescribed her antidepressants to help her cope. There was no mention of either the victims or the actual offence in the psychiatric, medical, or pre-sentence reports on the offender.

In his reasons for sentencing, the judge quoted extensively from the psychiatrist's report. He noted the family support for the offender and his medical problems. He also quoted the testimony of the offender's wife in terms of "the devastation that has been caused to their lives [and] the personal sickness and illness resulting by way of stress that has been caused to her husband."

The judge cited the impact on the victim as outlined in the mother's testimony and her report. He concluded by stating that "there was not the depravity of the type noted in other cases in respect to fellatio or sodomy or anything of that nature." He also cited the diagnosis of pedophilia as a mitigating circumstance: "A distinction must be made in respect to pedophilia which is a differently motivated child sexual assault involving an accused who has a compulsion as opposed to individuals who are child sexual assaulters absent a compulsion." The judge stated his belief that pedophilia is an illness requiring treatment and that "this treatment is not usually found in correctional institutions." He concluded that "public deterrence is partially satisfied by the publicity, shame and loss of status of the offender." He cited an absence of "violence" in the commission of the offences and concluded that "[the offender] is a person of general good character with the exception of this aberration and has the support of his family and his community." The Court of Appeal agreed with the trial judge for many of the same reasons and dismissed the Crown's appeal.

The second case, *R. v. Simard* (1990), dealt with an upper-middle-class offender whose assault on a child who was a stranger to him met all the criteria for a pedophilic assault. In his report, the psychiatrist described the offender's background and indicated that the offender was bisexual by his own claim. He informed the court that phallometric testing indicated some arousal to rape stimulus and some attraction to children whom he perceived to be "consenting." The report concluded that, in spite of pedophilic arousal, the offence was probably the result of excessive consumption of alcohol.

The trial judge's interpretation of the psychiatrist's report ignored the presence of pedophilia: "He presents no continuing danger to young children and the circumstances of the commission of this offence are unlikely to ever be repeated again." After the young man was convicted of forcible seizure and sexual interference, the judge imposed a suspended sentence in addition to a term of three years of probation. The Court of Appeal supported the trial judge's sentence without comment other than to say that it could find no fault with it. The diagnosis of pedophilia appeared to be irrelevant, unlike the mixed attention that it received in other cases.

When was pedophilia relevant? In these data, it depends on other factors, such as when intercourse occurred and when the offender was not supported by a clinical assessment. In the last two cases described above, it did not seem to be relevant if the offender was of high social status. Both of these offenders had the benefit of high-profile forensic psychiatrists testifying and/or submitting reports on their behalf. These psychiatrists predicted in their input that the offenders would not reoffend. This opinion, as noted earlier, is a theme in these data. This notion existed in most cases in spite of considerable behavioural evidence that the perpetrator might well present a future risk.

In many cases, the reports about the offender included factors considered by the clinician writing them to minimize and explain the offender's behaviour and in some cases excuse the offender from responsibility. In addition to the assumption that the offender would not reoffend, in eleven of the reports the clinician described the offender as not being a typical sex offender.

Both themes were present in *R. v. L., G.A.* (1990). The trial judge followed the general direction of the psychologist's report in a case involving intercourse by a father, forty-six to fifty years of age, of a daughter who was from eleven to fifteen years of age at the time. The intercourse took place twice a week over a four-year period. The psychologist concluded in her report that

> Mr. X's personality profile is by no means suggestive of an individual with assaultive potential. He does not fit any particular psychiatric diagnostic category. His is not the typical "sexual offender profile: although his narcissism and poor impulse control are potential problems and should therefore continue to be the major focus of his continued treatment. With continued psychotherapeutic intervention, it is highly unlikely that he would repeat.
>
> Mr. X has suffered great emotional turmoil and personal loss as a result of his actions. While it is clear that he did commit a punishable offence, I do not see the potential benefit of incarceration in this case. It is my opinion that he would benefit from continued therapy.

Although it might seem somewhat contradictory even to a casual observer to describe someone who has sexually assaulted a child twice a week over a four-year period as having a personality profile that is "by no means suggestive of assaultive potential," the trial judge accepted and acknowledged the report in his reasons for the sentence: "The only thing about this situation that saves you from the penitentiary is the fact that the psychologist has in effect gone to bat for you. She feels that you are making strides and that you are not going to be a real danger in the future."

The Crown appealed the sentence, partially claiming that "the judge erred in law in failing to give adequate consideration to the serious nature of the offence and in giving undue weight to the principle of rehabilitation." The Court of Appeal granted the Crown's appeal, and the sentence was increased to two years less one day. This left it within the provincial range, even though this was not consistent with the guidelines set by the Court of Appeal for such cases. The Court of Appeal gave no reasons for its decision. It certainly did not challenge the judge's dependence on the psychologist's report. Even though a challenge may be implicit in the fact that the court raised the sentence, it is difficult to know where it stood with respect to construction of the offender.

It appears, then, that both being a pedophile and not being a typical sex offender can be constructed positively on behalf of the offender by the clinicians assessing him and by the judges sentencing him. This is difficult to explain rationally and impossible to explain based on the research literature existing at the time, which, as Langevin (1993) clearly stated, indicates that the vast majority of sexually abusive behaviour is not connected to a diagnosis of pedophilia. That is, most men who commit sexual assaults on children are not "typical sex offenders" because there is no such thing as a "typical sex offender."

Similarly, the predictions in eleven of the cases that offenders would not reoffend are difficult to support. In contrast, in three of the reports, the offender was identified as a possible future risk. There are no qualitative differences between the cases in either group. The only difference appears to be in the interpretation of the person writing the report. The major features of the cases are the same in terms of age of victim, socioeconomic status of offender, relationship of victim to offender, type of abuse, and duration of abuse.

Only one of these reports, in *R. v. F.D.* (1991), mentioned the effect of the abuse on the victim. It was one of the reports that identified the offender as presenting a risk to reoffend. Mention of an offender's sense of entitlement to engage in sexual activity with a child was also seldom made in these reports. One psychiatrist referred to the offender as being macho, promiscuous, self-absorbed, unchanging, and demeaning toward women. This view of the offender was not as prevalent as a more sympathetic view in which the offender was seen as suffering from some form of pathology, usually based in his personality, over which he was seen as having little control.

In one case, *R. v. R., P.* (1991), the psychiatrist's description of the offender's sense of entitlement was put in terms that the judge did not seem to fully understand. (This case was discussed in Chapter 5.) The abuse was disclosed when the child was diagnosed as having herpes. A report was presented to the court concerning the child's resulting medical condition and the physical, social, and emotional toll that it was having on her and would likely have on her in the future.

The psychiatrist assessing the offender described what he referred to as the thirty-two-year-old offender's "cognitive distortions" – that is, his perception that the six-year-old child, his niece, was seductive and cooperative and his sense that his behaviour was understandable because his wife was pregnant and he was sexually frustrated. The psychiatrist explained that the offender further rationalized his behaviour by saying that he had been drinking at the time of the offences. Phallometric testing indicated a preference for adult females, but the offender told the psychiatrist that he found himself attracted to children. In spite of this self-report, the psychiatrist concluded that he did not present a risk to reoffend.

Although he described the offender's "cognitive distortions," the psychiatrist did not comment on them in terms of the offender's acceptance of responsibility. The psychiatrist never highlighted – in fact he downplayed – the man's view of women and the overriding importance that the offender placed on his entitlement to act on his sexual urges.

His macho view of sex never seemed to be a significant issue. The judge interpreted these "cognitive distortions" as excusing the offender from responsibility for the offence and its impact on the victim.

The judge's interpretation of the "psychological weakness" of the offender indicates how the focus on the individual pathology of an offender deflects from an analysis of the offence itself. It also indicates a willingness to label – and write off – this man's and other men's concepts of the value of women and children as pathology instead of ideology. Pathologizing leads to excusing from responsibility.

This is evidence of a social control function that Conrad and Schneider (1985, 244) refer to as "gatekeeping," as noted earlier: "The medical profession is the official designator of the 'sick role.'" This function imbues the physician with the authority to define particular kinds of deviance as illness and exempt the patient from certain role obligations. These are generally gatekeeping and social control tasks. In an analysis of the following two cases, it is obvious that the official designators of the sick role sometimes differ in their interpretations of similar situations, and as a result the outcome at sentencing differs.

In the first case, *R. v. Pascoe* (1990), an offender with a significant prior record of sexual offences was convicted of sexual assault (s. 271) and breach of recognizance (s. 145[3]) and sentenced to two years less one day and three years of probation to follow concurrent on each charge for fondling a seven-year-old boy who was a casual acquaintance. The Crown appealed the sentence on the following grounds:

1 The judge erred in principle in holding that a treatment oriented reformatory sentence and probation would best protect the public. It is submitted that this disposition fails to protect the community from the "horrendous effect" of such paedophiliac assaults because it fails to acknowledge: the utter ineffectiveness of the numerous treatment and probation orders that have emanated from this Honourable Court on two prior occasions and various other Courts, and; the virtual certainty that the respondent will reoffend.
2 The sentence imposed fails to embody the daunting conglomeration of aggravating circumstances in this case.

The offender had twelve previous convictions, nine of which were for fondling young boys and three of which were for failing to comply with probation conditions to stay away from children. He served four periods of incarceration ranging from twelve months to two years less one day. The thirty-eight-year-old man was described in psychiatric and pre-sentence reports as being a low-functioning homosexual pedophile who had been in a number of treatment facilities. A report on his last episode of treatment was not positive and outlined the offender's serious limitations in his ability to take part in treatment.

The victim impact was described as being dramatic in terms of the behavioural change in the boy, who went from being a quiet to an argumentative and uncooperative child with a serious sleep disturbance. He also reportedly suffered from enuresis and sexualized behaviour with his younger brother.

The trial judge gave as his rationale for a provincial sentence the various psychiatric reports about the offender, which clearly stated that the offender had not benefited from past attempts to treat him and that he would certainly offend again even if he received treatment. The psychiatrists advocated, however, for a provincial sentence for this offender so that he might receive more treatment; they reasoned that when he offended he did little harm, and if he were sent to the penitentiary he would likely be abused by other inmates. The judge acknowledged that the offender would likely offend again but agreed about the penitentiary. Additionally, he agreed, in contradiction to the victim impact statement, that when the offender abused boys he did little damage. In reference to the offender's diagnosis of pedophilia, the trial judge stated, "I believe it is clear, given the man's unfortunate condition, that the possibility of a reoccurrence is almost definite. However, it appears that he is unlikely to perform physically aggressive acts." In the Crown appeal, the Court of Appeal did not accept the Crown's arguments: "We are not persuaded the trial judge erred in delivering proper sentence. The appeal fails and is dismissed." In reviewing the case, it appears as if the number and type of supporting reports from various professionals advocating for the provincial system for more treatment of the offender were what influenced the court.

In the second case, *R. v. M., M.* (1992), an offender was sentenced to five years in the penitentiary after a conviction for gross indecency involving the abuse, on three separate occasions, of the five-year-old grandson of the thirty-three-year-old offender's homosexual partner. The offender had a previous criminal record of eight convictions, three of which were for similar sex offences. The sentence was suspended and a term of probation was ordered in the previous cases. The psychiatric report pointed out the offender's limitations and the issues related to treatment. The offender was described as mildly intellectually delayed, illiterate, and demonstrating little insight into his current difficulties. Phallometric testing was reported as indicating that he had an "inability to suppress aggressive impulses concerning homosexual pedophilic activity." He was also described as having "no potential for rape and assault."

The trial judge interpreted the psychiatric report differently than did the judge in the first case. The report, while saying substantially the same things that the psychiatric reports in the first case did, did not advocate as strongly for the offender to receive treatment in the provincial system, questioned the likelihood that he could be treated because of his intellectual limitations, and did not minimize the harm done by his assaultive behaviour.

Even though both offenders were seen to be intellectually limited and had been on the receiving end of many attempts at treatment, this trial judge made a different interpretation of the diagnosis of pedophilia, of the offender's prior record, and of the harm done by his sexual assaults than did the judge in the previous case. This variance is most likely attributable to the difference in emphasis of the reports in the cases.

The offender appealed the sentence of five years in the penitentiary, but the Court of Appeal was not receptive: "The appellant has been diagnosed as a homosexual pedophile. He has a number of prior convictions for related offences. We are advised that he refuses to undertake treatment for his condition and so it is apparent that he has refused to come to terms with his sexual impulses. We consider this appellant to be a continuing danger to society and a period of custody of 5 years is fully justified in the circumstances. Leave to appeal is allowed but the appeal is dismissed." Both the trial judge and the Court of Appeal expressed concern that the offender would reoffend and about his lack of interest in treatment. In the first case, although the certainty of reoffence was acknowledged and his unresponsiveness to treatment recognized, these were not primary factors in decision making.

There are many similarities between these cases. Both offenders had records of fondling boys (the first being more significant than the second), both were identified in the proceedings as being intellectually limited, and both had previous opportunities for treatment that they did not use. The difference in the cases is that the second offender, while he had essentially the same history, diagnosis, and prognosis, had less support from the professionals writing the pre-sentence assessments, and victim harm was given more notice. He was also considered to be in a position of trust because his victim was his partner's grandson. However, a discrepancy of three years in sentencing is difficult to justify on that one basis. The tone of the first case was affected by a number of psychiatric and psychological reports, which advocated for treatment for the offender, even though he had been involved in a number of treatment programs, was unmotivated to change, and was likely (by the account of everyone involved) to commit similar offences again. He had a much more significant record for similar offences, and he had abused more boys over a longer period of time. The difference seems to be in the judges' approach to or perception of pedophilia and victim harm at both the trial and the appellate levels.

In nine of the reports, the clinicians recommended to the court that the offender not be incarcerated. In 87 percent of these cases, the recommendation was ignored; however, all of the offenders incarcerated in these cases were given provincial sentences. In eleven of the reports, the clinicians recommended that, if the offender was incarcerated, he should be given a provincial sentence to facilitate his involvement in treatment/rehabilitation. In 81.6 percent of these cases, the recommendation was followed by the trial judge and not overturned by the Court of Appeal. In the 18.4 percent of the cases in which the trial judge ignored the recommendation and imposed a penitentiary sentence, the Court of Appeal did not disagree with the sentence.

As we noted in the previous chapter, involvement in treatment/rehabilitation was cited as a mitigating circumstance by trial judges (16 percent) and by justices of the Court of Appeal (22 percent). Trial judges gave rehabilitation as a reason for the sentence in 28.8 percent of the cases, and the Court of Appeal cited it as a reason in 15 percent of the cases. The analysis of medical/psychiatric and psychological reports contained in this chapter raises issues about the use of this reason. What do judges understand treatment to be? What would it be directed at? The reports in these data seem to view treatment of the offender as indicated because of particular issues such as stress, self-image, and other circumstances within his personality or situation to which the cause of offending is attributed. There is no significant discussion on what treatment or rehabilitation would involve other than face-to-face meetings with clinicians. Treatment programs for men who have committed sex offences vary considerably, as do their reported rates of "success" (Harris, Rice, and Quinsey 1998). Conflicting views about offenders, some of which have been seen in this analysis, result in conflicting notions about what constitutes reasonable treatment.

1998-99

Comparing the 1990-93 data to the 1999 data, there are significant differences in most of the reports presented to the courts. By the time the second set of appeals took place, there was no discussion at sentencing on whether or not the offender was a "typical" sex offender. Some of these discussions, however, took place in the actual trials. Although not part of these studies, there were a number of cases during the same time period in which use of expert witnesses in the actual trials was a source of dispute in appeals against conviction. Some of these cases involved psychiatric evidence as to whether or not the offender met the criteria for a "typical" sex offender.

In relative terms, considering the number of cases in each time period, the most distinct differences show up in the area of whether or not the offender should be considered a risk to reoffend (11 percent in 1990-93 compared with 24 percent in 1999), and pathologizing the individual offender (24 percent versus 17 percent). There were fewer cases in which the professional described the offender's behaviour as emanating from stress or depression. There was more discussion of victim impact (3 percent in 1990-93 versus 7 percent in 1999) and more likelihood that the "expert" would consider the offender a risk to reoffend (3 percent versus 12 percent). Although some of these differences appear to be marginal, there is greater evidence of a more balanced approach to the assessment of offenders, and there is evidence of somewhat more discrimination by judges as to their use of expert reports.

For example, in *R. v. Elder* (1999), an offender who was from thirty-one to fifty-one years of age at the time of the offences was convicted of sexually assaulting ten young men over a period of ten years, each for a single time. The offences consisted of five instances of genital fondling and five instances of the offender performing fellatio on the victims, as well as one failed attempt at anal intercourse. The offender was a fifty-eight-year-old sports figure who enjoyed a good reputation in the media, and the victims were, for the most part, street-involved youth. Fifty-seven reference letters, written by prominent members of the community in which he lived, testified to his good character.

In passing sentence, the trial judge cited the victim impact statements, the psychiatric report, the pre-sentence report, and the character references. She stated that few of the letters acknowledged E's wrongdoing: "While he was being a generous and loyal friend and an accomplished [sportsman], young men were fleeing his house in the middle of the night. While he was taking in so many lost young men and helping them straighten out their lives, he was taking in others and assaulting them in their sleep." The judge gave little credibility to the psychiatric report, which said that "his sexual preferences and activities are not, from a psychiatric perspective, abnormal. The socio-cultural context of the time when he was involved episodically with adolescent boys was certainly receptive to this behaviour; it would not have been considered deviant ... From a psychiatric perspective, this man is not mentally ill and does not show evidence of thoughts or behaviour which would leave him disposed or vulnerable to future antisocial or criminal behaviour. He has a well-developed moral code and sense of ethical responsibility and has not shown a pattern of persistent flaws in character." Someone had circled these quotations in the appeal book on file and written "crap" and "what crap" around them. Construction of the offender as having no character flaws was not received warmly at the appeal process.

Another significant distinction between the 1990-93 and the 1998-99 data is that in the latter set were two appeals that dealt with "dangerous offender" designations. This was likely the result of changes to the *Criminal Code* in 1997 that altered the provisions dealing with dangerous offenders and added the concept of "long-term offender." There were no appeals dealing with long-term offenders. Much of the hearing into whether or not a dangerous offender designation should be made revolves around how to interpret "expert" input into the process.

The two appeals demonstrate how the term "dangerous offender" is defined and what criteria must be met in order for someone to be so designated. In the first case, *R. v. S., K.* (1999), the thirty-eight-year-old offender entered a guilty plea to five charges, which included sexual assault, sexual interference, anal intercourse, making obscene material, and attempting to obtain sexual services of a minor. These charges concerned nine victims, eight boys and one girl, ranging in age from nine to fourteen years. At sentencing, an application was made by the Crown to declare him a dangerous offender. The behaviour consisted primarily of single incidents of fondling; performing oral sex on boys; and having boys and at least one girl engage in sexual activities, including simulated intercourse, while he watched and made videos. There were also incidents of mutual masturbation, anal intercourse, and fellatio. The offender had a criminal record dating back to 1965, consisting of sixteen previous convictions for sexual assaults on young males.

The original hearing was held in 1993, at the request of the Crown, to determine whether or not the convicted offender met the criteria and could be sentenced to an indefinite term of imprisonment. Ultimately, the judge decided that the offender did meet the criteria. To arrive at that decision, he needed the testimony of two psychiatrists. As a result of the 1997 amendments, the testimony of only one psychiatrist is required. However, the case at appeal in 1999 was first tried in 1993, and the sentencing hearing was held under the old rules, which required the evidence of two psychiatrists. In giving his reasons, in part, the trial judge made the following comments, which speak to the definition of dangerousness:

> He is proven to be a middle-age homosexual pedophile who from a young age has dedicated his life to the sexual abuse of boys for his own sexual gratification. There is no evidence to even suggest that the accused would stop. He does not believe the conduct to be wrong or that it may cause harm to the victims ... It must be said of the accused, however, [that] he is not a violent man. Some of the victims reported that if the activity was particularly offensive or caused pain, they would refuse to engage in the activity, and the accused would respect their wishes. His approach to the victims was repetitive over the years. He would target a vulnerable subject, shower him with attention, treats in the form of meals and snacks, trips to places of interest, gifts and trips to out of town cities.
>
> ...
>
> The experts all agree that a significant number of children abused as the accused abused his victims would suffer severe psychological damage, sometimes short-term and sometimes long–term. Th[e] definition of a dangerous offender fits the accused exactly ...
>
> The second definition of a dangerous offender in subsection (b) [of the *Criminal Code*] requires that the Crown prove that the accused is a person who constitutes a threat to the mental well-being of other persons and that his conduct in any sexual matter, including that involved in the commission of the offences for which he has been convicted, has shown a failure to control his sexual impulses, and there is a likelihood of his causing injury, pain or other evil to persons through failure in future to control his sexual impulses. While the accused, I find, will certainly continue his abusive conduct if free to do so, there is no likelihood that he will cause physical injury to his victims. However, I interpret the phrase "causing injury, pain or other evil" to include psychological harm. The evidence establishes that the accused is indeed an evil man who will, if allowed to do so, inflict great harm to the children and will by seduction involve them in his evil activities. Therefore I find beyond a reasonable doubt that the accused has been proven to be a dangerous offender on either definition found in s.753.

As noted above, the judge relied on the testimony of two psychiatrists who assessed the offender for the purpose of the hearing. The psychiatrist for the accused testified that "at this time, from a psychiatric perspective, we have no purposeful recommendations to offer. Mr. S. suffers from a deeply ingrained sexual deviation which, in my opinion, puts him at continued, very real and serious risk for further pedophilic, sexually assaultive behaviour. Furthermore, Mr. S. seems to have benefited little from past detention (jail) with respect to its having any sustained deterring effect on his behaviour. As a result, it is my conclusion that overall, his prognosis is quite poor."

In his evidence, the psychiatrist for the accused explained the definition of pedophilia to the court and stated that it can be managed but not cured. He discussed how he used the behavioural history of the offender to formulate his diagnosis, and he educated the court about the minimizations, denials, and rationalizations that these offenders frequently use. He explained further that, although there was no overt violence, there were threats of harm of various types and that "his 'kindnesses' are part of a seduction strategy." The psychiatrist supported the dangerous offender application in that he said the offender represented "a very serious and ongoing risk for further sexually assaultive behaviour involving pubescent and prepubescent males." It is very unusual to have a psychiatrist, hired by the defence, recommend incarceration, particularly indefinite incarceration. These two dangerous offender appeals were the only instances of this in the data in my two studies.

In addition to the psychiatrist for the accused and the psychiatrist for the Crown, who, as well as speaking about the offender testified about victim impact, a third psychiatrist was accepted as an expert on the effects of abuse on victims of these types of assaults. He "testified generally about the effects of child abuse and of his examination of the boy victims" in two of the charges before the court. In addition, the offender's previous parole officer was recognized as being a "graduate psychologist," and she testified about her contact with him over the years. The judge cited her in his remarks on sentencing: "She said it all when she reported for her superiors it was foolhardy to think that this man's career has ended." At that time, the accused's lawyer told him that another conviction of this nature would earn him a dangerous sexual offender sentence. She explained this sentence to him. He told her that he would apply in five years for a pardon so that, if he were caught again, he would be dealt with lightly, or he might move to a country where the laws are less severe.

Four victims also testified about the effects of the offender's behaviour on them. The youngest victim who testified was ten, and the oldest, who obviously had been victimized many years previously, was thirty-nine. Finally, the probation report contained evidence of the offender's previous experience with incarceration, and a file of reports from a provincial treatment institution was entered as evidence. The reports documented his difficulties in treatment, his misconduct in the institution, and a discharge summary that noted "worse to no improvement" and "little commitment to change." He was reported to have refused to take sex-drive reduction medication.

The Court of Appeal saw no reason to interfere with the trial judge's decision in this case to designate the offender dangerous and to impose an indeterminate sentence. It is difficult to see how this case differs significantly from a 1990 case described earlier, *R. v. Pascoe,* before the rules changed, in which the offender had essentially the same history and profile. What *is* different is the way in which the offenders were viewed by the experts, who were given essentially a similar set of facts but a different policy and legal context. Both offenders were seen to be essentially "non-violent." In the first case, the trial judge saw the offender's behaviour as minimally harmful in spite of testimony to the contrary. He recognized that the offender would likely offend again, but with the support of the expert reports he concluded, "I believe it is clear, given the man's unfortunate condition, that the possibility of a re-occurrence is almost definite. However, it appears that he is unlikely to perform physically aggressive acts." In the 1999 case, the experts helped the judge reach a different conclusion concerning a very similar offender.

In the second dangerous offender case in 1999, *R. v. S., K.,* a forty-four-year-old man was designated a dangerous offender after conviction on a charge of sexual interference (s. 151). He touched a twelve-year-old girl sexually after forcibly removing some of her clothing. He was reported to have an extensive history as a juvenile offender and to have spent time in two different training schools. He had nineteen previous convictions for personal injury crimes, some of which were sexual assaults. His most recent conviction, prior to this one, was for a sexual assault with a weapon on a young boy.

The trial judge based his decision on information provided through an assessment conducted at a maximum security forensic mental health facility by a team of "experts," including a psychiatrist. The assessment was based on a number of psychological tests, phallometric tests, and clinical interviews. The results showed the man to have superior intelligence, an elevation in rape scores, and an elevation in scores on attraction to children of both sexes and to coercive sexual activity with female children. The report indicated that the offender denied ever having engaged in inappropriate sexual activity. The psychiatric report outlined a long history of intervention with no success and reviewed reports written by a variety of psychiatrists, psychologists, and others about the offender's lack of response to treatment and his continuing violence. The assessment concluded that he continued to present a risk to re-offend.

The probation report contained extensive information about the offender's background, his alcohol abuse, the problems in his family of origin, his evasiveness about the current offence, and his incarceration history and management problems in institutions. It described his inability to successfully complete any term of probation/parole or community supervision. The report, which cited numerous unsuccessful attempts at treatment, concluded that the offender presented a continuing risk, especially to vulnerable and unsupervised "street kids."

In giving his reasons for the sentence, the judge described the demeanour of the victim as she cried on the witness stand:

> Only the most hard-hearted of persons could fail to be moved by her plight ... Judges are part of a society in which there is an increasingly widespread dissemination of knowledge, studies and literature which overwhelmingly support the soundness of the idea that adverse psychological effects often befall the victim of sexual assault and more especially so, the young and vulnerable victim. The notion is no longer startling.
>
> The prospect – indeed the possibility – that child sexual assault victims should be required to undergo psychological testing or be required to re-attend in court still again, runs counter to the numerous steps taken in the past decade to make the criminal justice system a less stressful process for children. Borrowing again from the approach adopted by the Supreme Court of Canada in *McCraw,* this Court believes that the ordinary and reasonable person looking at the impact of the prisoner's conduct on O.S. (as manifested by her plight in the witness box) would conclude that she sustained severe psychological damage. Nor is it logical to believe that adverse psychological effects only occur in or are limited to the court proceedings.

The judge concluded that "even the defence psychiatrist finds the offender to be a serious risk to reoffend." He cited the victim impact statements from the offender's previous victims. He listed all of them and spoke to the impacts on them. He cited all the psychiatric and psychological reports, adding up their similar conclusions about the risk to reoffend sexually and sadistically.

When the offender appealed the dangerous offender designation, the Court of Appeal dismissed the appeal: "The appellant submitted that the predicate offence [sexual interference] did not constitute a serious personal injury offence because it did not involve violence and that there was no evidence upon which the trial judge was entitled to conclude that there was severe psychological damage. In our view, in this case, the predicate offence did involve physical violence (s. 752[a][i]). The appellant forcibly removed some of the complainant's clothing. The complainant screamed for assistance, and the appellant continued to force himself upon her. Thus, we see no merit in the submission that the predicate offence did not meet the requirements of s. 752." The trial judge carefully considered the appropriate sentence to be imposed upon the appellant: "In our opinion, it was open to him to impose an indeterminate sentence particularly in light of the experts' evidence. This sentence is not demonstrably unfit. Accordingly, appeal against the dangerous offender finding and sentence is dismissed."

Five of the professional reports written in the 1999 data were written for the two dangerous offender hearings. These reports were the most extensive and clear in terms of relating their findings to current literature. In less high-profile cases, some of the psychiatric testimony seemed to demonstrate questionable expertise in terms of the research on sex offenders when the testimony was given or the report was submitted. In *R. v. B., J.S.* (1998), in which an offender appealed a sentence of two years less one day, a psychiatrist was qualified by the judge to testify as an expert witness about child sexual abuse largely because he had been recognized by other courts in the past. The psychiatrist had done some training years before in a forensic clinic but had been working primarily as a child psychiatrist for a school board. He stated that at the time of the trial he had a private practice in which he worked with children who had been sexually abused and with men who had been abusers. When cross-examined by the Crown about his credentials, he responded to the Crown's question "you would agree with me, doctor, by a review of the curriculum vitae it would be hard to determine the area of your expertise as being that of child sexual abuse?" by saying, "Yes, you're quite right. I do that deliberately so as not to advertise it, as otherwise I'm going to be called by every defence lawyer or Crown attorney for miles around." The Crown continued his cross-examination by asking the witness whether or not he knew certain people the Crown named for him who were prominent experts in the field, both in practice and in the research literature. The witness said that he did not. The Crown then asked the witness, "Are you familiar, doctor, with the writings of authors in the area of child sexual abuse and can you tell me some of the more prominent authors of issues dealing with child sexual abuse?" The witness answered:

> I have written many pamphlets and guidelines as part of my work at the school board. I was also active in the collaboration of the investigation team at the ... Hospital.
>
> Crown: Yes?
>
> Witness: And was fortunate enough during my tenure as psychiatrist in chief at the ... School Board to have the benefit of the newly fledgling [political party] department as they were being elected as school trustees, who were agreeing with me in their social activism, and through the auspicious [sic] of the student services we successfully put out a lot of publications and implemented screening programs to screen for children. So, yes, I have been familiar for over twenty years with the writings of the various people in the field.
>
> Crown: Could you advise his Honour, sir, as to who you would consider well-known authors of articles that deal with the issue of child sexual abuse as it relates to the survivor and/or the offender?
>
> Witness: Well, there are several areas to that. That's a very broad question. If you are canvassing me on authors who have done epidemiological studies of the incidents [sic] of sexual abuse, that's one question. If you are canvassing me on the different patterns that abusers fall into. There is [sic] very few, about half a dozen ...
>
> Crown: Perhaps we can stop at that point, sir. With respect to that issue, can you advise me as to who are the leaders in the field that you have just spoken to?
>
> Witness: There's no single paper that I could point you to around patterns of abusers.
>
> Crown: All right?
>
> Witness: But there's lots of papers I can point you to around patterns of abusers.
>
> Crown: And those would be?
>
> Witness: They fall again into about half a dozen different common patterns.
>
> Crown: Which papers can you point me to, sir?
>
> Witness: Most of it has come out of California, largely as a result of some of the ritualistic sexual abuse cases there. There is a great

wealth of literature that came out of the committee on mind abuse. This is a committee that was started by Premier ... government some, I don't know, 17 years ago. I was on that committee for approximately ten years until it was shut down four or five years ago. During that time I was associated with that committee and ... we made a detailed study of the various Satanic cult groups around southern Ontario, working in collaboration with the [police]. And actually, that was some of the time I was doing under cover work for the internal affairs of the [police] to try to learn more about Satanic cults and their various types of ritualistic sex abuse they engaged in. So you will find in ... Ministry of Attorney General publications ... a great deal about patterns of victims.

Crown: Are you familiar, sir, with the term "child abuse accommodation syndrome"?

Witness: Oh, yes, my goodness, it's an old term.

Crown: And the author of that, the writings dealing with the syndrome itself, who is credited with the development of that syndrome?

Witness: I forget the name of the paper but it was published in 1981.

Crown: Now, doctor, are you familiar with the various programs available at both reformatory institutions and penitentiary institutions as it relates to treatment for child abuse offenders?

Witness: No, I have lost touch with what is currently available.

Crown: So you have no experience in the recent past in terms of what treatment, if any, is available in either the reformatory or the penitentiary system?

Witness: No.

Crown: Are you familiar, sir, with any of the statistics dealing with the rate of recidivism as it relates to child abuse offenders?

Witness: Depends on the category ... I mentioned earlier that there are several patterns that we find that are typical in the sex abuse, sex abuser syndromes. And recidivism rate depends on the patterns.

Crown: I certainly wasn't looking for a half hour lecture, doctor. I was simply interested [in] your knowledge of the issues of recidivism with respect to child abuse offenders.

The questions and answers go on like this until the judge intervenes to ask what the defence wants the witness qualified for. The defence counsel answers, "as an expert with regards to child sexual abuse both in the treatment of abusers as well as victims." The judge responds, "I have no difficulty in qualifying Dr. W. on the basis of his expertise, his experience and his general knowledge in the field of child sexual abuse, particularly with respect to both abuser and victim." This was the case of a child, who, from the age of four to fourteen years, was abused by her stepfather. The abuse involved fondling, vaginal touching, sucking the victim's breasts, forced fellatio, verbal insults such as "slut" and "whore," and death threats. In giving his reasons for sentencing the offender to two years less a day, the judge relied heavily on the psychiatrist's report and testimony:

> There is no psychiatric disorder or paedophiliac [sic] tendency; The offender accepted responsibility for his actions and was very remorseful for the harm he caused the victim. Indeed, Dr. W. testified that the offender wept copiously and said he wished that there was some way he could make it up to the victim ... The doctor was subjected to close and long cross-examination by the Crown on his testimony, his notes and his methodology. While there were shortcomings in his testimony, I am satisfied that generally his conclusions are sound and trustworthy. I observed that Dr. W. administered the standard mental status examination and that the examination lasted three hours. In addition, Dr. W. has been involved with at least 192 sexual assault cases over the years and has appeared 66 times as an expert witness before the court. I found his credentials and experience impressive.

Looking at the transcript of this trial, it is difficult to imagine how Dr. W. could have qualified as an expert witness. The judge clearly had no idea what is required to conduct a reasonable assessment and did not seem to grasp the "expert's" inability to speak to the literature on assessment and treatment of offenders. The credit that the judge gave to the mental status examination is completely unsupported by the literature in this area and appears to demonstrate that the judge was out of his depth in trying to understand the issues involved in these assessments. It is equally difficult to imagine how this "expert" was qualified sixty-six times to testify in court. Perhaps on other occasions he provided expertise on matters on which he had genuine expertise. Or, having qualified one or more times as an "expert" witness, perhaps he was simply accepted by various courts without subsequent proof of his "expertise."

Pre-Sentence Reports

As noted at the beginning of this chapter, there were pre-sentence reports written by probation officers and presented to the trial judges in 83 of the 103 cases in the 1990-93 data and in 36 of the 41 cases in the 1999 data. Section 721(1) of the *Criminal Code of Canada* outlines the expectations of pre-sentence reports: "Where an accused, other than a corporation, pleads guilty to or is found guilty of an offence, a probation officer shall, if required to do so by a court, prepare and file with the court a report in writing relating to the accused for the purpose of assisting the court in imposing sentence or in determining whether the accused should be discharged pursuant to section 730." Table 6.4 shows the themes present in the pre-sentence reports written by probation officers about the offenders at the request of trial judges. One feature of these reports that stands out in both the 1990-93 data and the 1998-99 data is their variability in approach. Even though the reports have a standard appearance, there is considerable difference in how they are written. This may be more obvious in Court of Appeal data than in other research because the cases came from a range of geographical areas within Ontario.[1]

In cases with both pre-sentence reports and psychiatric or psychological reports, the pre-sentence report simply reported on and usually quoted the clinician's report. In cases in which the reports were positive toward the offender, community supervision was recommended as a disposition. For example, in *R. v. H.* (1991), which involved an offender

Table 6.4

Pre-sentence reports

Content of report	1990-93 N = 83 of 103 cases	1999 N = 36 of 41 cases
Pathologizes offender	22	5
Positive toward offender	29	6
Negative toward offender	17	11
Neutral	27	9
Mentions victim	7	5
Raises questions about guilt of offender	6	1

1 For a comprehensive discussion on the role of the probation officer and probation reports at sentencing, see Cole and Angus (2003).

who was sixty-two years of age at the time of trial, the probation officer stated that "he transfers some blame for his actions back to the victims, and his intentions of removing them as beneficiaries from his Will would seem to indicate a lack of remorse ... Since his family have already placed conditions on the offender to minimize him as a risk at home and in the community, the writer believes he would successfully complete a further period of probation." In this case, the offender, over a period of thirty years, had sexually assaulted his daughter for seven years and three granddaughters for varying periods of time. He had a previous conviction for sexual assault. The trial judge sentenced the offender to six months of incarceration, due largely to the following reasons: "the serious breach of trust, vis a vis the accused and his daughter and granddaughters; the ages of the victims at the time of the offences; the length of time he subjected his daughter to many revolting acts; and the effect upon her, which may last the rest of her life." The offender appealed the sentence, but his appeal was not supported by the Court of Appeal.

In cases with reports noted as negative toward the offender, incarceration was recommended. For example, in another 1990 case, *R.v. A., T.L.*, an offender appealed a three-year sentence imposed on him by the trial judge when he was convicted of having sexual intercourse with his twelve-year-old cousin when she was unconscious due to alcohol consumption. In his report, the probation officer described the offender's alcohol problem and his chaotic family background, including the observation that the offender had four children from two different relationships and that three of the children were in the care of a child welfare agency. The probation officer was not positive about the offender's chances for rehabilitation on probation. He observed that the offender had not made any effort to deal with his obvious alcohol problem, and noted that he was developing a pattern of assaulting family members. He concluded that, "due to the subject's previous response to community supervision and the nature of the offence, it is the writer's opinion that a period of probation would not prove to be beneficial or adequately serve as an appropriate disposition in accordance with community sentiment. It is therefore respectfully submitted that the court may wish to consider a sentence that would serve as a specific deterrent and be reflective of the nature of the incident." The trial judge's sentence of three years of incarceration was upheld by the Court of Appeal.

In cases with reports noted as neutral toward the offender, the probation officer did not make a recommendation. Reports that mentioned victim impact were more likely to be neutral or negative toward the offender. Reports that were positive toward the offender did not mention victim impact, but some did question the guilt of the offender even though the offender had entered a guilty plea or had been found guilty. For example, in 1998, in *R. v. B., J.S.*, the case noted above, the probation officer wrote that "the subject described some of the allegations made with regard to these charges as 'absolutely ludicrous.' Sources contacted by the writer appear supportive of the subject in this regard." The probation officer did not include any victim impact information and indicated that he had not been able to contact the police to get information from the police report about the offence. He did not express any caution about the absence of that information when he made his recommendation: "The writer can see no reason why this individual would not respond to probation supervision, should the court be considering that course of action."[2]

Although there is still considerable variability in how such reports are written, those in the 1999 data appear to be more standardized in terms of the information they contain and are less likely to be positive toward the offender or to question his guilt or responsibility for the offence. There seems to be more thoroughness in terms of citing the sources of the information received and the limitations of the information received. One case in the 1999 data contained a report that is the exception. It gave a basic social history and indicated that the offender ran a group home during the period when the offences took place. It indicated as well that the offender was a recovered alcoholic who had a strong religious affiliation and said that he had rehabilitated himself. It did not recommend anything but said that the offender claimed he would abide by any community supervision conditions. The writer then went on to suggest some. The report did not include any victim impact information or input, just as few pre-sentence reports did in the 1990-93 data. The probation officer was subpoenaed and grilled about her report and the fact that she did not really write an assessment under the title "assessment" on the form but just reported the offender's words. The judge was not satisfied either with the report or with the probation officer's defence of it and ordered a second report to be written. It was written by a different probation officer and included a Crown brief, victim input, and many character references concerning the offender, including one from the mayor of the town where the offences took place. The report described the offender as a "born again Christian" since 1991 who had quit drinking and was running a boarding home for men as well as a

2 Cole and Angus (2003) contains an interesting section on code language in pre-sentence reports.

twelve-step program and a Bible study group. The writer went on to say that

> these offences now before the Court represent a tremendous breach of trust that occurred in 1973 and 1974. J. does not demonstrate an understanding of the impact his behaviour may have had on these four women. While stating that he is very sorry these events happened, when asked who he was sad for, he quickly replied "for me!" He later stated that he was sorry for the girls as well. He blames his criminal acts on alcohol use and has distanced himself from any personal blame or responsibility. J. feels that the girls and women had "no bad feelings with him" when he left the group home. He states that he left because he knew he had "lost it." He was afraid the girls would take advantage of him as they knew they had "something on him." Troublesome is the lack of victim empathy. [He] seems mainly interested in how these crimes have affected him. True remorse is for the victims, not for one self and the consequences which may occur for one's actions. This writer saw no remorse for the victims, nor empathy for the damage done by his actions.
>
> Although J. has turned his life around by quitting alcohol and serving the community, this in no way addresses his previous sexual crimes or makes ammends [sic] to the specific victims. (*R. v. M., J.* [October 1998])

In arriving at the sentence, the trial judge explained the issue of the pre-sentence reports and appeared inclined to agree with the writer of the second. He stated that the offender had made "great strides in rehabilitating" himself and mentioned his attempts to help others with alcohol problems. He said that the offender's guilty plea saved him from a penitentiary sentence. In citing the breach of trust, the apparent lack of remorse, and the duration of the abuse, the judge said that

> the mere passage of time cannot, in my view, wipe the slate clean ... In this case I took the unusual step of ordering a second pre-sentence report. You will recall that the officer who prepared the first pre-sentence report, which is Exhibit One in these proceedings, was called to the stand to testify. From her testimony it became clear that she had spoken to only your friends, your associates or your clients, and your relatives ... It was my view that we should have a more balanced report rather than what was, in my view, simply a self-serving report for the most part, echoing your pleas ... Quite frankly, I do not accept that this

> period in your life, these incidences that have given rise to the charges before the court, are solely the result of alcohol abuse. I am not satisfied that you realize, even though you protest here today that you do, ... the harm that you've done to those young women.

The Ontario policy manual for probation officers outlines under what circumstances a probation officer can make recommendations in the pre-sentence report: "If the [probation officer] recommends community supervision, the rationale should be included along with specific factors that address the offender's criminogenic risk factors. It is not appropriate for the [probation officer] to specifically recommend probation or Conditional Sentence. The [probation officer] may comment on the suitability/amenability of the offender for community supervision but not on the specific type of community supervision (i.e. probation or Conditional Sentence)" (cited in Cole and Angus 2003, 41).

Cole and Angus (2003, 302) claim that research has demonstrated that pre-sentence reports have a powerful influence on "the nature, length and conditions attached to the sentence ultimately imposed. Rates of concurrence between the recommendations of probation officers and the sentence imposed are very high." This does not appear to be the case in these data in either time period. The relative importance of the pre-sentence reports is evidenced by the rate at which they are cited compared with the rate at which they are prepared for the court. Although pre-sentence reports were the most frequently written reports, they were cited only 24 percent of the time by the trial judges and only 3.6 percent of the time by the Court of Appeal in the 1990-93 data. In the 1999 data, these reports were cited at the same rate, 24 percent of the time, by trial judges and not at all by the Court of Appeal. The judges did not seem to value the opinions of this group of people as highly as they did those of the clinical professionals who submitted reports.

Conclusion

In this chapter, we have examined reports presented to the court at sentencing. Although pre-sentence reports make up the majority of the reports, they are the least cited by judges. Professionally written statements are the most frequently cited. The reports that get the most notice from judges in terms of being cited and appearing to influence the decision are those written by professionals, usually psychiatrists.

Conrad and Schneider's (1985, 248) comments quoted at the beginning of this chapter that "medicalization is primarily a definitional phenomenon – that is, one of how a problem is collectively defined, by whom and with what consequences" – are significant in these data. Attempts by clinicians, usually psychiatrists, to define whom individual offenders are for the courts often ignore the illegal behaviour. Conflicting views about pedophilia and efforts to identify someone as not being a "typical sex offender" are indicative of definitional confusion.

These attempts to construct the offender as typical or atypical illustrate that the courts lack education about sexual abuse and the men who sexually abuse children. Langevin (1990, 1993) and Finkelhor et al. (1990) have clearly identified that the vast majority of men who sexually abuse children are otherwise "normal." That is, they are not pedophiles, nor do they have a diagnosable disorder.

Analysis of the reports prepared for the court on behalf of the offender at sentencing demonstrates construction of the offender as someone who is experiencing some form of individual pathology. The reports, not surprisingly, given that they are commissioned and paid for by the defence, support the idea of the offender as not entirely responsible or not fully accountable. They feed into a construction of the offender that Scully and Marolla (1984, 530) describe as a "negotiation of identity" and a "neutralization" of the offender's liability. They produce a view of men who sexually abuse children, in many cases over a period of years, as exhibiting individual pathology. Construction of the male offender as not able to help himself or unable to resist the child continues a social construction of the child as "sexual." This construction facilitates the explanations and excuses proffered for the behaviour. It acts in combination with comparable understandings of the offender as a "good" man possessing a respectable work record to minimize the emphasis on the victim and the harm done by the abuse.

How these reports are received by judges illustrates the need to further examine the input of "experts" into the court process. It also demonstrates a need for judicial education about these offences and offenders. This need will be discussed in the next and final chapter.

7
The Court as a Site of Struggle

The purpose of my studies was to explore the influences on trial court judges and on the Court of Appeal of Ontario in sentencing offenders who have sexually offended against children. In one of the earliest criticisms of changes to sexual assault laws, Roberts and Gebotys (1993) commented that, although the 1983 and 1988 changes had resulted in more victims coming forward with complaints, the system had not changed how it responded to those complaints. On one hand, these data demonstrate that this may still be a reality. On the other, there have been some changes in how victims and offenders are viewed.

I posed a number of questions at the end of Chapter 1 that I have examined throughout the book. I summarize the results of this examination below and then summarize the courts' views of the offender, the victim, and the offence.

1 *What is the relative importance of the victim, the offender, and the offence?* From the data examined in this book, it is clear that the offender is the dominant person in sentencing deliberations. This is not surprising since the offender is the one being sentenced. What is concerning, however, is the degree to which the offence and its effects are overlooked even in the 1999 data. The offence appears to come second and the victim third. It is not possible to be precise about this assessment since the data yielded no statistically significant predictors of sentence. A qualitative analysis of those cases that had their original sentences appealed illustrates that the tendency in many of the cases was to discuss the sentence relative to the offender and not to the offensive behaviour or the harm done to the victim.
2 *Is judicial comment overly sympathetic to the accused?* There were many cases in the earliest data (1990-93) in which the judicial comment

could be described as overly sympathetic to the accused. By the 1999 data, this tendency was much less obvious, although it was present in some cases.

3 *Are judges overly concerned with the accused's background and the effect of the sentence/charge on him?* In the earliest data, 1990-93, they were more so than in the most recent data. In the 1999 data, there were some cases in which this was an issue but not in as many as in the 1990-93 data. The problem with formulating responses to this question (and others) is the small number of Crown appeals in the 1999 data. For example, in the earliest data, there was concern about re-incarcerating offenders who had already served the short sentences handed down. This kind of concern could only arise in the case of a Crown appeal. In the 1999 data, this was not a factor, but there were cases in which offenders who had been given conditional sentences were incarcerated after appeal.

4 *Do they downplay or trivialize the severity of the offence?* By 1999, most trials and appeals reflect an appreciation for the seriousness of the offence. It depends on what the offence was, however. In cases that did not involve penetration, the tendency to downplay the offence was sometimes evident.

5 *Is sexual assault considered a violent act in and of itself, or is violence viewed as an additional factor?* Yes and no. If the sexual assault was intercourse, then in most cases violence was recognized. If it was not, then the inherent violence may or may not have been clear to the courts.

6 *What consideration is there of the victim in the sentencing process?* The victim is more present in victim impact statements and in judicial comment in the 1999 cases, probably as a result of changes to the *Criminal Code of Canada,* but the victim still seems to be a minor player in these proceedings.

7 *To what degree is the "patriarchal dividend" evident in this consideration?* The term "patriarchal dividend" was coined by Connell (1995). The term is meant to recognize that, although many men do not benefit from the masculine construction of law, to some extent all men are advantaged by it in comparison to most women and children. The patriarchal dividend is evident in these data in the continued emphasis on penetration and in how some men are credited for their performances in their public male roles. Their roles as fathers or caregivers are not emphasized.

8 *What kinds of mitigating and aggravating circumstances are accepted in sentencing?* All kinds. Tables 4.1 and 4.2 list the mitigating

circumstances at trial and appeal in both the 1990-93 and the 1998-99 time periods. In 1990-93, trial judges' top ten mitigating circumstances were work record, no previous related offence, positive report, good character/reputation, guilty plea, no violence, involved in rehabilitation, age of accused, remorse, and type of abuse (not intercourse). In 1998-99, the top ten mitigating circumstances cited by trial judges were support of family and friends, situational crisis/health problems, no previous offence, employed, from a dysfunctional family, counselling, guilty plea, no danger/risk to reoffend, no violence, and alcohol abuse. In 1990-93, the Court of Appeal of Ontario listed receiving treatment, no previous offence, hardship of re-incarceration, positive report, previous good character, age of offender, delay in processing the appeal, guilty plea, pre-trial custody, and minimal/no impact on the victim as its top ten mitigating reasons. In 1998-99, the same court listed type of abuse, no criminal record, no risk to reoffend, pre-trial custody, gainfully employed, sought treatment, compliance with bail conditions, out of character, primary source of family income, and wife dependent on him as its top-ten mitigating circumstances.

The top ten aggravating circumstances listed by trial judges in the 1990-93 data were position of trust, victim impact, nature of abuse (penetration), age of victim, duration of abuse, no remorse, negative report, no treatment, age of offender, planned, previous offence, previous sexual offence, and impact on family. The top ten aggravating circumstances listed by the Court of Appeal of Ontario in 1990-93 were position of trust, duration of abuse, intercourse, age of victim, victim impact, relationship to the victim, previous sexual offences, number of victims, age of the offender, and pedophile. The top ten aggravating circumstances in the 1998-99 data were position of trust, duration/frequency of abuse, type of abuse (penetration), seriousness of offence, relationship to victim, age of victim, victim impact, criminal record, treatment unsuccessful, and premeditation. An examination of the actual cases has illustrated that, although the mitigating and aggravating circumstances are cited by the judges of both trial and appeal courts, sometimes the same circumstances are explained and used differently by different judges. Young's (1988, 10) comment earlier about the "myriad of factors" has proven to be true in these data.

9 *What role does psychiatry play in delineating these variables?* As predicted in Chapter 1, psychiatry and to some extent psychology play a pivotal role in the gatekeeping function of the court, particularly

in dangerous offender cases. While the psychiatric input in those cases appeared to be consistent with current research findings and showed concern for public safety and for victims and potential victims, in other cases the psychiatric and psychological input is less likely to reflect up-to-date views of research results and assessment processes. It is important to keep in mind that the majority of clinical professionals who presented reports on sentencing in these data were solicited by the offenders through their defence attorneys, and that these clinicians were testifying on behalf of the offenders.

10 *What is the language of the court?* The 1999 data indicate that the language of the court has become more consistently respectful of the victim and that there is less evidence of egregious comments in terms of victim blame or minimization of victim harm. But there is still evidence of minimization of the victim's reality. These data are not good indicators of progress, however, because they consist mainly of offender appeals, and cases that might previously have been appealed by the Crown are no longer being appealed.

The Courts' View of the Offence

In Chapter 2, Mohr and Roberts (1994, 5) were quoted as saying that "the drafters of the 1983 sexual assault provisions did not define 'sexual assault.' It is judges who, by default, become the law-makers as far as the definition of the offence itself is concerned."

In Chapter 3, I asked the following questions. What is child sexual abuse? Who decides? In making the decision, from whose perspective is the abuse viewed? How do judges decide which sexual acts are more or less offensive? In that chapter, we saw that the Court of Appeal of Ontario set a benchmark for deciding sentences in child sexual abuse that emphasized three elements in determining the most serious cases: (1) if the assault involves intercourse and (2) it is committed by a person in a position of trust with reference to the victim of the assaults, then (3) the sentence is supposed to be three years in the penitentiary. That appellate court decided that intercourse was the most significant form of abuse, particularly if it was committed by a parent or step-parent. The data in these studies indicate, however, that there is a great deal of variability in how judges at both the trial level and the Court of Appeal level view the offence. In both the 1990-93 and the 1998-99 studies, the standard deviations in all sentence conditions, as noted in tables, were high. In some cases, they were as high as the means. Qualitative attempts to explain this variability have raised some potential explanations, which I offered in Chapters 4, 5, and 6. In 2002, after these data were collected,

Moldaver JA in *R. v. D.D.* (2002) articulated a higher range of sentence for child sexual abuse cases but nonetheless retained the construct of penetration as a benchmark indicator. He was comparing the case in front of the court to the *R. v. Stuckless* (1998) decision:

> *Stuckless* does not stand for the proposition that 6 years represents the high end of the appropriate range of sentences for like offenders convicted of like offences. On the contrary, it seems to me that in similar circumstances, mid to upper single digit penitentiary terms will, as a general rule, represent the appropriate sentencing range.
>
> Cases like the present one however, which involve repeated acts of anal intercourse, as well as the use of other physical violence, threats of physical violence and extortion are in a different category. Such cases, in my view, call for a higher range of penalty because of the enhanced gravity and seriousness of the crimes and the greater degree of moral culpability attributable to the offender. As a rule, I believe that upper single digit to low double digit penitentiary terms are called for in these circumstances.

Moldaver went on to say, "I wish to emphasize that the ranges which I have identified are not meant to be fixed and inflexible. On the contrary, sentencing is not an exact science and trial judges must retain the flexibility needed to do justice in individual cases. The suggested ranges are merely guidelines designed to assist trial judges in their difficult task of fashioning fit and just sentences in similar cases."

The Courts' View of the Offender

In the 1990-93 data, construction of the offender illustrated patriarchal thinking about male sexuality and appeared to be influenced by traditional notions of male rights in terms of domestic privacy. This construction is consistent with the findings of early studies about the change in the legislation (Marshall 1985; Brown 1991; METRAC 1992) that the offence is downplayed and the accused's background or character is the focus. In cases in which the offence was not intercourse, other factors were emphasized as more relevant than the offence. These factors were related to the offender as a person, usually from the perspective of his public persona. Focus on the offender took the form of an analysis of mitigating circumstances. These circumstances usually portrayed the offender as a man of "good character" or as someone who would suffer unduly from incarceration. As noted in Chapter 4, the offender's responsibility was minimized and/or neutralized, and his presence in society as a "good" man in terms of work record was considered important as to whether or not he should be held fully accountable.

In terms of the extent to which judges accept the excuses and justifications of men who have sexually abused children, an analysis of the mitigating factors in these data demonstrated that they lessened the responsibility or accountability of the offender. That is, in the 1990-93 period, the tendency appeared to be to treat children as less important than the offenders who had abused them. It can be argued that an emphasis on these factors was an attempt to reinforce the concept of adult-child relationships as private, particularly if they occurred within a family. This understanding of sexuality and sexual contact is consistent with a belief in a different standard in a domestic sphere in which women and children are subordinated to the person in control in that sphere, the man. Offenders' "antecedents" were considered to be relevant, as was the impact of the disclosure of the abuse on offenders and their families. Victim issues faded into the background.

In the 1999 data, which consisted primarily of offender appeals, the picture was somewhat different. There was a much stronger emphasis on the offence itself and on the impact on the victim, and more consistency in sentencing when the offence involved intercourse, even though there was no statistical significance to these factors as predictors in a quantitative analysis. The focus on the "good man" was gone for the most part, and the majority of the cases both at trial and at appeal demonstrated this change in focus. Not known is how representative this change is of cases of child sexual abuse sentencing in general. It is known that Crown resources were significantly cut back in the mid- to late 1990s in Ontario. Perhaps cases that contained an emphasis on the offender as a credit to his male role and that could have been appealed were not.

The Courts' View of the Victim

In considering the 1990-93 data, the old cliché that "children should be seen and not heard" is relevant. The child's experience of abuse was the reason for the trial, but at the sentencing stage the child was not present in any substantial way. The Court of Appeal also did not challenge trial court judges' negative comments about victims or their absence of attention to victim impact. Cases in which the Court of Appeal emphasized the seriousness of the offence in terms of its impact on the victim were rare. When the victim was mentioned, it was usually in cases of intercourse. In cases in which the offence was not intercourse, the victim, if mentioned at all, was noted peripherally and discounted, similar to how the offence was discounted or downplayed in favour of a discussion of the offender as a person. These data support West's (1987, 82) contention that "women's gender specific injuries are dismissed as trivial," as well as Mitchell's (1985, 96) contention that we do not hear all sides of the story.

In the 1999 data, there were more victim impact statements, and they did receive more notice. Again, however, the notice depended on the details of the offence. The victim's view of the offence is not the dominant consideration in the sentencing proceedings. Victims' experiences of the crimes were subjugated to a different order of understanding of the behaviour. Different judges heard them differently, and most judges heard other voices speaking more loudly to the issues in front of the court. Although victim impact had been given a clearer place in the *Criminal Code,* in the majority of cases in which victim impact was mentioned, there was a "yes, but" quality to the judicial notice. As Bacchus (1999, 217) has pointed out, "although in the vast majority of cases victims are the criminal justice system's *raison d'être,* their voice has traditionally been restricted."

In most cases, victim input took the form of handwritten, difficult-to-read statements characterized by poor spelling and bad grammar. This method of presenting victim impact seems to set it up for failure in an atmosphere that is otherwise quite formal. In instances in which professional reports were written about victims, the reports were the results of referrals made by the victim's parent or a child welfare agency. Referrals of victims are hampered by waiting lists for the assessment and treatment of children who have been sexually abused. The Crown cannot delay the process by asking for the court to wait until these assessments are done. It could be construed as systemic delay.

The convicted offender does not seem to have this problem in obtaining reports. There do not appear to be similar waiting times for these assessments, possibly because there are clinicians who specialize in providing them to the court. Professional reports about the victim seemed to make a qualitative difference in some cases in terms of the court's view of the offence. Such reports seem to give the victims a presence that their own victim impact statements do not. Should a child need a professional or "expert" advocate about the harm done to her? Is the court system inherently biased against the small voices of children? Children who have been sexually abused are not in a position to make the system work for them by engaging a professional to help them document their trauma. They are already disadvantaged since they are children and are without much status. If they are lucky enough to have a middle- or upper-class parent who can negotiate more powerful input for them, then their voices may be heard. If they come from poor families, then their chances of having a voice are further diminished. In our system, the only role that these children have is as witnesses, even though they are allowed to make input to sentencing. They do not have legal representation. The Crown counsel is not their lawyer and is not acting on their behalf.

The role played by the Crown in soliciting and facilitating victim impact statements could not be assessed in these data. It is a useful area to explore as part of a larger project that examines how victim impact is constructed by trial judges in a variety of offences. Such a study may shed some light on whether victim invisibility is related to the fact that the victims in these data are children or that these offences are sexual. Analysis of a broader range of offence categories may be more helpful in determining what weight victim impact statements have. Erez and Laster (1999), Erez and Rogers (1999), and Roberts and Edgar (2002) have surveyed judges to determine how they perceive victim impact. Although there is much positive comment about victim impact, there are also comments that illustrate the evidence that these data show. For example, Roberts and Edgar (2002, 197) quote a judge who said:

> It is often more therapeutic for the victim than it is helpful for the court to hear what the victim has to say ... a sentencing court will know the principles of sentencing with or without a VIS, and it must be careful to discharge its mandate properly rather than allow the victim to dictate what the sentence should be. Circumstances are often most compelling and heart breaking, but the court must temper its sentences according to jurisprudence, common sense, the submissions of counsel on both sides, the circumstances of the accused and indeed the victim, the crime itself and its own life experience and values. Sometimes a VIS can be helpful but care must be taken not to abuse it.

This quotation illustrates what Erez and Laster (1999) speak about when they refer to the need of the court to "objectify" victim impact. It assumes that victims have a particular result in mind, which these data and the other research to date do not support. It also speaks to a belief by judges and possibly by those who think that vigorously prosecuting child sexual abuse cases is a good thing – that is, that the law knows best.

The possibilities for challenge to the absence of proportionality in sentencing, at least from the victim's viewpoint, appear to be diminishing. If appeals are increasingly unlikely and joint submissions more and more possible, then how does a victim respond to this systemic invisibility? Child victims' needs are not fully met by the prosecution of those who have offended against them. A resort to law to remedy the social problem of the sexual abuse of children clearly has limited utility. What good was the Ramsay sentence, described in Chapter 1, to the (now) young women who were abused by him? How much benefit did they get from the sentencing hearing? They were clearly chosen for their vulnerability and the prospect that they would not report the offences. What services are available to them and to other children who are sexually abused? It can be argued that these victims may not have been victims had there been more social supports for them earlier in their lives. Regardless of whether a child comes from a chaotic family background or a relatively stable one, she will not get the support she needs through publicly accessible programs because their numbers have been cut. The social value of children is not evident in the number of programs readily available for abused children. Programs that did exist have been severely cut since the mid-1990s when the Canada Assistance Plan was replaced by the Canada Health and Social Transfer system. They continue to be cut and/or underfunded.

The government expectation that children should be put through a prosecution and trial is premised on some ideological notion of justice that society is best served by bringing the offenders to court. It is understandable that we, as a society, would want to identify and incapacitate those who sexually abuse children, but what else do we want? To date, children have been sacrificed to the process. If governments truly valued children, then there would be many other programs immediately available to help them heal. Perhaps the days when prosecutors argued against getting children into treatment until the trial was completed are over, but perhaps it is not much of an issue anymore because beyond the most rudimentary child protection investigation other programs do not exist for most children. It appears that Finkelhor's (1984, 199) words reported in Chapter 5 are true as well in this context: "The impact of an event on childhood itself is treated as less important. It is only 'childhood,' a stage which, after all, everyone outgrows."

Expert Input into Judicial Construction

The expert role as evidenced in these data was very consistent with Conrad and Schneider's (1992) description of it as "gatekeeping." Experts inform the court about who is a "real" offender and who is not. They also recommend how the offender should be managed. These data demonstrate a great deal of variability in the approach to assessing offenders and in the opinions presented about relatively similar men who offend against children.

The experts' reports on behalf of offenders were attempts at risk assessment. As such, many are questionable. As noted earlier, judges at both levels of the court appeared to heavily depend for their understanding of risk to reoffend on the opinion of the clinician who wrote a report for the defence. Many of the assessments available to the court in these data do not conform to current research findings or to the assessment procedures recommended by their peers who specialize in research into these kinds of offences. Their focus on individual pathology or life stresses on the offender reflects Scully and Marolla's (1984, 540) comments about constructions of the offender that describe his behaviour as "mild, transient and curable." In cases in which an offender was not diagnosed as a pedophile (the majority), most clinicians did not recognize Langevin's (1990) research in which he points out that most offenders are not pedophiles and offend for reasons other than sexual attraction. When they attempt to explain the offender's behaviour, they do so in terms of a medical model that locates the problem in the offender's stress level, depression, or some personality trait that may make the behaviour understandable to the judge. They do not assess the offender's view of women and children as sex objects to which the offender may feel he is entitled. When they encounter such sentiments of entitlement, they do not deal with them, or they label them as cognitive distortions. For the most part, the court seems to accept these constructions of offenders uncritically.

Rehabilitation

The experts frequently recommended treatment for offenders whom they had assessed. The Court of Appeal supported this notion, citing the fact that the offender was receiving treatment as a mitigating factor. All of this discussion about psychiatric input into the sentencing process prompts questions. What is rehabilitation for men who sexually abuse children? Where do the rehabilitators/treaters stand in terms of the formulation that Scully and Marolla (1984) present about excuses, justifications, and accounts? In some cases, the focus of the clinical reports would have the reader believe that the emphasis should be on psychotherapy to improve elements of individual functioning such as low self-esteem. It might also involve treatment for alcoholism or compulsion. Nothing in the research on these men indicates that these are productive strategies. Quinsey (1994) recommended a cognitive behavioural model of treatment that would emphasize the offensive behaviour and be consistent with the kind of intervention supported in the literature about effective treatment of men who commit other crimes. Because sex offenders are by definition criminal offenders, it is reasonable to expect that principles of treatment that apply to offenders in general also apply to sex offenders (Quinsey 1994, 7). Harris et al. (1998) were quoted in Chapter 1 as indicating that even that treatment has little evidence of success at this point. They support the notion that child sexual abuse is an antisocial act that requires the offender to rethink his value system, including his sense of entitlement to children (his own or members of his extended family in these data) as appropriate objects through which to achieve sexual gratification. In other words, the offender's social construction of children needs to be challenged.

Because clinicians believe that men who sexually abuse children within their own families do not present a risk to repeat their offences, little has been done to study this population. Questions are not generally asked in the treatment literature on these offenders about the problems associated with children reporting this kind of abuse. As a result, the assumption is made that, in the absence of further reports of abuse, no problems exist. In the population studied here, much of the abuse committed by these offenders took place over a period of years and was undetected. In the clinical reports, duration of abuse often was not taken into consideration in the assessment of the offender. This alone is sufficient to question the clinician's commonsensical ideas about sexual abuse within families.

The Problem of Incarceration

Length of sentence or period of incarceration was used in this study as a measure of the seriousness with which the offence is viewed. This is the societal measure of seriousness. To some extent, it makes sense in terms of denunciation. That is, to date we have not come up with another way of stating in clearer terms that something is offensive to society. However, there is an element of "be careful what you wish for" in this approach. In the cognitive-behavioural or relapse prevention programs that Quinsey (1994) reviews, there is an emphasis at times on what is called pro-social behaviour. It is not always clear what this means. Sometimes, but not often, it includes challenges to these men's beliefs about entitlement to control women and children. If the program is offered in a traditional correctional institution, then it is unlikely that such an emphasis will be possible or reinforced by the inmate's surroundings. One of the serious problems with incarcerating men for sexual abuse in the expectation that they will be rehabilitated is that the prison environment is almost uniformly negative in terms of pro-social concepts. Prison values are not defined along feminist lines of thought either by the keepers or by the kept. The entire basis of prison life is paramilitary, and conformity to power is valued. The keepers expect inmates to conform to their exercise of power, and the rules of the inmate subculture dictate that inmates follow a "survival of the fittest" notion in which physical power is the ideal. This is not an environment in which "cognitive defects" about men's entitlement to desired sexual objects are likely to be challenged. Even though the popular perception that child molesters are viewed as the lowest form of life in prisons is largely accurate, this is not because the inmate subculture values children and rejects the notion of children or women as property. It is simply because prison life is based on a hierarchy of power, and the stereotypes of the child molester as an intellectually deficient stranger or a homosexual are accepted in prison, just as they often are elsewhere. If an otherwise powerful inmate, such as a member of a motorcycle gang, has been convicted of assaulting a child, especially a female child, chances are that it will be overlooked. This is not an environment from which feminists should expect much. If long sentences are supported for the purposes of rehabilitation, then advocates for change in the lives of women and children will have to advocate for change in prisons. If such advocates think that penitentiary sentences should be imposed on men who sexually assault children, then they should be aware of the potential cost of the denunciation through long-term incarceration. This cost may be paid in the ultimate release of a man who is stronger in his sense of antagonism toward women and his belief that his gender entitles him to take his sexual gratification wherever he may seek it. There is no simple solution to this problem.

Variability

If there is one thing to which these data speak loudly, it is variability in sentencing. Many have claimed that variability is the result of judges carefully considering the merits of each case. These data do not support that claim. The possibility that arises out of this research is that proportionality is an elusive goal because sentencing, as Hogarth pointed out in 1971, has more to do with the judge than any other factor. As the judge cited above by Roberts and Edgar (2002) says, the court must temper its judgment based on, among other things, "its own life experience and values." What happens when judges make decisions from their points of view? Cases in which the factors were substantially similar had different outcomes. By 1999, there was less variability, but there were also fewer Crown appeals, which may have significantly skewed the evidence of variability. What is the solution to this problem?

As noted in Chapter 1, Doob and Brodeur (1996) claim that Canadians are confused by sentencing. It is not a big surprise that the variability seen in these data is confusing. The challenge lies in what to do about it. In advocating sentencing guidelines, Mohr and Roberts (1994, 183) conclude that a criminal law response to a social problem is limited but that "its symbolic significance, however, cannot be ignored." Victims' needs are not well served by the prosecution of the offender. But the least that may be possible would be to send a clearer message in denunciation. That message does not have to involve longer sentences, and it should include some consideration of rationalized sentences. Perhaps to some extent the courts reflect our lack of consensus as a society about these issues and how to deal with them. Who would design the sentencing guidelines? In the past, such tasks have been assigned to judges, lawyers, and academics. Perhaps inclusion of voices from the ranks of victims would be desirable. Research cited here has demonstrated that the majority of victims do not want vengeance; sometimes they do not even want the offender to be incarcerated. If guidelines are the way to go, then victims should be part of the process.

Another relevant consideration is that the comment that goes with the sentence is as important as, if not more so than, the sentence itself. Emphasis on the sentence without an even stronger emphasis on the comment that accompanies it is problematic. Mitra (1987, 130) concluded in her study that, "although the rhetoric employed was condemnatory, the sentences passed did not always reflect such sentiments." In the data studied here, the rhetoric was condemnatory most often when judges saw the offensive behaviour as meeting a certain standard. Perhaps longer sentences are not necessary as long as the factors considered in arriving at them were consistently concerned with the actual offence and its effects on the victim. A reduction in the focus on the offender, less excusing, justifying, and minimizing, and a clearer denunciation of the conduct in judicial comment might be satisfactory to victims. A tariff may be necessary, but it will not be sufficient. No sentence will ever be long enough if the reasons for it do not clearly outline the repugnance that we as a society and the courts as our agents have for it.

Suggestions for Change

One of the common suggestions for change in how courts operate is the recommendation that more women be appointed to the bench. Some have challenged this as a viable solution. In discussing the entrenched gendered nature of the legal profession and by extension judges, Sheehy (1989, 154) commented that "the belief systems generated by such institutions reproduce relations of dominance, and are employed by most decision-makers within these institutions, regardless of the individual's sex, race or class." This observation seems to be relevant in the case noted in Chapter 1, decided by Madam Justice Verrault in Quebec. Others, however, believe that at least in appointing more women to decision-making positions there is more likelihood that a patriarchal approach can be changed. Grant and Smith (1991, 58) identify the Canadian judge as "a white man." They list some possible reasons for considering gender representation on the bench:

1 Those who are bound by a system should be participants in it.
2 Public confidence in the system would be enhanced.
3 Female judges serve as important role models.
4 Female judges could make a unique and important contribution to the adjudication process.

Part of their argument for increased representation of women on the bench is predicated on the reality that men and women have a different set of experiences and understandings in life and that there has been a tendency to equate men's reality or perspective with a "neutral, human perspective" (Grant and Smith 1991, 67). They also quote Madam Justice Bertha Wilson, who contends that the judge must "enter into the skin of the litigant and make his or her experience part of [the judge's] experience" (74). They use this quotation to argue that real objectivity requires the judge to see the world from the perspective of the individual being judged. In these data, this did not seem to be a problem. The problem, in fact, was that the judges could not see the offence for the offender. The focus on the offender was often to the exclusion of consideration of the offence and the victim's experience of it. Would more female justices make the chances greater that the offence would be seen in context? Minow (1987, 315) concludes that "justice is engendered when judges admit the limitations of their own viewpoints, when judges reach beyond those limits by trying to see from contrasting perspectives."

There are issues raised in this study about the ability of judges to see child sexual abuse from the perspective of the victim. If judicial awareness can be achieved through the appointment of a more diverse group of judges, then such a process is desirable. One essential problem, however, is that we will likely never have a child as a judge. While women's "gender-specific injuries" may someday be ameliorated as a result of increasing political activity by women and appointing more women to the bench, childhood-specific injuries may never be similarly addressed. Obviously, appointing a child is not an option, so other solutions must be sought. Wilson and others who subscribe to feminist notions that women are more sensitive to and aware of children's issues because of their traditional roles as primary caregivers would contend that more female judges would be a benefit to children. Sheehy's (1989) caution is one to remember, however. Childhood, as Finkelhor (1984) points out, is frequently discounted, and children will always be powerless. They will always be dependent on the kindness of adults for proper treatment. At the beginning of this study, I posed questions about the utility of the law as a mechanism for ensuring the protection of children. Law relies on people for its construction and interpretation. These people are adults who may never have experienced abuse as children or who may have forgotten the vulnerability of childhood and perhaps romanticized situations in which a parent or someone else exercised power over them as constructive "trips to the woodshed."

Laws can be helpful in conveying particular messages about how children should be treated, but they are not enough. Laws have to be interpreted with clear understandings of what children's vulnerabilities are, not with a focus on what adult interests are. We have not yet succeeded in achieving this goal. The focus of child custody cases is frequently adult interests, although some progress has been made in advancing the interests of children. The focus of child sexual abuse is still, for the most part, as noted in these data, on adult interests, those of the offender. But who will *consistently* speak for the child in these situations? Perhaps children who are victims of sexual abuse should be represented in court by a lawyer whose job would be to advocate for the best possible treatment for the child throughout the process, from plea bargaining related to the original charges to advocating for the child's voice to be heard concerning victim impact. Children can be represented in other types of court proceedings that affect their lives. Perhaps it is time to study the possibility of representation for them in criminal cases as well. Child welfare workers who deal with the aftermath of the abuse in some of these cases are generally unfamiliar with the criminal court process, and their opinions are not valued in it (Erez and Rogers 1999). They are therefore limited in their ability to advocate for children in this arena.

They are relatively powerless to help beyond attempting to secure some specialized post-abuse support programs for the child, which, as noted earlier, are increasingly difficult to access.

In addition to the possibility of appointing lawyers to protect children's interests in the court, there is an obvious need, beyond the appointment of more women to the bench, to help some members of the judiciary rethink their construction not only of sexual abuse but also of childhood. Mendes (1991), in an article focusing on gender and Native issues, titled in part "Promoting Heterogeneity of the Judicial Mind," suggested that a task force be struck to investigate "vulnerability awareness." This task force would ask the following questions:

1 Do articulated or unarticulated myths, biases and stereotypes affect the content of law and in particular judicial decision-making?
2 Does gender, minority or native status affect the treatment of individuals in the legal and judicial environment (e.g. in the courtroom, chambers, professional associations, law schools)?
3 How can judges affirmatively ensure equal treatment for women, natives and minorities in the courts? (106)

Mendes recommended a committee similar to the medical profession's ethics committees that judges could consult about issues of vulnerability. He also recommended that training about vulnerability be included in all judicial orientation and training programs. This training should include the vulnerability of children, which some may think is obvious but which, as demonstrated in these data, is frequently overlooked. Childhood vulnerability is invisible except in situations in which the physical impact of abuse is obvious in ways that make sense to adults. As Summit (1988, 41), quoted previously, has said, "It is adult skepticism that blinds us to all but the most blatant sexual assaults." Judges should be trained about the damages to children that are not so visible.

Bala et al. (2004, 5) contend that, "in the last 25 years, however, the nature of law has changed dramatically. Law has become a social policy tool, affecting virtually every aspect of Canadian society." Social policy in the area of child sexual abuse still needs work. The law as an agent of social policy in this area may give many citizens a sense of complacency that something is being done to ameliorate the situations of children who have been abused. The results of this study indicate, however, that only some children are constructed as genuine victims or deserving of recognition because one type of abuse is recognized as more significant than many others. Some children seem to be revictimized by the process and by a less than whole-hearted understanding of what positions of trust mean to children and what we should expect from adults in those positions. Child victims need people in positions of authority such as judges and Crown attorneys to acknowledge their pain and the efforts that they have made in pursuing justice for themselves, as was sometimes evident in these data. This acknowledgment should be part of the judge's explanation of the sentence. Even if it is not widely reported in the media, it constitutes recognition of the importance of the court process to the child.

What does this study tell us? It does not give answers about the solution to the social problem of child sexual abuse. It does appear to reinforce the conclusion that changing the law alone is not enough. If the intent or spirit of the law is not clearly visible at the level of the Court of Appeal, then what is it like at the front lines of the justice system? How are the police, the Crown attorneys, and the trial judges interpreting it? These data give no general information about those parts of the process. One can reasonably inquire, however, about what may be happening at these levels based on what these data show about the social construction of child sexual abuse at the appeal court level.

At the least, this study supports calls for further research into the practices of Crown attorneys and trial judges in cases of child sexual abuse. If the findings of this study are reproduced in that population, then serious questions must be asked about the utility of a criminal justice response for victims of child sexual abuse. A legal response is only one of many that must be put in place, but it is an important part of the process of denouncing abusive behaviour. When its response is inconsistent or seen to perpetuate myths and stereotypes that excuse offenders, that response is not what victims have the right to expect from the courts as important components of our social structure.

The difficulties in conducting sentencing research in this area should also be the subject of future discussion and action. Individual women and women's organizations have reported cases that involve questionable judicial comment to the media, but judicial accountability should not depend on anecdotal evidence or on sporadic volunteer court-watch programs. The federal and provincial governments should ensure that court records are kept in such a way that they are readily accessible to researchers. We need to be able to find out in more detail and with more accuracy on a broader basis how the judiciary makes decisions.

To summarize, we began with a discussion of the history of women and children as the domestic property of the male head of the household. I cited Roman civil and criminal law to explain the concept of *patriae potestas* or "power of the father," which gave the male head of the household total power and control over the family. Some of this power has been eroded by the proclamation of laws that legislators describe as criminalizing abuse of women and children. This study has demonstrated that, although we may believe we have protections in law, there are still many vestiges of the *patriae potestas* concept in how the law is interpreted. These vestiges need to be addressed both in society at large and in those institutions supposed to be fundamental to justice in society. Governments must appoint judges who can see the vulnerability of children and understand what a position of trust means. They must also understand the importance of their positions as positions of trust and that their response is extremely significant to the victims of these cases. If they are to decide cases of child sexual abuse, then we should be able to rely on them for a social construction of children that meets the needs and interests of children. To meet these needs and take care of these interests, they will have to understand the potential for tyranny in domestic privacy.

We must also be careful not to be complacent about child sexual abuse; it is a crime. After new laws were passed in the 1980s, there was a great deal of discussion about and media scrutiny of child sexual abuse cases. Where has that discussion gone? There is little now except in terms of length of sentence in a few high-profile cases. What of the many cases about which we never hear? It is obvious in these data that many myths about childhood and gender are perpetuated through some of our fundamental social structures. We should not think that we are centuries removed from the Roman concept of the power of the father or people in positions of authority in relation to children. Many victims' experiences with the court tell us that we are not.

References

Books, Articles, and Government Documents

Abel, G., J. Becker, and J. Cunningham-Rathner. 1984. "Complications, Consent, and Cognitions in Sex between Children and Adults." *International Journal of Law and Psychiatry* 7: 89-103.

Abel, G., M. Mittleman, and J. Becker. 1985. "Sexual Offenders: Results of Assessment and Recommendations for Treatment." In *Clinical Criminology: The Assessment and Treatment of Criminal Behaviour,* ed. M.H. Ben-Aron, S.J. Hucker, and C.D. Webster, 191-205. Toronto: M and M Graphics.

Adler, Z. 1987. *Rape on Trial.* London: Routledge and Kegan Paul.

Auburn, T., and S. Lea. 2003. "Doing Cognitive Distortions: A Discursive Psychology Analysis of Sex Offender Treatment Talk." *British Journal of Social Psychology* 42: 281-98.

Bacchus, S. 1999. "The Role of Victims in the Sentencing Process." In *Making Sense of Sentencing,* ed. J. Roberts and D. Cole, 217-29. Toronto: University of Toronto Press.

Badgley, R.F. 1984. *Sexual Offences against Children: Report of the Committee on Sexual Offences against Children and Youths.* Ottawa: Department of National Health and Welfare.

Bagley, C., and R. Ramsay. 1986. "Sexual Abuse in Childhood: Psychosocial Outcomes and Implications for Social Work Practice." *Journal of Social Work and Human Sexuality* 5: 33-47.

Bala, N., M.K. Zapf, R.J. Williams, R. Vogl, and J.P. Hornick. 2004. *Canadian Child Welfare Law: Children, Families, and the State.* 2nd ed. Toronto: Thompson Educational Publishing.

Becker, J.V., and V.L. Quinsey. 1993. "Assessing Suspected Child Molesters." *Child Abuse Neglect* 17, 1: 169-74.

Berger, P.L., and T. Luckmann. 1966. *The Social Construction of Reality: A Treatise on the Sociology of Knowledge.* Garden City, NY: Anchor Books.

Blanchard, G. 1985a. "The Addictive Personality in Child Sexual Abuse." *Protecting Children* 2.

–. 1985b. "Counselling the Sexually Addicted Incest Offender." *Protecting Children* 2.

Boudreau, F.A., R.S. Sennott, and M. Wilson. 1986. *Sex Roles and Social Patterns.* New York: Praeger Scientific.

Briere, J., and D.M. Elliott. 2003. "Prevalence and Psychological Sequellae of Self-Reported Childhood Physical and Sexual Abuse in a General Population Sample of Men and Women." *Child Abuse and Neglect* 27: 1205-22.

Briere, J., and M. Runtz. 1989. "University Males' Sexual Interest in Children: Predicting Potential Indices of 'Pedophilia' in a Nonforensic Sample." *Child Abuse and Neglect* 13: 65-75.

Brown, M. 1991. *Gender Equality in the Courts: Criminal Law.* Winnipeg: Manitoba Association of Women and the Law.

Browne, A., and D. Finkelhor. 1986. "Impact of Child Sexual Abuse: A Review of the Research." *Psychological Bulletin* 99: 66-77.

Burgess, A.W., ed. 1985. *Rape and Sexual Assault: A Research Handbook*. New York: Garland Publishing.

Canadian Sentencing Commission. 1988. *Sentencing in the Media: A Content Analysis of English-Language Newspapers in Canada*. Ottawa: Department of Justice.

Carmody, M. 2003. "Sexual Ethics and Violence Prevention." *Social and Legal Studies: An International Journal* 12, 2: 199-216.

Carnes, P. 2002. *Clinical Management of Sex Addiction*. New York: Brunner-Routledge.

–. 2004. Dr. Carnes' Resources for Sex Addiction and Recovery. http://www.sexhelp.com.

Chunn, D. 2002. "Secrets and Lies: The Criminalization of Incest and the (Re) Formation of the 'Private' in British Columbia, 1890-1940." In *Regulating Lives: Historical Essays on the State, Society, the Individual, and the Law*, ed. J. McLaren, R. Menzies, and D. Chunn, 120-44. Vancouver: UBC Press.

Chunn, D., and D. Lacombe, eds. 2000. *Law as a Gendering Practice*. London: Oxford University Press.

Cole, D., and G. Angus. 2003. "Using Pre-Sentence Reports to Evaluate and Respond to Risk." *Criminal Law Quarterly* 47: 302-64.

Cole, M. 2003. "Perceptions of the Use of Victim Impact Statements in Canada: A Survey of Crown Counsel in Ontario." Master's thesis, University of Ottawa.

Comack, E., ed. 1999. *Locating Law: Race/Class/Gender Connections*. Halifax: Fernwood.

Comack, E., and G. Balfour. 2004. *The Power to Criminalize: Violence, Inequality, and the Law*. Halifax: Fernwood.

Connell, R.W. 1995. *Masculinities*. Cambridge, UK: Polity Press.

Conrad, P., and J. Schneider. 1992. *Deviance and Medicalization: From Badness to Sickness*. Philadelphia: Temple University Press.

Conte, J., and J. Schuerman. 1987. "The Effects of Sexual Abuse on Children: A Multidimensional View." *Journal of Interpersonal Violence* 2, 4: 380-91.

Craig, W.C. 2004. "Seven-Year Sentence Sent a Weak Message to Sexual Predators." *Vancouver Sun* 11 June: A11.

Cramer, D. 1994. *Introducing Statistics for Social Research*. London: Routledge.

Cressey, D. 1960. "The Theory of Differential Association: An Introduction." *Social Problems* 8, 1: 2-6.

Criminal Code of Canada. R.S.C. 1985, c. C-46. Available at http://laws.justice.gc.ca/en/C-46/index.html.

DeMause, L. 1975. "Our Forebearers Made Childhood a Nightmare." *Psychology Today* April: 85-88.

DeYoung, M. 1982. *The Sexual Victimization of Children*. Jefferson, NC: McFarland.

Dobash, R.E., and R.P. Dobash. 1992. *Women, Violence, and Social Change*. London: Routledge.

Dominelli, L. 1991. *Gender, Sex Offenders and Probation Practice*. Norwich, UK: Novata Press.

Doob, A.N., and J.P. Brodeur. 1996. "Achieving Accountability in Sentencing." In *Accountability for Criminal Justice: Selected Essays*, ed. P. Stenning, 376-96. Toronto: University of Toronto Press.

Du Mont, J. 2003. "An Exploratory Examination of Charging and Sentencing in Sexual Assault Cases." *Canadian Journal of Women and the Law* 15, 2: 305-43.

Du Mont, J., and T.L. Myhr. 2000. "So Few Convictions: The Role of Client-Related Characteristics in the Legal Processing of Sexual Assaults." *Violence against Women* 6, 10: 1109-36.

Eberle, P., and Eberle, S. 1986. *The Politics of Child Abuse*. Secaucus, NJ: L. Stuart.

Erez, E. 1999. "Who's Afraid of the Big Bad Victim? Victim Impact Statements as Victim Empowerment *and* Enhancement of Justice." *Criminal Law Review* 1: 545-77.

Erez, E., and K. Laster. 1999. "Neutralizing Victim Reform: Legal Professionals' Perspectives on Victims and Impact Statements." *Crime and Delinquency* 45, 4: 530-53.

Erez, E., and L. Rogers. 1999. "Victim Impact Statements and Sentencing Outcomes and Processes: The Perspectives of Legal Professionals." *British Journal of Criminology* 39, 2: 216-39.

Erickson, W.D., M.C. Luxenberg, N.H. Walbek, and R.K. Seeley. 1987. "Frequency of MMPI Code Types among Sex Offenders." *Journal of Clinical and Consulting Psychology* 55, 4: 566-70.

Finkelhor, D. 1984. *Child Sexual Abuse*. New York: Free Press.

–. 1988. "The Trauma of Child Sexual Abuse: Two Models." *Journal of Interpersonal Violence* 2, 4: 348-66.

Finkelhor, D., G. Hotaling, I.A. Lewis, and C. Smith. 1990. "Sexual Abuse in a National Survey of Adult Men and Women: Prevalence, Characteristics, and Risk Factors." *Child Abuse and Neglect* 14: 19-28.

Finkelhor, D., and I.E. Lewis. 1988. "An Epidemiologic Approach to the Study of Child Abuse." In *Human Sexual Aggression: Current Perspectives*, ed. R.A. Prentky and V.L. Quinsey, 64-78. New York: New York Academy of Sciences.

Foucault, M. 1968. *The History of Sexuality*. Vol. 1. London: Allen Lane.

Freidland, N. 1990. "The Combined Effect of the Severity and the Certainty of Threatened Penalties." *Journal of Applied Social Psychology* 20: 1358-68.

Gardner, R.A. 1987. *The Parental Alienation Syndrome and the Differentiation between Fabricated and Genuine Child Sex Abuse*. Cresskill, NJ: Creative Therapeutics.

Garner, B.A., and H.K. Black, eds. 1999. *Black's Law Dictionary*. 7th ed. Saint Paul, MN: West Group.

Gelles, R.J. 1973. "Child Abuse as Psychopathology: A Sociological Critique and Reformulation." *American Journal of Orthopsychiatry* 43: 611-21.

–. 1975. "The Social Construction of Child Abuse." *American Journal of Orthopsychiatry* 45: 363-71.

Gibbons, D.C. 1992. *Society, Crime, and Criminal Behaviour*. Englewood Cliffs, NJ: Prentice-Hall.

Gil, D.G. 1971. "Sociocultural Perspective on Physical Child Abuse." *Child Welfare* 50: 389-95.

–. 1975. "Unraveling Child Abuse." *American Journal of Orthopsychiatry* 45: 346-56.

Gittens, M., and D. Cole. 1994. *Racism behind Bars: The Treatment of Black and Other Racial Minority Prisoners in Ontario Prisons. Interim Report of the Commission on Systemic Racism in the Ontario Criminal Justice System.* Toronto: Queen's Printer for Ontario.

Globe and Mail. 1984. "Abuse That Hides (1 and 2)." Editorials, 1-2 October.

Grant, I., and L. Smith. 1991. "Gender Representation in the Canadian Judiciary." In *Appointing Judges: Philosophy, Politics, and Practice,* 57-90. Toronto: Ontario Law Reform Commission.

Greene, I., C. Baar, P. McCormick, G. Szablowski, and M. Thomas. 1998. *Final Appeal: Decision-Making in Canadian Courts of Appeal.* Toronto: Lorimer.

Griffiths, C.T., and S.N. Verdun-Jones. 1994. *Canadian Criminal Justice.* Toronto: Harcourt Brace.

Groth, A.N., and H.J. Birnbaum. 1978. "Adult Sexual Orientation and Attraction to Underage Persons." *Archives of Sexual Behavior* 7, 3: 175-81.

Gunn, R., and R. Linden. 1993. "Evaluating the Impact of Legal Reform: Canada's New Sexual Assault Laws." In *Evaluating Justice: Canadian Policies and Programs,* ed. J. Hudson and J. Roberts, 135-54. Toronto: Thompson Educational Publishing.

Gusfield, J. 1992. Foreword. In *Deviance and Medicalization: From Badness to Sickness,* by P. Conrad and J. Schneider, v-x. Columbus: Merrill.

Haller, J.S., and R.M. Haller. 1974. *The Physician and Sexuality in Victorian America.* Urbana: University of Illinois Press.

Hansen, I. 1993. *Report of the Bell Cairn Centre Enquiry.* Toronto: Queen's Printer.

Hanson, R.K., R. Gizzarelli, and H. Scott. 1994. "The Attitudes of Incest Offenders: Sexual Entitlement and Acceptance of Sex with Children." *Criminal Justice and Behavior* 21: 187-202.

Harris, G., T. Rice, M.E., and V.L. Quinsey. 1998. "Appraisal and Management of Risk in Sexual Aggressors: Implications for Criminal Justice Policy." *Psychology, Public Policy, and Law* 4, 1-2: 73-115.

Herman, J.H. 1990. "Sex Offenders: A Feminist Perspective." In *Handbook of Sexual Assault: Issues, Theories, and Treatment of the Offender,* ed. W.E. Marshall, D.R. Laws, and H.E. Barbaree, 177-93. New York: Plenum Press.

Hickl-Szabo, R. 1984. "Reports of Sexual Abuse Rise Sharply in Toronto." *Globe and Mail* 23 August: M5.

Hogarth, J. 1971. *Sentencing as a Human Process.* Toronto: University of Toronto Press.

Hornick, J.P., and F. Bolitho. 1992. *A Review of the Implementation of the Child Sexual Abuse Legislation in Selected Sites.* Ottawa: Justice Canada.

Houston, S.E. 1974. "The Impetus to Reform: Urban Crime, Poverty, and Ignorance in Ontario 1850-1875." PhD diss., University of Toronto.

Hucker, S.J., and J. Bain. 1990. "Androgenic Hormones and Sexual Assault." In *Handbook of Sexual Assault: Issues, Theories, and Treatment of the Offender,* ed. W.L. Marshall, D.R. Laws, and H.E. Barbaree, 93-102. New York: Plenum Press.

Hudson, J., and J. Roberts, eds. 1993. *Evaluating Justice: Canadian Policies and Programs.* Toronto: Thompson Educational Publishing.

Jones, G.P. 1982. "The Social Study of Pederasty: In Search of a Literature Base: An Annotated Bibliography of Sources in English." *Journal of Homosexuality* 8: 61-95.

Knight, R., and R. Prentky. 1990. "Classifying Sexual Offenders: The Development and Corroboration of Taxonomic Models." In *Handbook of Sexual Assault: Issues, Theories, and Treatment of the Offender,* ed. W.L. Marshall, D.R. Laws, and H.E. Barbaree, 23-52. New York: Plenum Press.

Kong, R., H. Johnson, S. Beattie, and A. Cardillo. 2003. "Sexual Offences in Canada." *Juristat: Canadian Centre for Justice Statistics* 23, 6: 1-26.

Krippendorff, K. 2004. *Content Analysis: An Introduction to Its Methodology.* Thousand Oaks, CA: Sage Publications.

Langevin, R. 1990. "Sexual Anomalies and the Brain." In *Handbook of Sexual Assault: Issues, Theories, and Treatment of the Offender,* ed., W.L. Marshall, D.R. Laws, and H.E. Barbaree, 103-13. New York: Plenum Press.

–. 1993. "A Comparison of Neuroendocrine and Genetic Factors in Homosexuality and Pedophilia." *Annals of Sex Research* 6: 67-76.

Law Reform Commission of Canada. 1974. *The Principles of Sentencing and Dispositions.* Working Paper 3. Ottawa: Information Canada.

Lombroso, C., with G. Lombroso. 1911. *Criminal Man, According to the Classification of Cesare Lombroso.* New York: Putnam.

MacKinnon, C. 1983. "Feminism, Marxism, Method, and the State: Toward Feminist Jurisprudence." *Signs* 8, 2: 635-58.

–. 1987. *Feminism Unmodified: Discourses on Life and Law.* London: Harvard University Press.

–. 1989. *Toward a Feminist Theory of the State.* Cambridge, MA: Harvard University Press.

MacMillan, H.L., et al. 1997. "Prevalence of Child Physical and Sexual Abuse in the Community: Results from the Ontario Health Supplement." *Journal of the American Medical Association* 278: 131-35.

Mair, K.J. 1993. "The Nature of the Act: A Neglected Dimension in the Classification of Sex Offenders." *British Journal of Criminology* 33, 2: 267-75.

Mandel, M. 1991. "Democracy, Class, and Canadian Sentencing Law." In *The Social Basis of Law: Critical Readings in the Sociology of Law,* 2nd ed., ed. E. Comack and S. Brickey, 142-62. Halifax: Fernwood.

Manson, A., P. Healy, and G. Trotter. 2000. *Sentencing and Penal Policy in Canada: Cases, Materials, and Commentary.* Toronto: Emond Montgomery Publications.

Marshall, P. 1985. "Sexual Assault, the Charter, and Sentencing Reform." *Criminal Reports* 63: 216-35.

Martin, S.L. 1993. "Proving Gender Bias in the Law and the Legal System." In *Investigating Gender Bias: Law, Courts, and the Legal Profession,* ed. J. Brockman and D. Chunn, 19-36. Toronto: Thompson Educational Publishing.

Mendes, E.P. 1991. "Promoting Heterogeneity of the Judicial Mind: Minority and Gender Representation in the Canadian Judiciary," 91-108. *Appointing Judges: Philosophy, Politics, and Practice.* Toronto: Ontario Law Reform Commission.

Messerschmidt, J. 1997. "Varieties of 'Real Men.'" In *Gender Violence: Interdisciplinary Perspectives,* ed. L.L. O'Toole and J.R. Shipman, 92-109. New York: New York University Press.

METRAC. 1992. *Breach of Trust in Sexual Assault.* Toronto: Ontario Women's Directorate.

Mills, C.W. 1940. "Situated Actions and Vocabularies of Motive." *American Sociological Review* 6: 904-13.

Miner, M.H., and E. Coleman. 2001. "Advances in Sex Offender Treatment and Challenges for the Future." *Journal of Psychology and Human Sexuality* 13, 3-4: 5-24.

Minow, M. 1987. "The Supreme Court 1986 Term, Foreword: Justice Engendered." *Harvard Law Review* 101: 10-96.

Mitchell, A. 1985. "Child Sexual Abuse." In *No Safe Place: Violence against Women and Children,* ed. C. Guberman and M. Wolfe, 87-110. Toronto: Women's Press.

Mitra, C.L. 1987. "Judicial Discourse in Father-Daughter Incest Appeal Cases." *International Journal of the Sociology of Law* 15: 121-48.

Mohr, R.M., and J.V. Roberts, eds. 1994. *Confronting Sexual Assault: A Decade of Legal and Social Change.* Toronto: University of Toronto Press.

Nadin-Davis, R.P. 1983. "Making a Silk Purse? Sentencing: The 'New' Offences." *Criminal Reports* 32, 1: 28-46.

Naffine, N. 1990. *Law and the Sexes: Explorations in Feminist Jurisprudence.* North Sydney, Australia: Allen and Unwin.

Norman, G.R., and D.L. Streiner. 1986. *PDQ Statistics.* Toronto: B.C. Decker.

Norusis, M.J. 1993. *SPSS for Windows: Base System User's Guide.* Chicago: SPSS.

Olafson, E., D.L. Corwin, and R.C. Summit. 1993. "Modern History of Child Sexual Abuse Awareness: Cycles of Discovery and Suppression." *Child Abuse and Neglect* 17: 7-24.

Pelton, L.H. 1978. "Child Abuse and Neglect: The Myth of Classlessness." *American Journal of Orthopsychiatry* 48, 4: 608-17.

Platt, A. 1977. *The Child Savers: The Invention of Delinquency.* Chicago: University of Chicago Press.

Polan, D. 1982. "Towards a Theory of Law and Patriarchy." In *The Politics of Law: A Progressive Critique,* ed. D. Kairys, 294-303. New York: Pantheon.

Ptacek, J. 1988. "Why Do Men Batter Their Wives?" In *Feminist Perspectives on Wife Abuse,* ed. K. Yllo and M. Bograd, 133-57. Newbury Park, CA: Sage Publications.

Quinsey, V.L. 1986. "Men Who Have Sex with Children." In *Law and Mental Health: International Perspectives,* vol. 2, ed. D. Weisstub, 140-72. New York: Pergamon Press.

–. 1994. "Assessment, Management, and Treatment of Sex Offenders." IARCA unpublished paper, Lacrosse, WI.

Reuters. 1994. "Stepfather's Light Sentence Sparks Outcry." *Toronto Star* 15 January: A2.

Roberts, J.V. 1996. "Sexual Assault in Canada." *Queen's Law Journal* 21: 395-422.

Roberts, J.V., and A. Edgar. 2002. *Victim Impact at Sentencing: Perceptions of the Judiciary.* Ottawa: Department of Justice.

Roberts, J.V., and R.J. Gebotys. 1993. "Evaluating Criminal Justice Legislation: Effects of Rape Reform in Canada." In *Evaluating Justice: Canadian Policies and Programs,* ed. J. Hudson and J. Roberts, 155-69. Toronto: Thompson Educational Publishing.

Rodriques, G.P., and J. Ouellet. 1993. *Pocket Criminal Code.* Scarborough: Carswell.

Rooke, P.T., and R.L. Schell. 1982. *Discarding the Asylum: From Child Rescue to the Welfare State in English Canada (1800-1950).* New York: University Press of America.

Rothman, D.J. 1971. *Discovery of the Asylum: Social Order and Disorder in the New Republic*. Boston: Little, Brown.

Ruby, C.C. 1994. *Sentencing*. 4th ed. Toronto: Butterworths.

–. 1999. *Sentencing*. 5th ed. Toronto: Butterworths.

Ruebsaat, G. 1985. *The New Sexual Assault Offences: Emerging Legal Issues*. Ottawa: Department of Justice, Communications and Public Affairs.

Rush, F. 1980. *The Best Kept Secret: Sexual Abuse of Children*. New York: McGraw-Hill.

Scott, M., and S. Lyman. 1968. "Accounts." *American Sociological Review* 33, 1: 46-62.

Scully, D. 1990. *Understanding Sexual Violence*. Boston: Unwin Hyman.

Scully, D., and J. Marolla. 1984. "Rapists' Vocabulary of Motive." *Social Problems* 31, 5: 530-44.

Segal, Z., and L. Stermac. 1990. "The Role of Cognition in Sexual Assault." In *Handbook of Sexual Assault: Issues, Theories, and Treatment of the Offender,* ed. W.E. Marshall, D.R. Laws, and H.E. Barbaree, 161- 74. New York: Plenum Press.

Sheehy, E. 1989. "Canadian Judges and the Law of Rape: Should the Charter Insulate Bias?" *Ottawa Law Review* 21, 1: 151-97.

Simon, L.M.J. 2000. "An Examination of the Assumptions of Specialization, Mental Disorder, and Dangerousness in Sex Offenders." *Behavioral Sciences and the Law* 18: 275–308.

Skinner, H.A., and R.K. Blashfield. 1982. "Increasing the Impact of Cluster Analysis Research: The Case of Psychiatric Classification." *Journal of Consulting and Clinical Psychology* 50: 727–35.

Smallbone, S.W., and R.K. Wortley. 2004. "Criminal Diversity and Paraphilic Interests among Adult Males Convicted of Sexual Offences against Children." *International Journal of Offender Therapy and Comparative Criminology* 48, 2: 175-88.

Smart, C. 1989. *Feminism and the Power of Law*. London: Routledge.

–. 1999. "A History of Ambivalence and Conflict in the Discursive Construction of the 'Child Victim' of Sexual Abuse." *Social and Legal Studies* 8, 3: 391-409.

Soothill, K., B. Francis, B. Sanderson, and E. Ackerley. 2000. "Sex Offenders: Specialists, Generalists – or Both? A 32 Year Criminological Study." *British Journal of Criminology* 40: 56-67.

Stake, R.E. 2006. *Multiple Case Study Analysis*. New York: Guilford Press.

Stermac, L.E., Z.V. Segal, and R. Gillis. 1990. "Social and Cultural Factors in Sexual Assault." In *Handbook of Sexual Assault: Issues, Theories, and Treatment of the Offender,* ed. W.L. Marshall, D.R. Laws, and H.E. Barbaree, 143–59. New York: Plenum Press.

Summit, R. 1983. "The Child Sexual Abuse Accommodation Syndrome." *Child Abuse and Neglect* 7: 177–93.

–. 1988. "Hidden Victims, Hidden Pain: Societal Avoidance of Child Sexual Abuse." In *Lasting Effects of Child Sexual Abuse,* ed. G. Wyatt and G.J. Powell, 39-60. Newbury Park, CA: Sage Publications.

Sutherland, E.H. 1961. *White-Collar Crime*. New York: Holt, Rinehart and Winston.

Sutherland, N. 1976. *Children in English Canadian Society: Framing the Twentieth Century Consensus*. Toronto: University of Toronto Press. (Re-issued, Studies in Childhood and Family in Canada series [Waterloo: Wilfrid Laurier University Press, 2000].)

Sykes, G., and D. Matza. 1957. "Techniques of Neutralisation: A Theory of Delinquency." *American Sociological Review* 22: 664-70.
Taylor, S.C. 2004. *Court Licensed Abuse: Patriarchal Lore and the Legal Response to Intrafamilial Sexual Abuse of Children*. New York: Peter Lang.
Trocmé, N., and N. Bala. 2005. False Allegations of Abuse and Neglect When Parents Separate. *Child Abuse and Neglect* 29: 1333-45.
Trocmé, N., J. Siddiqi, B. Fallon, B. MacLaurin, and S. Sullivan. 2002. *Maltreatment Rates: Ontario Incidence Study of Reported Child Abuse and Neglect, 1993-1998*. Toronto: Institute for the Prevention of Child Abuse.
Walker, N. 1985. *Sentencing: Theory, Law, and Practice*. London: Butterworths.
Walsh, C., E. Jamieson, H. MacMillan, and N. Trocmé. 2004. Measuring Child Sexual Abuse in Children and Youth. *Journal of Child Sexual Abuse* 13, 1: 39-68.
Ward, T., S.M. Hudson, L. Johnston, and W.L. Marshall. 1997. "Cognitive Distortions in Sex Offenders: An Integrative Review." *Clinical Psychology Review* 17: 479-507.
Weber, R.P. 1990. *Basic Content Analysis*. Newbury Park, CA: Sage Publications.
West, R. 1987. "The Difference in Women's Hedonic Life: A Phenomenological Critique of Feminist Legal Theory." *Wisconsin Women's Law Journal* 3: 81-146.
Whitfield, C.L. 2001. "The 'False Memory' Defense: Using Disinformation and Junk Science In and Out of Court." In *Misinformation Concerning Child Sexual Abuse and Adult Survivors,* ed. C.L. Whitfield, J. Silberg, and P.J. Fink, 53-78. New York: Hawthorn Press.
Yin, R.K. 1989. *Case Study Research: Design and Methods*. Newbury Park, CA: Sage Publications.
–. 1993. *Applications of Case Study Research*. Newbury Park, CA: Sage Publications.
Yochelson, S., and S. Samenow. 1976-86. *The Criminal Personality*. 3 vols. New York: J. Aronson.
Young, A.N. 1988. *The Role of the Appellate Court in Developing Sentencing Guidelines*. Ottawa: Department of Justice Canada.
–. 2001. *The Role of the Victim in the Criminal Process: A Literature Review – 1989 to 1999*. Victims of Crime Research Series. Ottawa: Department of Justice Canada.

Cases Cited

Unreported ONCA Cases

R. v. A., H. (October 1998), ONCA C23088.
R. v. A., T.L. (June 1990), ONCA 406/90.
R. v. B., C.I. (January 1999), ONCA C25369.
R. v. B., J. (September 1998), ONCA C29313.
R. v. B., J.S. (November 1998), ONCA C24955.
R. v. B.S. (November 1998), ONCA C29947.
R. v. C., A. (January 1999), ONCA C24896.
R. v. C., M.E. (1993), ONCA C12603.
R. v. C., S. (January 1993), ONCA C11389.
R. v. D., J.G. (June 1993), ONCA C8761.
R. v. D., J.M. (March 1991), ONCA 1040/90.
R. v. Elder (January 1999), ONCA C29229.
R. v. E., P. (May 1991), ONCA 1215/90.

R. v. E., R.J. (November 1990), ONCA 727/90.
R. v. F., V. (March 1992), ONCA C6030.
R. v. F., G. (1991), OCJ 697/91.
R. v. G., D. (November 1990), ONCA 564/90.
R. v. G., J. (November 1998), ONCA C29056.
R. v. G., P.E.R. (October 1992), ONCA C8074 or 799/91.
R. v. G., T. (January 1992), ONCA C6105.
R. v. H. (January 1991), ONCA 393/90.
R. v. I., R. (May 1992), ONCA C8768.
R. v. K., D. (October 1991), ONCA 75/90.
R. v. K., M. (1993), ONCA C13049.
R. v. L., A.P. (December 1991), ONCA C6867.
R. v. L., G.A. (July 1990), ONCA 193/90.
R. v. L., H. (October 1991), ONCA C6131.
R. v. L., R.A. (1993), ONCA C13578.
R. v. M., J. (October 1998), ONCA C29506.
R. v. M., J. (October 1998), ONCA C29184.
R. v. M., M. (September 1992), ONCA C5916.
R. v. M., S.J. (February 1993), ONCA C6825.
R. v. McNall (June 1992), ONCA C10530.
R. v. N., W.R. (January 1999), ONCA C31068.
R. v. Pascoe (October 1990), ONCA 229/90.
R. v. P., R.B. (March 1992), ONCA C7241.
R. v. R., H. (December 1998), ONCA C22761.
R. v. R., P. (November 1991), ONCA 408/90.
R. v. Simard (October 1990), ONCA 577/90.
R. v. S., K. (March 1999), ONCA C23984.
R. v. T., A. (December 1991), ONCA 300/91.
R. v. T., J. (July 1992), ONCA C6133.
R. v. W., C.C. (March 1991), ONCA 657/90.
R. v. W., E. (November 1998), ONCA C27388.
R. v. W., W. (November 1992), ONCA C11464.

Reported Cases

R. v. B. (1990), 36 ONCA 307 9 W.C.B. (2d) 622.
R. v. C.A.M. (1996), 46 CR (4th) 269 (SCC).
R. v. Clubb (1984), 20 ONCA 157.
R. v. D.D. (2002), 163 C.C.C. (3d) 471 (Ont. C.A.).
R. v. D., P. (1999), ONCA 139 C.C.C. (3d) 274 c31319.
Regina v. F.D. (1991), 77 C.C.C. (3d) 575 c6765.
R. v. G., A. (1998), 130 C.C.C. (3d) 30 Affirmed 143 C.C.C. (3d) 46 c25403.
R. v. Inwood (1989), 48 C.C.C. (3d) 173.
R. v. M., G. (1991), 77 C.C.C. (3d) 310, 58 O.A.C. 390 c8836.
R. v. Mohan (1992), 8 O.R. (3d) 173 (Ont. C.A.) 104/91.
R. v. Morissette (1970), 1 C.C.C. (2d) 307, 12 CRNS 392, WWR 664.
Regina and Owens (1986), 33 C.C.C. (3d) 275.
R. v. Proulx (2000), 1 S.C.R. 61 SCC 5.
R. v. Ramsay (2004), B.C.S.C. 756, 22 C.R. (6th) 76 (B.C.S.C).
R. v. Stuckless (1998), 127 C.C.C. (3d) 225 (Ont. C.A.) c28532.

Index

Note: (t) after a page number denotes a table, (f) a figure